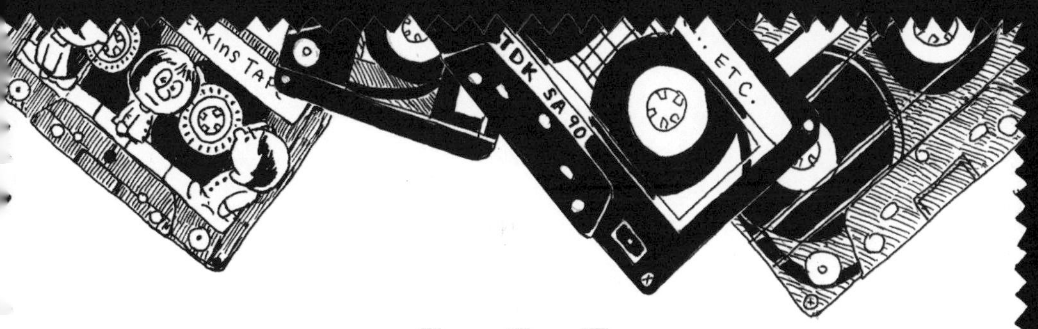
TDK SA 90
... ETC.

ALL THE SAD SONGS

Summer Pierre

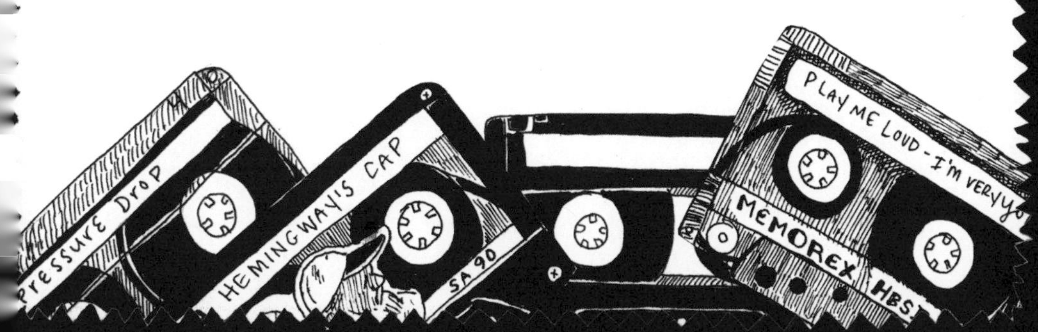
Pressure Drop
HEMINGWAY'S CAP
SA 90
PLAY ME LOUD - I'M VERY
MEMOREX
HBS

All the Sad Songs © 2018 Summer Pierre

ISBN 978-1-940398-76-1

Retrofit 71

No part of this book may be reproduced without permission of
the artist except small portions for the purposes of review.

Published by Retrofit Comics & Big Planet Comics
Washington, DC
retrofitcomics.com / bigplanetcomics.com

Distributed by SCB Distributors

Printed in Canada

FOR GRAHAM

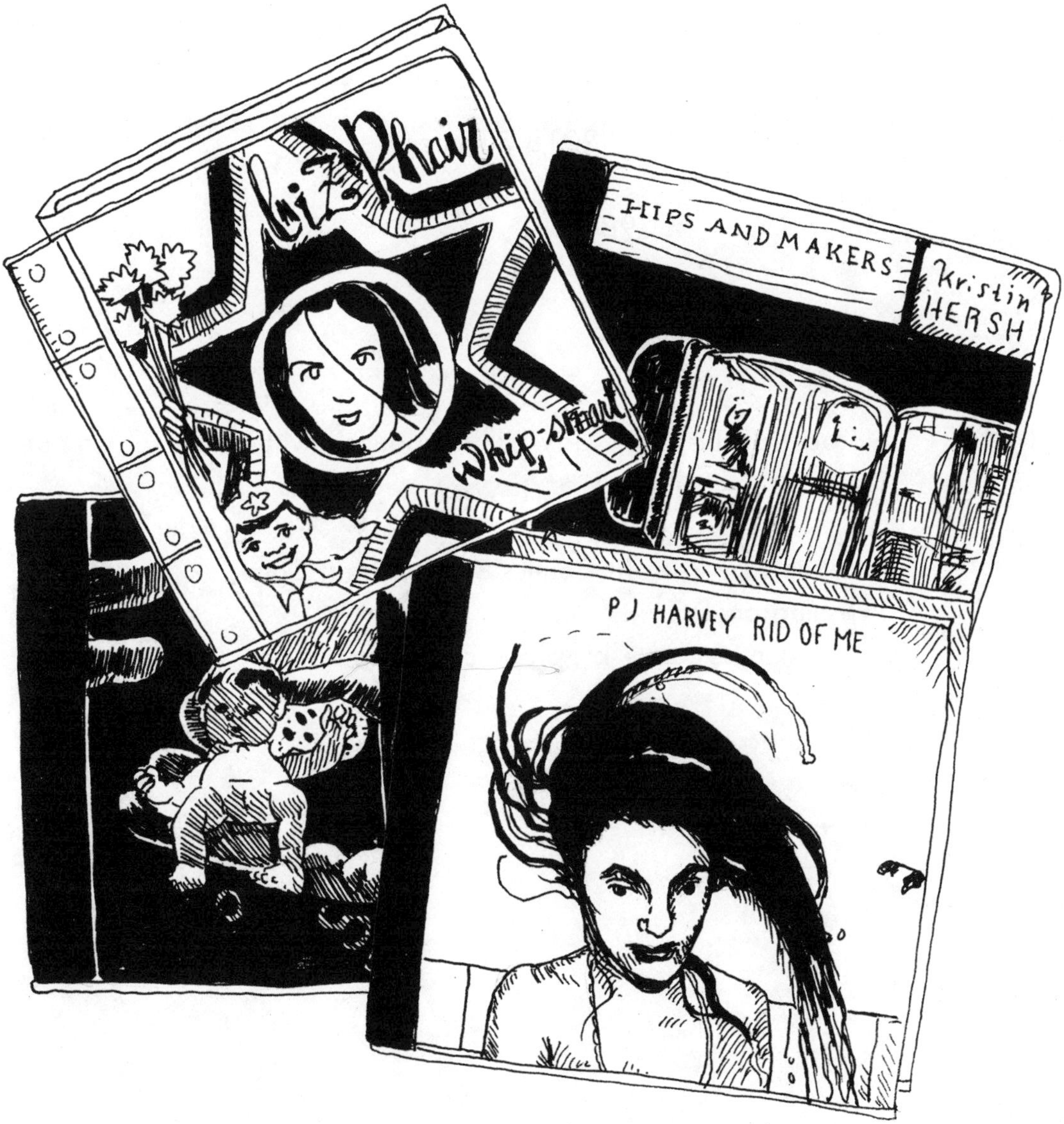
Liz Phair
Whip-smart
HIPS AND MAKERS
Kristin HERSH
PJ HARVEY RID OF ME

"I WANTED TO LIVE IN A
SONG AND NEVER COME BACK."
—TOM WAITS

PART ONE

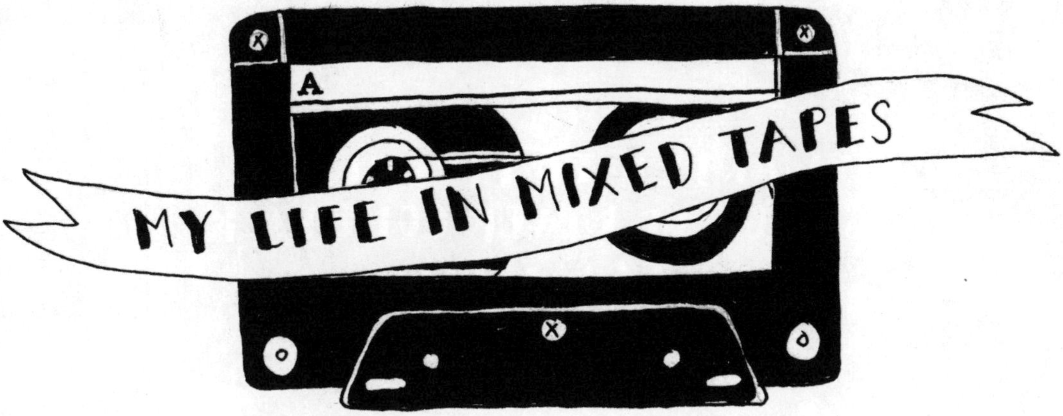
A
MY LIFE IN MIXED TAPES

THE
HUDSON VALLEY,
NEW YORK
2017

I'VE BEEN WORKING ON A COMIC ABOUT MUSIC THAT'S NOT GOING WELL --

-- SO THIS MORNING I WENT DOWN INTO THE BASEMENT TO FIND MY OLD STASH OF MIX TAPES.

THEY WERE THERE, BURIED AMONG MY JOURNALS, AND OLD NOTEBOOKS --

-- AND ALL THE OTHER THINGS I CAN'T SEEM TO LET GO OF.

P. Horos

LIKE A LOT OF PEOPLE MY AGE, I REGARD MIX TAPES LIKE HOLY RELICS --

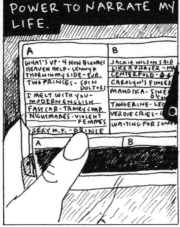

-- THAT ONCE HAD THE POWER TO NARRATE MY LIFE.

A

WHAT'S UP - 4 NON BLONDES
HEAVEN HELP - LENNY K
THORN IN MY SIDE - EUR.
TWO PRINCES - SPIN
　　　　　　　　　DOCTORS
I MELT WITH YOU -
　MODERN ENGLISH
FAST CAR - TRACEY CHAP.
NIGHTMARES - VIOLENT
　　　　　　　　FEMMES
SEXY M.F. - PRINCE

B

JACKIE WILSON SAID
LIKE A PRAYER - MA
CENTERFOLD - 0-6
CAROLYN'S FINGER
MANDIKA - SINE
　　　　　　　　　O'CON
TANGERINE - LE
VERDIE CRIES - 1
WAITING FOR SOM

A　　　　　　　B

IN A WAY, THEY STILL DO --

SPRING 1994

-- JUST IN THE PAST TENSE.

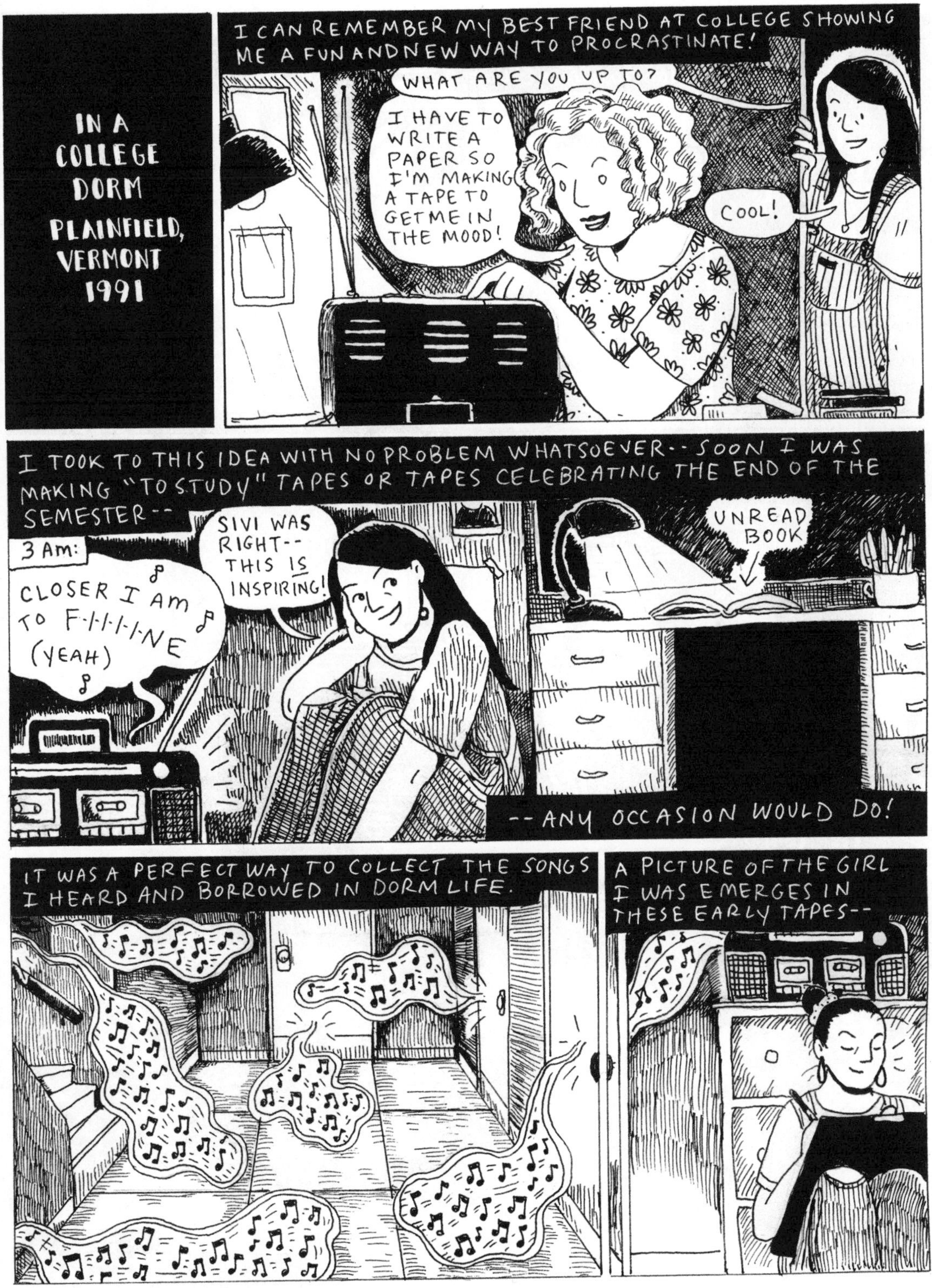
IN A COLLEGE DORM
PLAINFIELD, VERMONT 1991
I CAN REMEMBER MY BEST FRIEND AT COLLEGE SHOWING ME A FUN AND NEW WAY TO PROCRASTINATE!
WHAT ARE YOU UP TO?
I HAVE TO WRITE A PAPER SO I'M MAKING A TAPE TO GET ME IN THE MOOD!
COOL!
I TOOK TO THIS IDEA WITH NO PROBLEM WHATSOEVER-- SOON I WAS MAKING "TO STUDY" TAPES OR TAPES CELEBRATING THE END OF THE SEMESTER--
3 AM:
CLOSER I AM TO F-I-I-I-I-NE (YEAH)
SIVI WAS RIGHT-- THIS IS INSPIRING!
UNREAD BOOK
--ANY OCCASION WOULD DO!
IT WAS A PERFECT WAY TO COLLECT THE SONGS I HEARD AND BORROWED IN DORM LIFE.
A PICTURE OF THE GIRL I WAS EMERGES IN THESE EARLY TAPES--

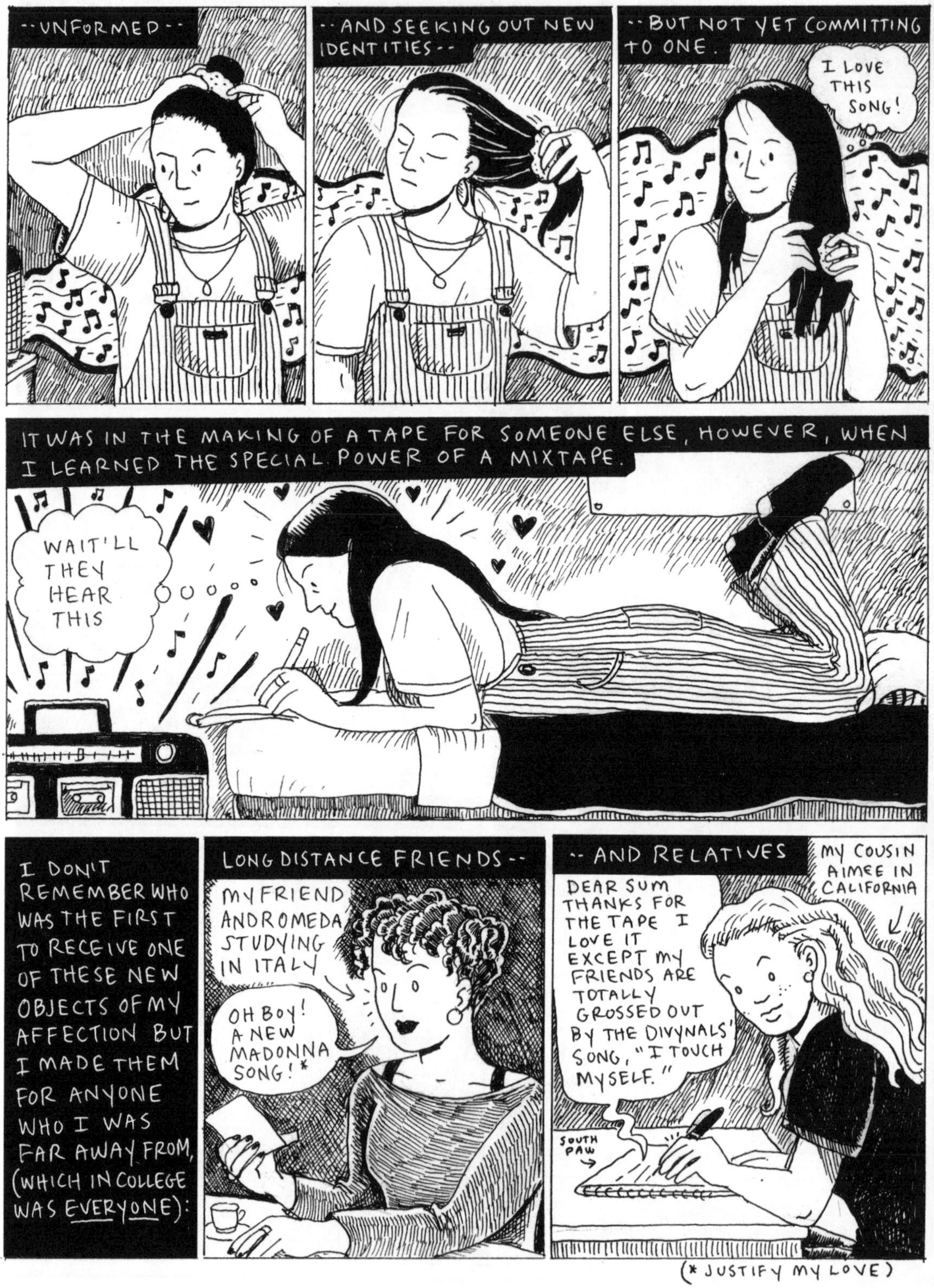
--UNFORMED--
--AND SEEKING OUT NEW IDENTITIES--
--BUT NOT YET COMMITTING TO ONE.
I LOVE THIS SONG!
IT WAS IN THE MAKING OF A TAPE FOR SOMEONE ELSE, HOWEVER, WHEN I LEARNED THE SPECIAL POWER OF A MIXTAPE.
WAIT'LL THEY HEAR THIS
I DON'T REMEMBER WHO WAS THE FIRST TO RECEIVE ONE OF THESE NEW OBJECTS OF MY AFFECTION BUT I MADE THEM FOR ANYONE WHO I WAS FAR AWAY FROM, (WHICH IN COLLEGE WAS EVERYONE):
LONG DISTANCE FRIENDS--
MY FRIEND ANDROMEDA STUDYING IN ITALY
OH BOY! A NEW MADONNA SONG!*
--AND RELATIVES
MY COUSIN AIMEE IN CALIFORNIA
DEAR SUM THANKS FOR THE TAPE I LOVE IT EXCEPT MY FRIENDS ARE TOTALLY GROSSED OUT BY THE DIVYNALS' SONG, "I TOUCH MYSELF."
SOUTH PAW
(* JUSTIFY MY LOVE)

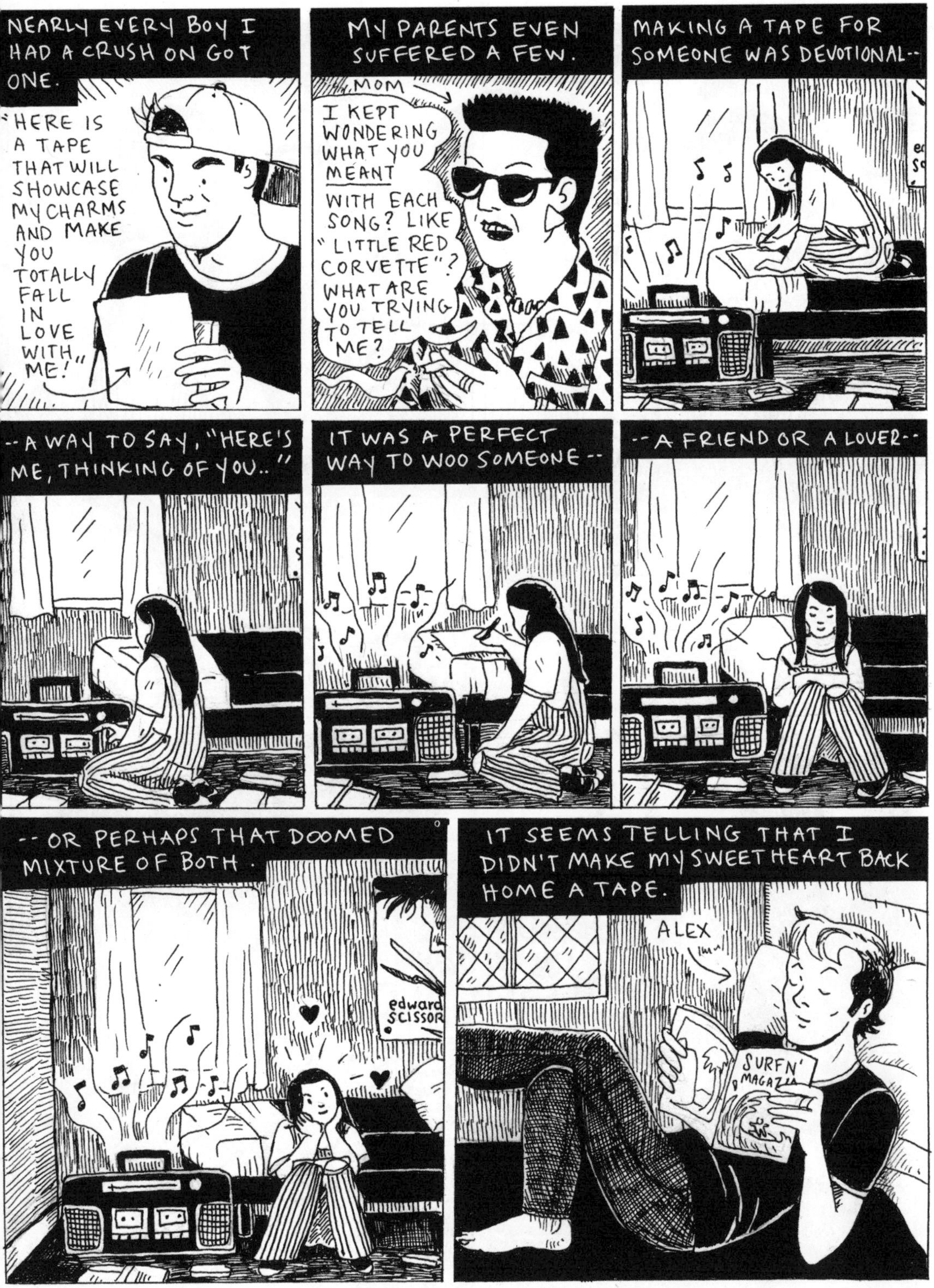
NEARLY EVERY BOY I HAD A CRUSH ON GOT ONE.
"HERE IS A TAPE THAT WILL SHOWCASE MY CHARMS AND MAKE YOU TOTALLY FALL IN LOVE WITH ME!"
MY PARENTS EVEN SUFFERED A FEW.
MOM
I KEPT WONDERING WHAT YOU MEANT WITH EACH SONG? LIKE "LITTLE RED CORVETTE"? WHAT ARE YOU TRYING TO TELL ME?
MAKING A TAPE FOR SOMEONE WAS DEVOTIONAL--
--A WAY TO SAY, "HERE'S ME, THINKING OF YOU.."
IT WAS A PERFECT WAY TO WOO SOMEONE--
--A FRIEND OR A LOVER--
--OR PERHAPS THAT DOOMED MIXTURE OF BOTH.
edward SCISSOR
IT SEEMS TELLING THAT I DIDN'T MAKE MY SWEETHEART BACK HOME A TAPE.
ALEX
SURFN' MAGAZI

I WENT TO COLLEGE IN VERMONT...

IT SNOWED TODAY!

← DORM PAY PHONE WAS NEAR THE FRONT DOOR, SO WAS ALWAYS FREEZING

-- WHILE HE LIVED AT HOME IN CALIFORNIA.

HA! IT'S 70 DEGREES HERE TODAY!

HIS STEP-MOTHER'S POODLE

FOR TWO YEARS WE SAW EACH OTHER AT CHRISTMAS AND IN THE SUMMER--

TWO SEPTEMBERS IN A ROW:

I DON'T WANT TO LEAVE YOU! (SOB)

IT'S THREE MONTHS, BUT IT FEELS LIKE FOREVER!

-- BUT BROKE UP WHEN I TOOK A YEAR OFF SCHOOL TO BE NEAR HIM WHEN HE WENT AWAY TO SCHOOL IN SANTA CRUZ.

JUST SHY OF A FOURTH SEPTEMBER:

MAYBE--

LET'S GET THIS OVER WITH!

GREW HIS HAIR LONG

--I'M CHANGING!

IN THE TAPE I HAVE FROM HIM, I HEAR THE MISMATCH.

SA TDK 90

A: FAITHFULLY

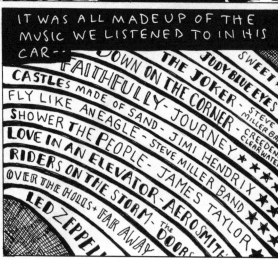

IT WAS ALL MADE UP OF THE MUSIC WE LISTENED TO IN HIS CAR--

SWEET

JUDY BLUE EYES

DOWN ON THE JOKER - STEVE MILLER BAND

FAITHFULLY

CASTLES MADE OF SAND - ON THE CORNER - CREEDENCE CLEARWATER

FLY LIKE AN EAGLE - JOURNEY

SHOWER THE PEOPLE - JIMI HENDRIX

LOVE IN AN ELEVATOR - JAMES TAYLOR

RIDERS ON THE STORM - AEROSMITH

OVER THE HILLS + FAR AWAY - THE DOORS

LED ZEPPELIN

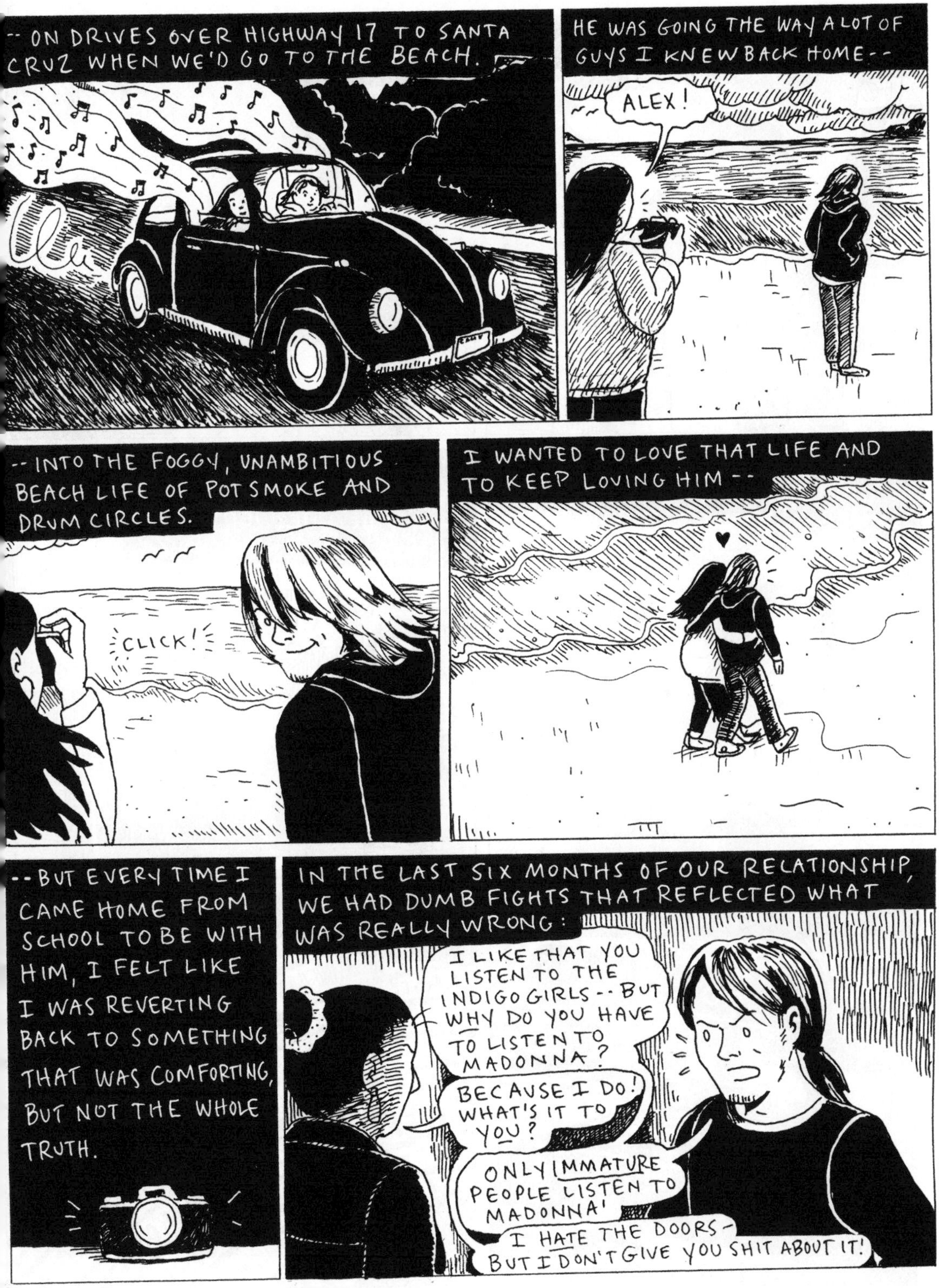
-- ON DRIVES OVER HIGHWAY 17 TO SANTA CRUZ WHEN WE'D GO TO THE BEACH.
HE WAS GOING THE WAY A LOT OF GUYS I KNEW BACK HOME--
ALEX!
--INTO THE FOGGY, UNAMBITIOUS BEACH LIFE OF POT SMOKE AND DRUM CIRCLES.
CLICK!
I WANTED TO LOVE THAT LIFE AND TO KEEP LOVING HIM--
--BUT EVERY TIME I CAME HOME FROM SCHOOL TO BE WITH HIM, I FELT LIKE I WAS REVERTING BACK TO SOMETHING THAT WAS COMFORTING, BUT NOT THE WHOLE TRUTH.
IN THE LAST SIX MONTHS OF OUR RELATIONSHIP, WE HAD DUMB FIGHTS THAT REFLECTED WHAT WAS REALLY WRONG:
I LIKE THAT YOU LISTEN TO THE INDIGO GIRLS -- BUT WHY DO YOU HAVE TO LISTEN TO MADONNA?
BECAUSE I DO! WHAT'S IT TO YOU?
ONLY IMMATURE PEOPLE LISTEN TO MADONNA!
I HATE THE DOORS- BUT I DON'T GIVE YOU SHIT ABOUT IT!

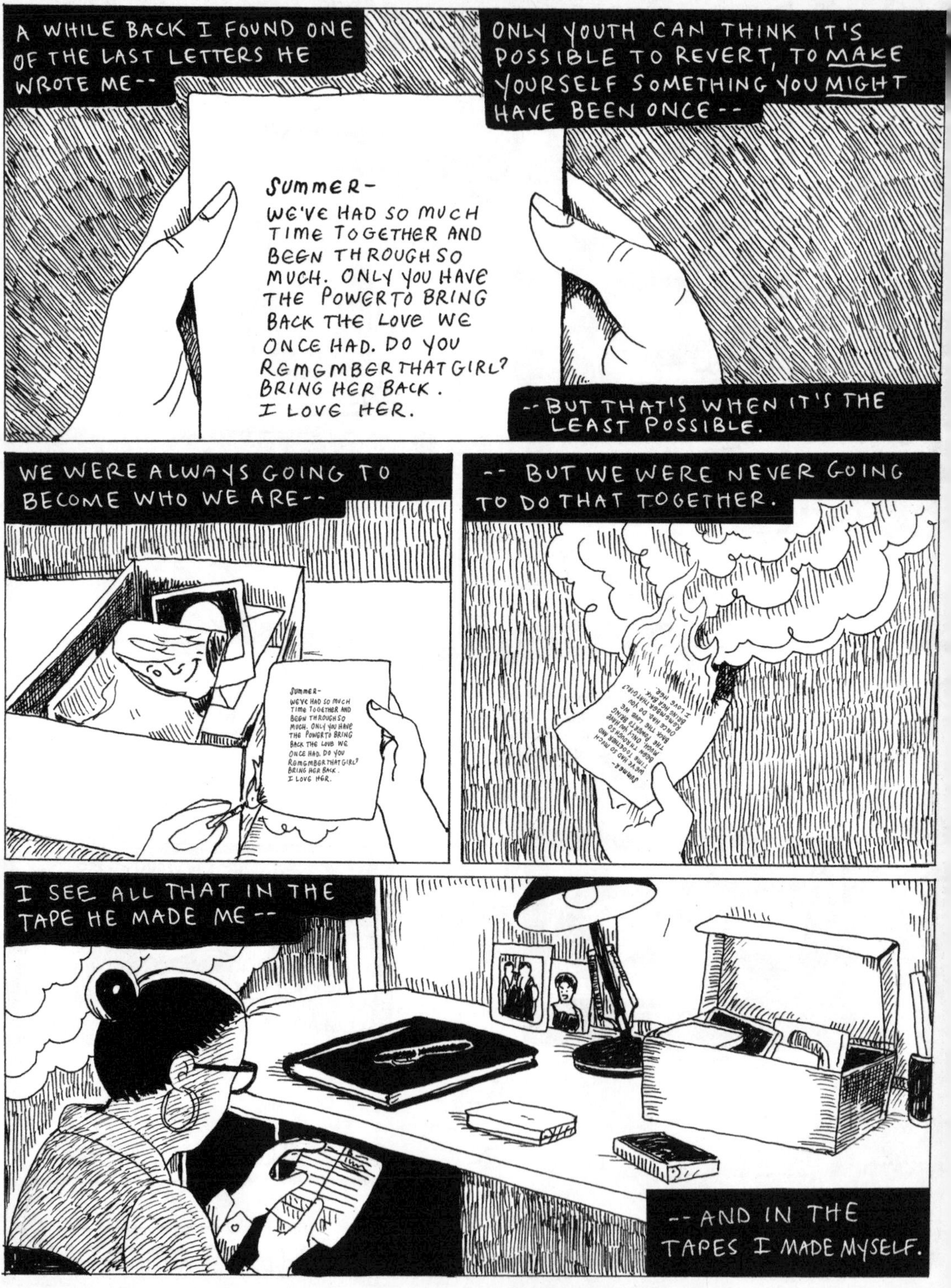
A WHILE BACK I FOUND ONE OF THE LAST LETTERS HE WROTE ME--
SUMMER-
WE'VE HAD SO MUCH TIME TOGETHER AND BEEN THROUGH SO MUCH. ONLY YOU HAVE THE POWER TO BRING BACK THE LOVE WE ONCE HAD. DO YOU REMEMBER THAT GIRL? BRING HER BACK. I LOVE HER.
ONLY YOUTH CAN THINK IT'S POSSIBLE TO REVERT, TO MAKE YOURSELF SOMETHING YOU MIGHT HAVE BEEN ONCE--
--BUT THAT'S WHEN IT'S THE LEAST POSSIBLE.
WE WERE ALWAYS GOING TO BECOME WHO WE ARE--
SUMMER-
WE'VE HAD SO MUCH TIME TOGETHER AND BEEN THROUGH SO MUCH. ONLY YOU HAVE THE POWER TO BRING BACK THE LOVE WE ONCE HAD. DO YOU REMEMBER THAT GIRL? BRING HER BACK. I LOVE HER.
-- BUT WE WERE NEVER GOING TO DO THAT TOGETHER.
I SEE ALL THAT IN THE TAPE HE MADE ME--
--AND IN THE TAPES I MADE MYSELF.

Ⓐ WILD, WILD LIFE - TALKING HEADS • TRY A LITTLE TENDERNESS - OTIS REDDING • WHERE THE STORY ENDS - THE SUNDAYS • HOLIDAY - MADONNA • BURNING DOWN THE HOUSE - TALKING HEADS • CLOSER TO FINE - INDIGO GIRLS • PEACE TRAIN - 10,000 MANIACS • WORLD CLIQUE - DEEE-LITE • ETC.

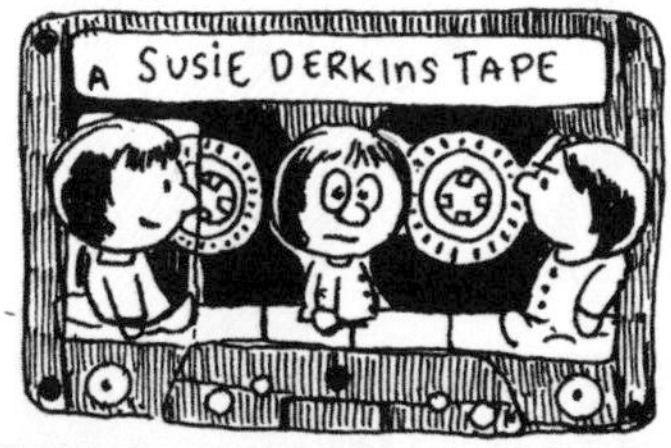
A SUSIE DERKINS TAPE

Ⓑ BEEN CAUGHT STEALN' - JANE'S ADDICTION • HANKY PANKY - MADONNA • BETTER BE HOME SOON - CROWDED HOUSE • JACKIE WILSON SAID - VAN MORRISON • HAVE A HEART - BONNIE RAITT • THORN IN MY SIDE - EURITHMICS • LOVE SHACK - B-52'S • LOVE LIKE WE DO - EDIE BRICKELL + THE NEW BOHEMIANS • KISS OFF - VIOLENT FEMMES • STARFISH + COFFEE - PRINCE • ABC - THE JACKSON 5 • BABY, I LOVE YOU - ARETHA FRANKLYN • PLEASE DO NOT GO - VIOLENT FEMMES

Ⓐ WHAT'S THE MEANING OF LIFE - SOUL II SOUL • BLACK OR WHITE - MICHAEL JACKSON • PROMISE OF A NEW DAY - PAULA ABDUL • WAITING FOR THAT DAY - GEORGE MICHAEL • PRINCE OF DARKNESS - INDIGO GIRLS • BEAST OF BURDEN • THE ROLLING STONES • YOU'RE THE ONE THAT I WANT - OLIVIA NEWTON-JOHN + JOHN TRAVOLTA • DANCE TO THE MUSIC - SLY + THE FAMILY STONE • ETC.

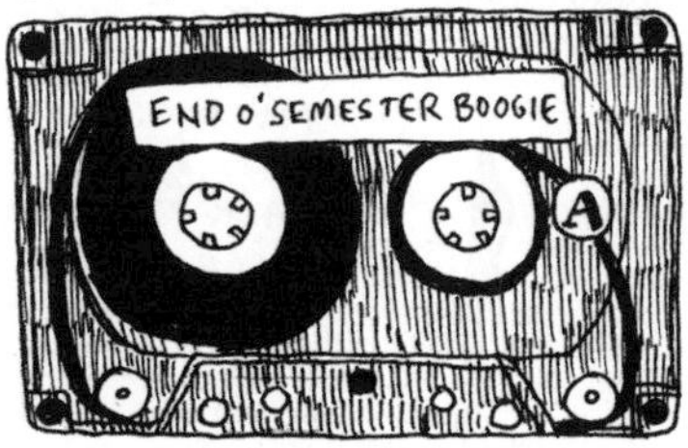
END O' SEMESTER BOOGIE
A

Ⓑ FREEDOM - GEORGE MICHAEL • SUMMER LOVN' - OLIVIA NEWTON-JOHN + JOHN TRAVOLTA • SHATTERED - THE ROLLING STONES • UNDER THE BRIDGE - RED HOT CHILI PEPPERS • LOVE COME THROUGH - SOUL II SOUL • OPEN YOUR HEART - MADONNA • EVERYDAY PEOPLE - SLY + THE FAMILY STONE • SARA - FLEETWOOD MAC • WAITING (REPRISE) - GEORGE MICHAEL • BLOOD + FIRE - INDIGO GIRLS • KEEP IT TOGETHER - MADONNA

SELECTED SOUNDTRACK

Ⓐ FEELING ALLRIGHT - JOE COCKER • BOHEMIAN RAPSODY - QUEEN • DOWN ON THE CORNER - CREEDENCE CLEARWATER REVIVAL • MERCY MERCY ME - MARVIN GAYE • SALSBURY HILL • PETER GABRIEL • WARM LOVE - VAN MORRISON • THE APARTMENT SONG - TOM PETTY • ROXANNE - THE POLICE • IN MY LIFE - THE BEATLES • LOLA - THE KINKS • MY BEST FRIEND'S GIRLFRIEND - THE CARS • BOYS OF SUMMER - DON HENLEY •

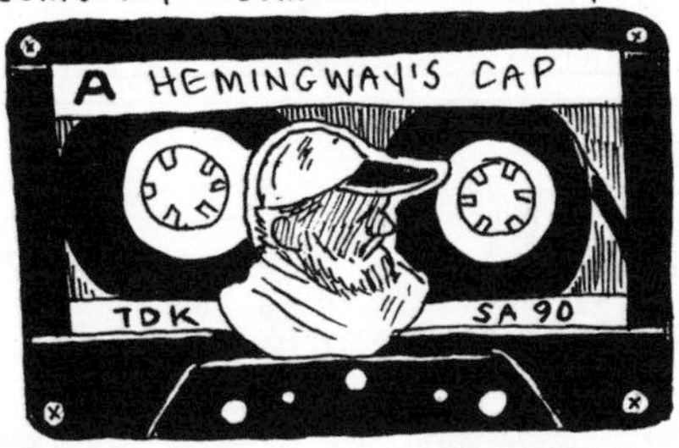
A HEMINGWAY'S CAP
TDK
SA 90

Ⓑ DÉJÀ VU - CROSBY, STILLS, NASH + YOUNG • BLACKBIRD - THE BEATLES • THE JOKER - STEVE MILLER BAND • OVER THE HILLS + FAR AWAY - LED ZEPPLIN • SLEDGE HAMMER - PETER GABRIEL • WITH A LITTLE HELP FROM MY FRIENDS - JOE COCKER • COULD HAVE LIED - RED HOT CHILI PEPPERS • SEXUAL HEALING - MARVIN GAYE • BROWN EYED GIRL - VAN MORRISON • MEXICO - JAMES TAYLOR • DREAMING - LOU REED

Ⓐ DANCING IN THE DARK - THE BOSS • I TOUCH MYSELF - THE DIVYNALS • HE'S SO FINE - THE CHIFFONS • TIME RUNS WILD - DANNY WILDE • HEY BABY - BRUCE CHANNEL • SHE TALKS TO ANGELS - THE BLACK CROWS • TRACKS OF MY TEARS • SMOKEY ROBINSON • GOOD LOVN' - THE RASCALS • RESPECT - ARETHA FRANKLYN • RIO - DURAN DURAN • I WANT YOUR SEX - GEORGE MICHAEL

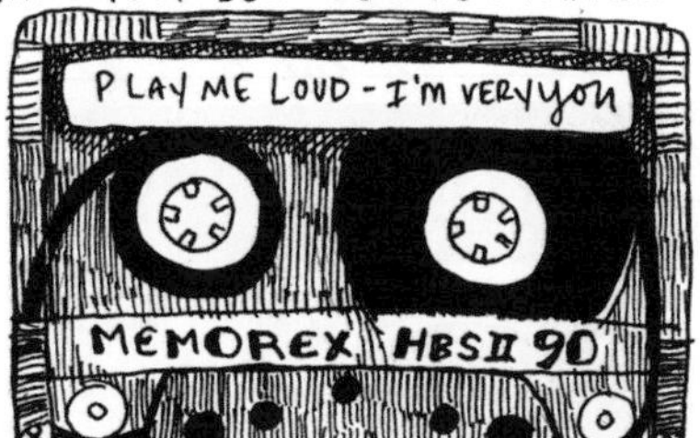
PLAY ME LOUD - I'M VERY YOU
MEMOREX HBS II 90

Ⓑ I WEAR YOUR RING - COCTEAU TWINS • NATURAL WOMAN - ARETHA FRANKLYN • TAKE ME WITH YOU - PRINCE • I'VE GOT DREAMS TO REMEMBER - OTIS REDDING • JOY TO THE WORLD - THREE DOG NIGHT • BATTLE STATIONS - WHAM! • I SECOND THAT EMOTION - SMOKEY ROBINSON • TRUE COLORS - CYNDI LAUPER • INTO THE MYSTIC - VAN MORRISON • NO MYTH - MICHAEL PENN • CRY TO ME - SOLOMON BURKE • LOVE IS STRANGE - MICKEY + SYLVIA • TRY ME ON - DEEE-LITE

PART TWO

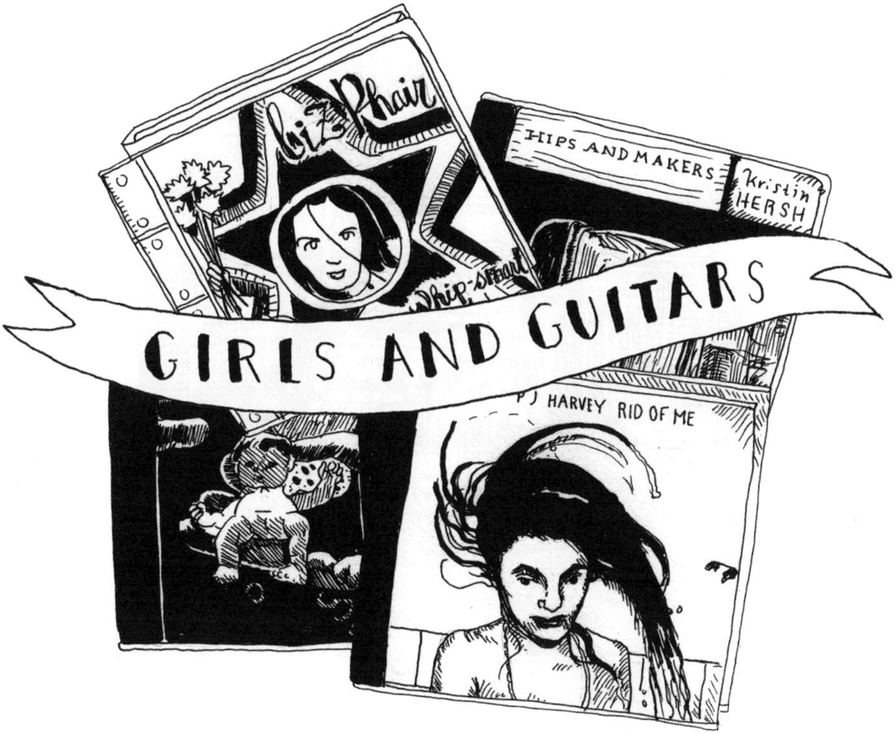
Liz Phair
Whip-smart
HIPS AND MAKERS
Kristin HERSH
GIRLS AND GUITARS
PJ HARVEY RID OF ME

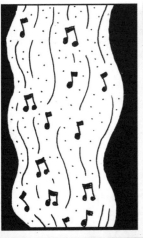

I GREW UP WITH A LOT OF MUSIC AROUND ME.

MY DAD IS AN ARTIST AND A MUSICIAN.

HIS SONG "LAUNDRY-MAT LINDA"

SHE'S A THREE CYCLE WASHING MACHINE--TRY IF YOU DARE SPEED QUEEN! SHE'LL WASH AWAY YOUR DIRTY BLUES AND SPIN YOU DRY BEFORE SHE'S THROUGH--OO! OO!

MY MOM WORKED IN THE ROCK N' ROLL INDUSTRY AS A STAGE HAND--

FUCKN' MICK JAGGER! HE ALWAYS WANTS THE SCRIM JUST RIGHT!

--AND MY STEPFATHER WAS A RECORD COLLECTOR AND REMAINS ONE OF THE MOST MUSICALLY CURIOUS PEOPLE I'VE EVER KNOWN.

NEVER TOUCH THE RECORD-- HOLD IT LIKE THIS!

STILL HAS FEARS OF SCRATCHING HIS LPS

MAYBE BECAUSE OF THIS I WAS A PASSIVE LISTENER. I LIKED MUSIC, HAD SONGS I LOVED--

03:45

--AND EVEN DREAMED OF MARRYING CERTAIN LEAD SINGERS--

DON'T WANT TO ARGUE, I DON'T WANT TO HEAR ABOUT OF FOOD YOU HATE-- YOU DON'T WANT TO DEBATE-- WHAT WON'T I KIND GET DESSERT 'TILL YOU CLEAN OFF YOUR PLATE-- SO EAT IT!

WHAM!

SIMON LE BON

USING MY DAD'S LP OF SGT. PEPPER'S LONELY HEARTS CLUB BAND AS A DRAWING BOARD

--BUT NONE OF IT WAS MINE.

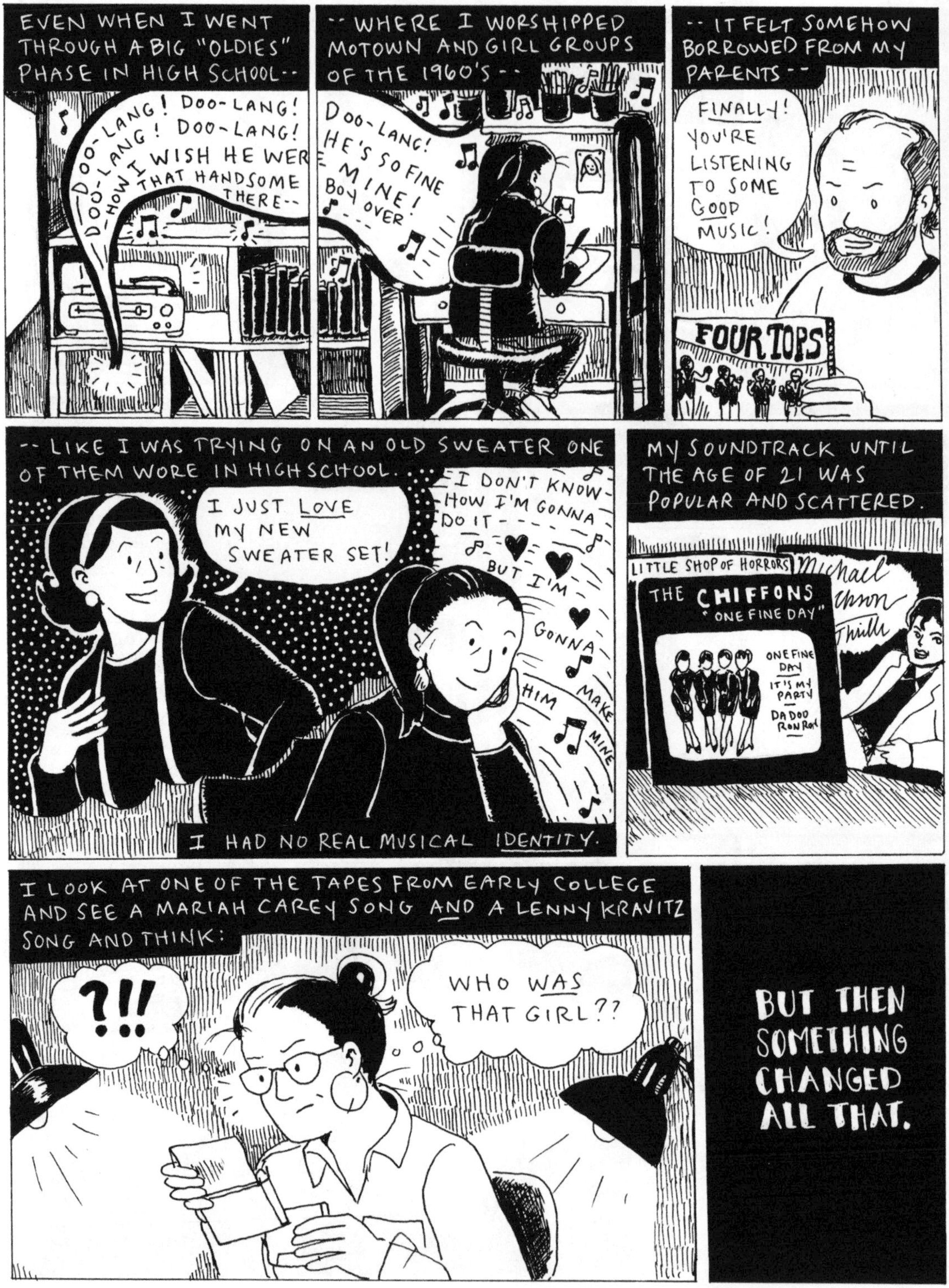
EVEN WHEN I WENT THROUGH A BIG "OLDIES" PHASE IN HIGH SCHOOL--
DOO-LANG! DOO-LANG! DOO-LANG! DOO-LANG! DOO-LANG! HOW I WISH HE WERE--HOW THAT HANDSOME BOY OVER THERE--
--WHERE I WORSHIPPED MOTOWN AND GIRL GROUPS OF THE 1960'S--
DOO-LANG! HE'S SO FINE MINE!
--IT FELT SOMEHOW BORROWED FROM MY PARENTS--
FINALLY! YOU'RE LISTENING TO SOME GOOD MUSIC!
FOUR TOPS
--LIKE I WAS TRYING ON AN OLD SWEATER ONE OF THEM WORE IN HIGH SCHOOL.
I JUST LOVE MY NEW SWEATER SET!
I DON'T KNOW HOW I'M GONNA DO IT--
BUT I'M GONNA MAKE HIM MINE
I HAD NO REAL MUSICAL IDENTITY.
MY SOUNDTRACK UNTIL THE AGE OF 21 WAS POPULAR AND SCATTERED.
LITTLE SHOP OF HORRORS
Michael Jackson Thriller
THE CHIFFONS "ONE FINE DAY"
ONE FINE DAY
IT'S MY PARTY
DA DOO RON RON
I LOOK AT ONE OF THE TAPES FROM EARLY COLLEGE AND SEE A MARIAH CAREY SONG AND A LENNY KRAVITZ SONG AND THINK:
?!!
WHO WAS THAT GIRL??
BUT THEN SOMETHING CHANGED ALL THAT.

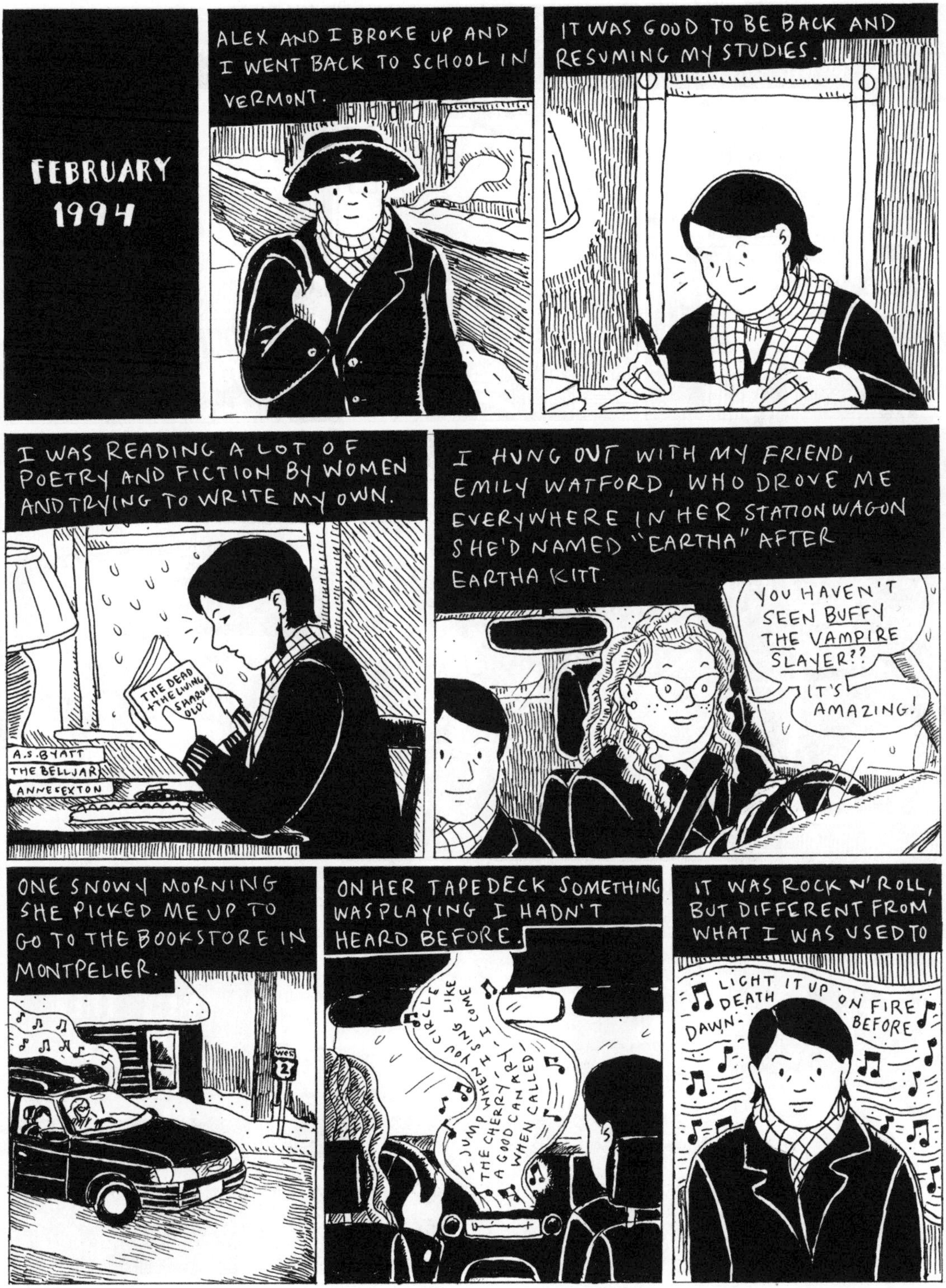
FEBRUARY 1994
ALEX AND I BROKE UP AND I WENT BACK TO SCHOOL IN VERMONT.
IT WAS GOOD TO BE BACK AND RESUMING MY STUDIES.
I WAS READING A LOT OF POETRY AND FICTION BY WOMEN AND TRYING TO WRITE MY OWN.
THE DEAD + THE LIVING SHARON OLDS
A.S. BYATT
THE BELL JAR
ANNE SEXTON
I HUNG OUT WITH MY FRIEND, EMILY WATFORD, WHO DROVE ME EVERYWHERE IN HER STATION WAGON SHE'D NAMED "EARTHA" AFTER EARTHA KITT.
YOU HAVEN'T SEEN BUFFY THE VAMPIRE SLAYER??
IT'S AMAZING!
ONE SNOWY MORNING SHE PICKED ME UP TO GO TO THE BOOKSTORE IN MONTPELIER.
WEST 2
ON HER TAPEDECK SOMETHING WAS PLAYING I HADN'T HEARD BEFORE.
LIKE I COME
YOU CIRCLE I SING
I JUMP WHEN THE CHERRY
A GOOD CAN
WHEN CALLED
IT WAS ROCK N' ROLL, BUT DIFFERENT FROM WHAT I WAS USED TO
LIGHT IT UP ON FIRE
DEATH
DAWN
BEFORE

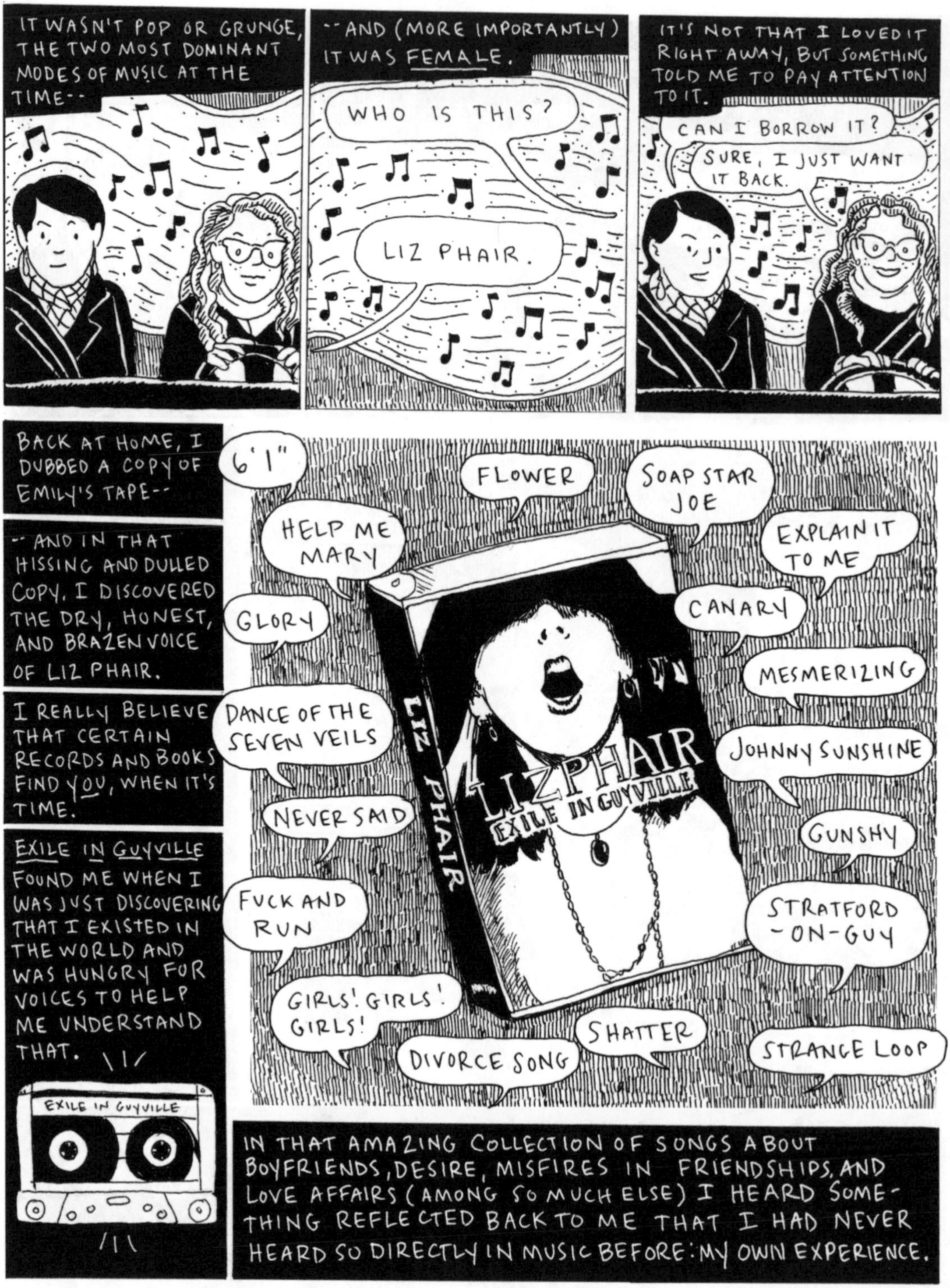

IT WASN'T POP OR GRUNGE, THE TWO MOST DOMINANT MODES OF MUSIC AT THE TIME--
--AND (MORE IMPORTANTLY) IT WAS FEMALE.
WHO IS THIS?
LIZ PHAIR.
IT'S NOT THAT I LOVED IT RIGHT AWAY, BUT SOMETHING TOLD ME TO PAY ATTENTION TO IT.
CAN I BORROW IT?
SURE, I JUST WANT IT BACK.
BACK AT HOME, I DUBBED A COPY OF EMILY'S TAPE--
--AND IN THAT HISSING AND DULLED COPY, I DISCOVERED THE DRY, HONEST, AND BRAZEN VOICE OF LIZ PHAIR.
I REALLY BELIEVE THAT CERTAIN RECORDS AND BOOKS FIND YOU, WHEN IT'S TIME.
EXILE IN GUYVILLE FOUND ME WHEN I WAS JUST DISCOVERING THAT I EXISTED IN THE WORLD AND WAS HUNGRY FOR VOICES TO HELP ME UNDERSTAND THAT.
EXILE IN GUYVILLE
6'1"
FLOWER
SOAP STAR JOE
HELP ME MARY
EXPLAIN IT TO ME
GLORY
CANARY
MESMERIZING
DANCE OF THE SEVEN VEILS
JOHNNY SUNSHINE
NEVER SAID
GUNSHY
FUCK AND RUN
STRATFORD-ON-GUY
GIRLS! GIRLS! GIRLS!
SHATTER
DIVORCE SONG
STRANGE LOOP
LIZ PHAIR
LIZ PHAIR EXILE IN GUYVILLE
IN THAT AMAZING COLLECTION OF SONGS ABOUT BOYFRIENDS, DESIRE, MISFIRES IN FRIENDSHIPS, AND LOVE AFFAIRS (AMONG SO MUCH ELSE) I HEARD SOMETHING REFLECTED BACK TO ME THAT I HAD NEVER HEARD SO DIRECTLY IN MUSIC BEFORE: MY OWN EXPERIENCE.

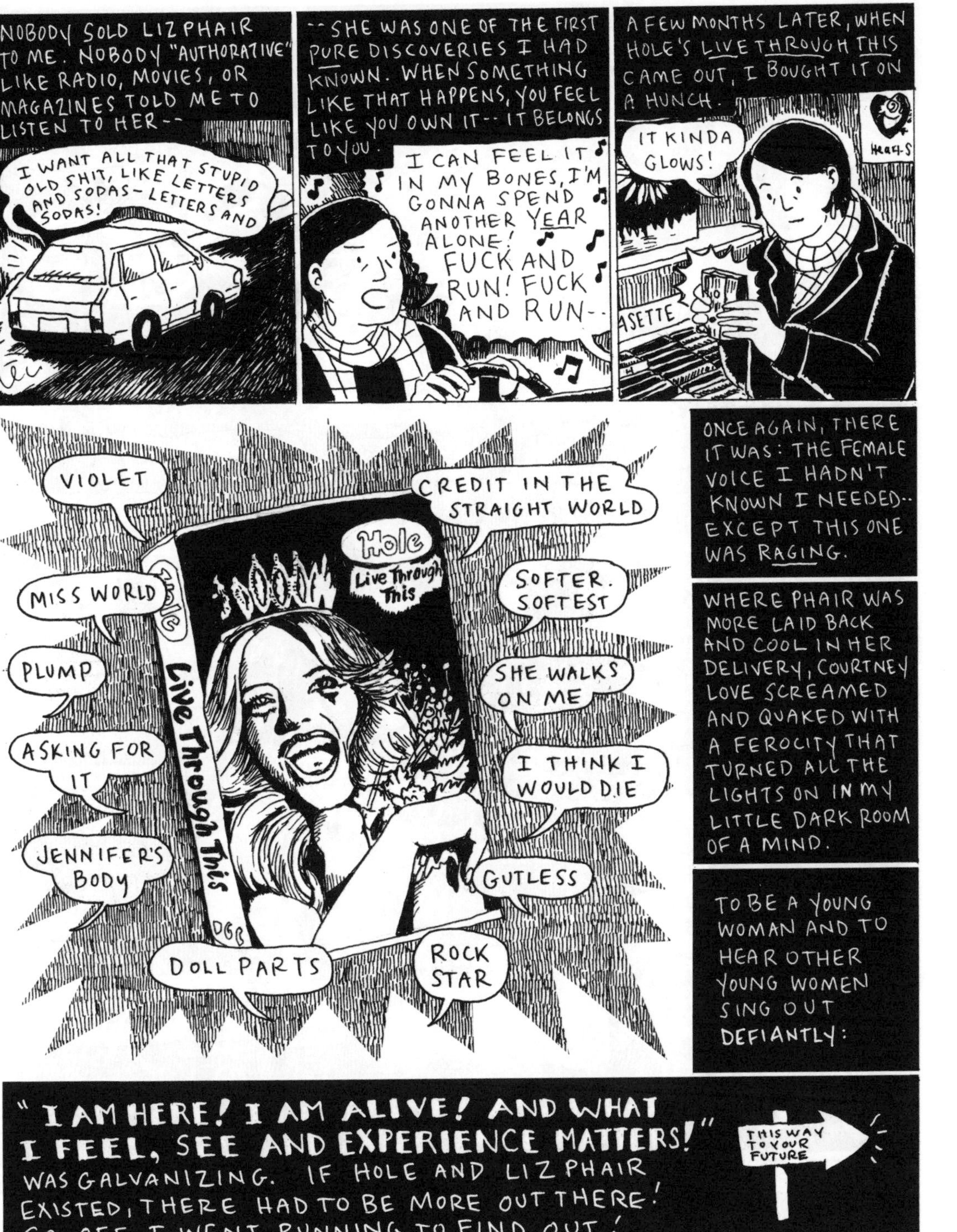
NOBODY SOLD LIZ PHAIR TO ME. NOBODY "AUTHORATIVE" LIKE RADIO, MOVIES, OR MAGAZINES TOLD ME TO LISTEN TO HER--
I WANT ALL THAT STUPID OLD SHIT, LIKE LETTERS AND SODAS- LETTERS AND SODAS!
--SHE WAS ONE OF THE FIRST PURE DISCOVERIES I HAD KNOWN. WHEN SOMETHING LIKE THAT HAPPENS, YOU FEEL LIKE YOU OWN IT-- IT BELONGS TO YOU.
I CAN FEEL IT IN MY BONES, I'M GONNA SPEND ANOTHER YEAR ALONE! FUCK AND RUN! FUCK AND RUN--
A FEW MONTHS LATER, WHEN HOLE'S LIVE THROUGH THIS CAME OUT, I BOUGHT IT ON A HUNCH.
IT KINDA GLOWS!
ASETTE
VIOLET
CREDIT IN THE STRAIGHT WORLD
Hole
Live Through This
MISS WORLD
SOFTER. SOFTEST
PLUMP
SHE WALKS ON ME
ASKING FOR IT
I THINK I WOULD DIE
JENNIFER'S BODY
GUTLESS
DOLL PARTS
ROCK STAR
ONCE AGAIN, THERE IT WAS: THE FEMALE VOICE I HADN'T KNOWN I NEEDED.. EXCEPT THIS ONE WAS RAGING.
WHERE PHAIR WAS MORE LAID BACK AND COOL IN HER DELIVERY, COURTNEY LOVE SCREAMED AND QUAKED WITH A FEROCITY THAT TURNED ALL THE LIGHTS ON IN MY LITTLE DARK ROOM OF A MIND.
TO BE A YOUNG WOMAN AND TO HEAR OTHER YOUNG WOMEN SING OUT DEFIANTLY:
"I AM HERE! I AM ALIVE! AND WHAT I FEEL, SEE AND EXPERIENCE MATTERS!" WAS GALVANIZING. IF HOLE AND LIZ PHAIR EXISTED, THERE HAD TO BE MORE OUT THERE! SO OFF I WENT RUNNING TO FIND OUT!
THIS WAY TO YOUR FUTURE

THERE WAS NO INTERNET THEN, SO ALL MY DISCOVERIES

HAPPENED

THROUGH CONVERSATIONS, SCOURING MAGAZINES AND

RECORD STORES, RAIDING MY COLLEGE RADIO STATION'S LIBRARY,

AND FRIENDS' AND ACQUAINTANCES' CD

COLLECTIONS. I MADE TAPES OF

EVERYTHING

AND BASKED IN THE VARIED SOUNDS OF GIRLS AND GUITARS.

LIZ PHAIR
HOLE
BABES IN TOYLAND
BIKINI KILL
SEVEN YEAR BITCH
THROWING MUSES
KRISTIN HERSH
L7
BELLY
THE BREEDERS
ELASTICA
PJ HARVEY
PATTI SMITH
SHONEN KNIFE
JOAN JETT
ALANIS MORISSETTE
LISA LOEB
JILL SOBULE
ANI DIFRANCO
BRATMOBILE
THE MUFFS
SLEATER-KINNEY
TIGER TRAP
PORTISHEAD
SONIC YOUTH
MARY LOU LORD
JEN TRYNIN
LUSCIOUS JACKSON
ANNIE LENOX
JULIANA HATFIELD
MICHELLE SHOCKED

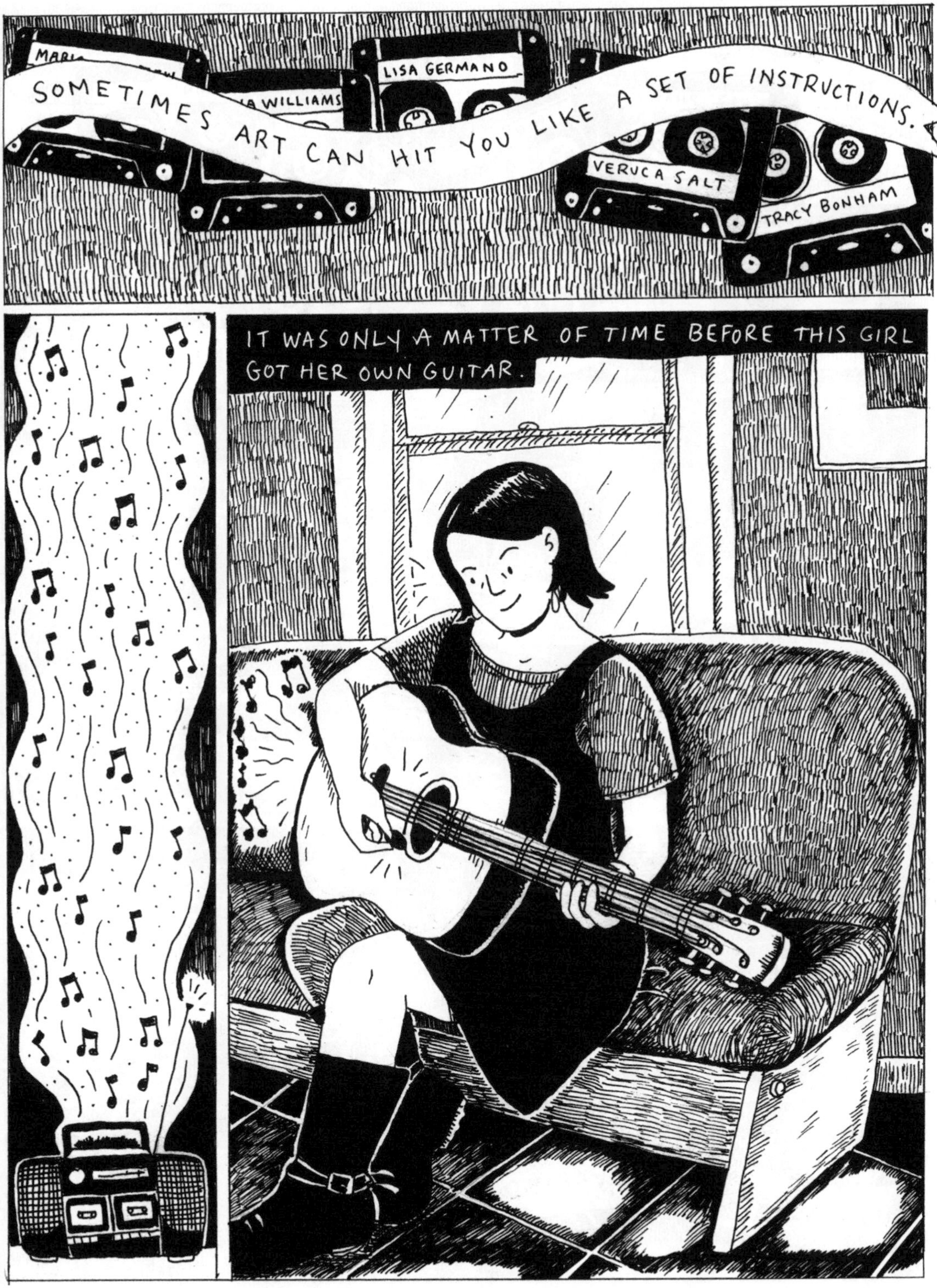
LISA GERMANO
SOMETIMES ART CAN HIT YOU LIKE A SET OF INSTRUCTIONS.
VERUCA SALT
TRACY BONHAM
IT WAS ONLY A MATTER OF TIME BEFORE THIS GIRL GOT HER OWN GUITAR.

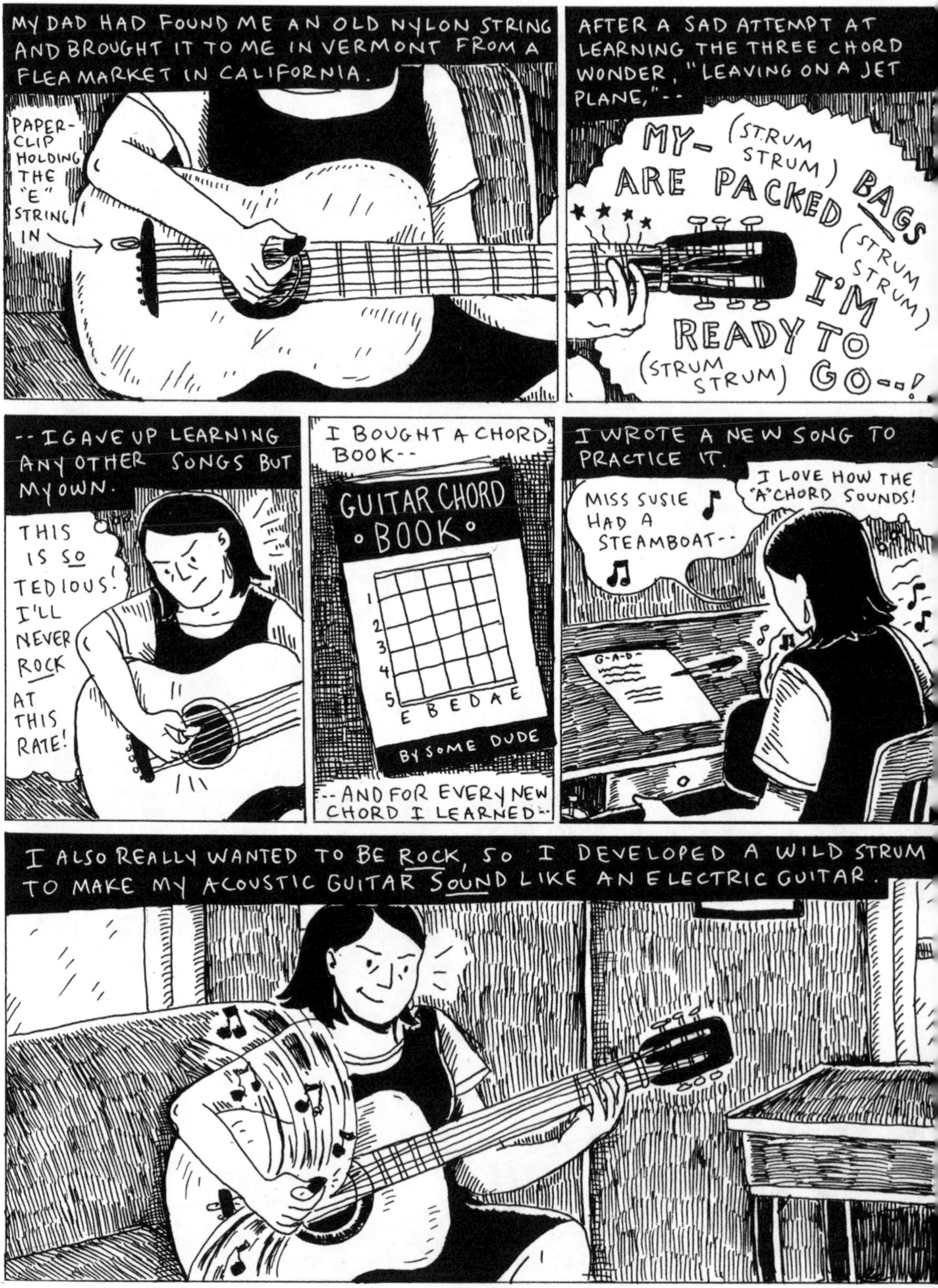
MY DAD HAD FOUND ME AN OLD NYLON STRING AND BROUGHT IT TO ME IN VERMONT FROM A FLEA MARKET IN CALIFORNIA.
PAPER-CLIP HOLDING THE "E" STRING IN
AFTER A SAD ATTEMPT AT LEARNING THE THREE CHORD WONDER, "LEAVING ON A JET PLANE,"--
MY- (STRUM STRUM) BAGS ARE PACKED (STRUM STRUM) I'M READY TO (STRUM STRUM) GO--!
--I GAVE UP LEARNING ANY OTHER SONGS BUT MY OWN.
THIS IS SO TEDIOUS! I'LL NEVER ROCK AT THIS RATE!
I BOUGHT A CHORD BOOK--
GUITAR CHORD BOOK
1
2
3
4
5
E B E D A E
BY SOME DUDE
--AND FOR EVERY NEW CHORD I LEARNED--
I WROTE A NEW SONG TO PRACTICE IT.
MISS SUSIE HAD A STEAMBOAT--
I LOVE HOW THE "A" CHORD SOUNDS!
G-A-D-
I ALSO REALLY WANTED TO BE ROCK, SO I DEVELOPED A WILD STRUM TO MAKE MY ACOUSTIC GUITAR SOUND LIKE AN ELECTRIC GUITAR.

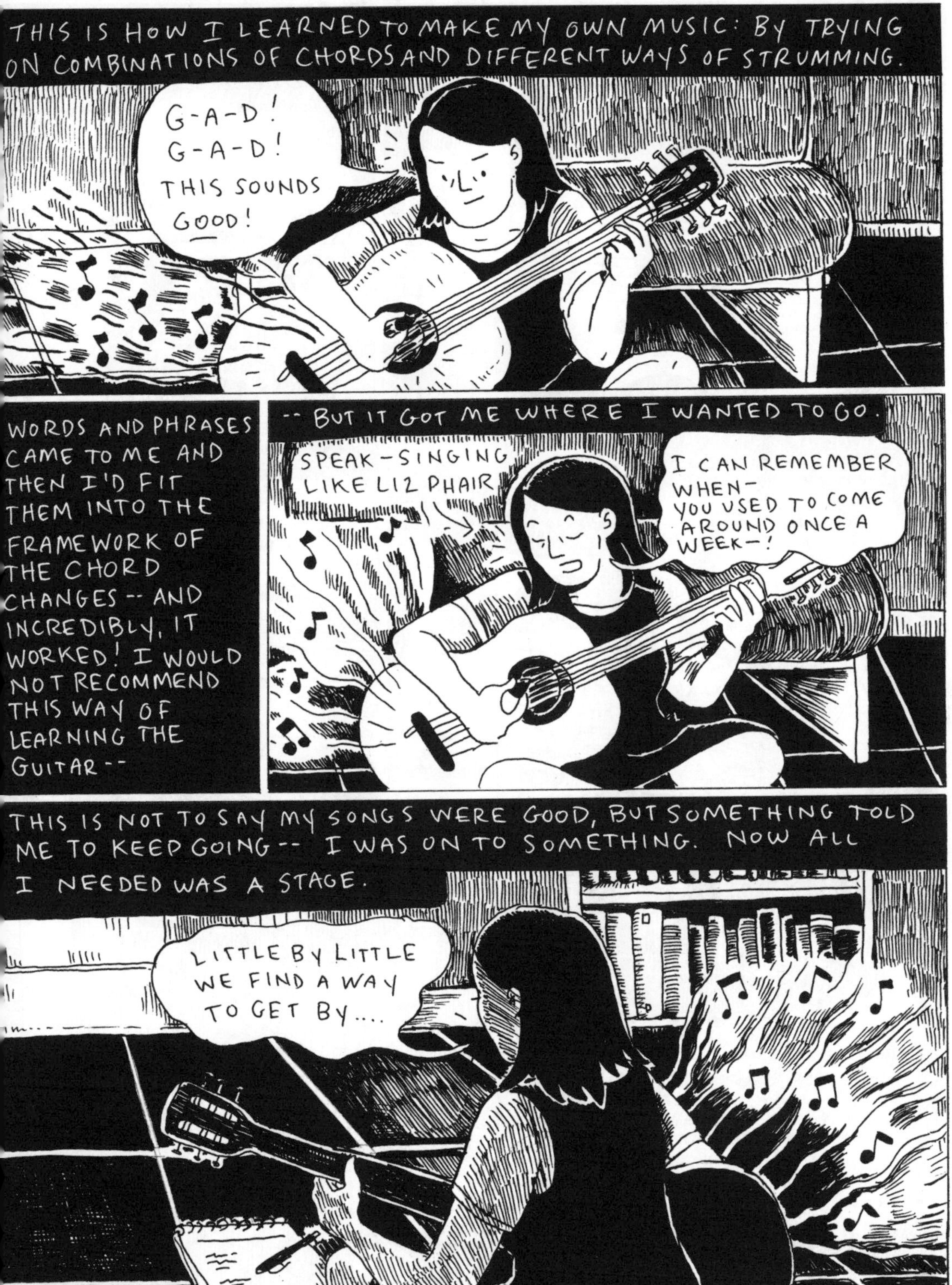
THIS IS HOW I LEARNED TO MAKE MY OWN MUSIC: BY TRYING ON COMBINATIONS OF CHORDS AND DIFFERENT WAYS OF STRUMMING.
G-A-D! G-A-D! THIS SOUNDS GOOD!
WORDS AND PHRASES CAME TO ME AND THEN I'D FIT THEM INTO THE FRAMEWORK OF THE CHORD CHANGES -- AND INCREDIBLY, IT WORKED! I WOULD NOT RECOMMEND THIS WAY OF LEARNING THE GUITAR --
-- BUT IT GOT ME WHERE I WANTED TO GO.
SPEAK-SINGING LIKE LIZ PHAIR
I CAN REMEMBER WHEN- YOU USED TO COME AROUND ONCE A WEEK-!
THIS IS NOT TO SAY MY SONGS WERE GOOD, BUT SOMETHING TOLD ME TO KEEP GOING -- I WAS ON TO SOMETHING. NOW ALL I NEEDED WAS A STAGE.
LITTLE BY LITTLE WE FIND A WAY TO GET BY....

SELECTED SOUNDTRACK

A C'MON BILLY - PJ HARVEY • STUCK HERE AGAIN - L7 • DO YOU LOVE ME NOW? - THE BREEDERS • STRATFORD-ON-GUY - LIZ PHAIR • ZOMBIE - THE CRANBERRIES • WON'T TELL - BABES IN TOYLAND • SILENT ALL THESE YEARS - TORI AMOS • WORKING FOR THE MAN - PJ HARVEY • TUNIC (SONG FOR KAREN) - SONIC YOUTH • VIOLET - HOLE • NO ALOHA - THE BREEDERS • MAY QUEEN - LIZ PHAIR

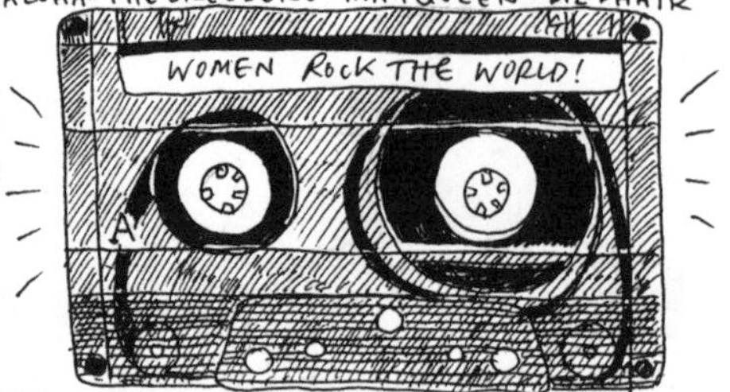
WOMEN ROCK THE WORLD!
A

B RAGWEED - BABES IN TOYLAND • SEND HIS LOVE TO ME - PJ HARVEY • THE LETTER - KRISTIN HERSH • MY SECRET REASON - LISA GERMANO • REDANDO BEACH - PATTI SMITH • ON TOP OF THE WORLD - SHONEN KNIFE • SURF COWBOY - THROWING MUSES • AGONY - THE MUFFS • ANNIE - ELASTICA • LEGS - PJ HARVEY • ROMEO AND JULIET - INDIGO GIRLS • KOOL THING - SONIC YOUTH

A NOT TOO SOON - THROWING MUSES • STUTTER - ELASTICA • IT'S A FIRE - PORTISHEAD • HAPPINESS IS A WARM GUN - THE BREEDERS • YOU OUGHTA KNOW - ALANIS MORISETTE • SHY - ANI DIFRANCO • SAN ANDREAS FAULT - NATALIE MERCHANT • RIGHT HAND MAN - JOAN OSBORNE • INSIDE - PATTI ROTHBERG • SUPPORT SYSTEM - LIZ PHAIR • MISSED - PJ HARVEY • ANCHORAGE - MICHELLE SHOCKED • ANDRES - L7

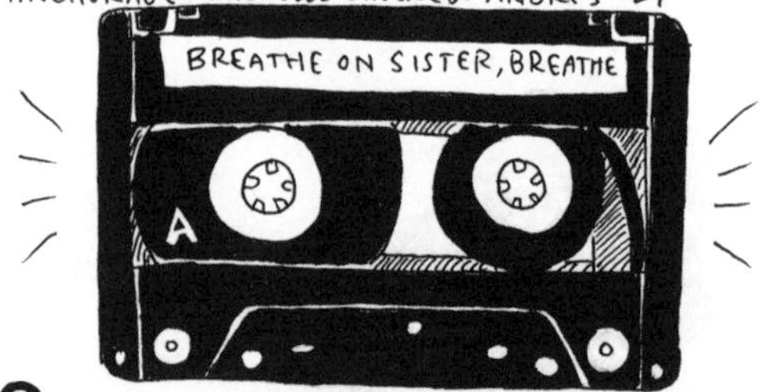
BREATHE ON SISTER, BREATHE
A

B BITTER - JILL SOBULE • BETTER THAN NOTHING - JEN TRYNIN • SLEEP TO DREAM - FIONA APPLE • MOTHER, MOTHER - TRACY BONHAM • PLANTS + RAGS - PJ HARVEY • WHAT YOU'VE DONE - THE MUFFS • OUT OF RANGE - ANI DIFRANCO • THE HARD WAY - MICHELLE SCHOCKED • PENSACOLA - JOAN OSBORNE • 6'1" - LIZ PHAIR • SMILE - ELASTICA • HAPPIER - JEN TRYNIN • FAREWELL REELE - PATTI SMITH

A SHE SAID - BRATMOBILE • COOL SCHMOOL - BRATMOBILE • MY SECRET - HEAVENS TO BETSY • I WANNA BE YOUR JOEY RAMONE • GO WAILING AGENTS - MIRANDA SEX GARDEN • 30-30 VISION - SLANT 6 • SUMMER - AUTOCLAVE • IMAGINATION - HAIL • TAKING BACK STAIRS - MECCA NORMAL • I PLANTED A VIOLET - MARTA SEBESTYÉN • RESUMÉ - BABE THE BLUE OX • LAMP - SUDDENLY TAMMY!

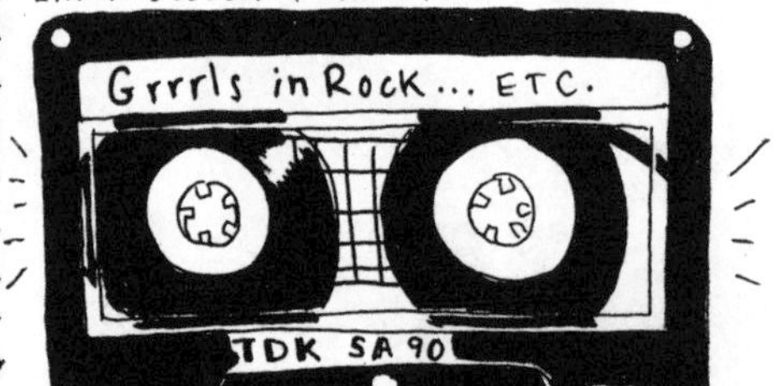
Grrrls in Rock... ETC.
TDK SA 90

B FUCK THE RULES - KICKING GIANT • QUEENIE - BRATMOBILE • CANDY - BIKINI KILL • STUMBLING BLOCK - UNNOUND • BOY - OKLAHOMA SCRAMBLE • ROMAN HOLIDAY - LUMIHOOPS • CHIA PET - CANANES • OUTA MONEY - CALAMITY JANE • 1 MORE SAFE - MECCA NORMAL • HOLLOWED OUT LOGS - BURL • SPRAY - COURTNEY LOVE • SECRET GOLDFISH - CRAYON • YOU NEED A FRIEND - MEMPHIS MINNIE • CIRCLE - VERSUS

A PRESSURE DROP - THE CLASH • COME ON EILEEN - DEXY'S MIDNIGHT RUNNER • MERRY XMAS, MR. JONES - THE NIELDS • DOLL PARTS - HOLE • FUCK AND RUN - LIZ PHAIR • EAT THE MUSIC - KATE BUSH • PAST THE MISSION - TORI AMOS • SITTING HERE IN LIMBO - JIMMY CLIFF • DANCE OF THE SEVEN VEILS - LIZ PHAIR • WHEN YOU COME BACK - WORLD PARTY • WHEN U WERE MINE - PRINCE

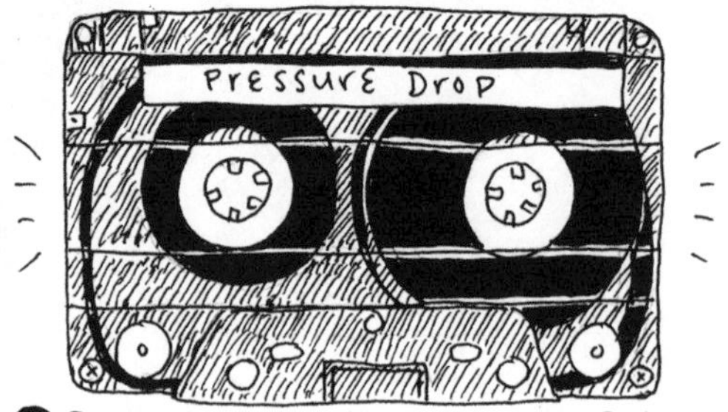
Pressure Drop

B PRESSURE DROP - JIMMY CLIFF • IF - JANET JACKSON • ROCKSTAR - HOLE • 6'1" - LIZ PHAIR • WHAT'S GOOD - LOU REED • FADE INTO YOU - MAZZY STAR • RASPBERRY BERET - PRINCE • YOU SEXY THING - THE HOT CHOCOLATES • CARAVAN - VAN MORRISON • PAINLESS - BABY ANIMALS • LET'S GO CRAZY - PRINCE

PART THREE

JUST LIKE HEAVEN

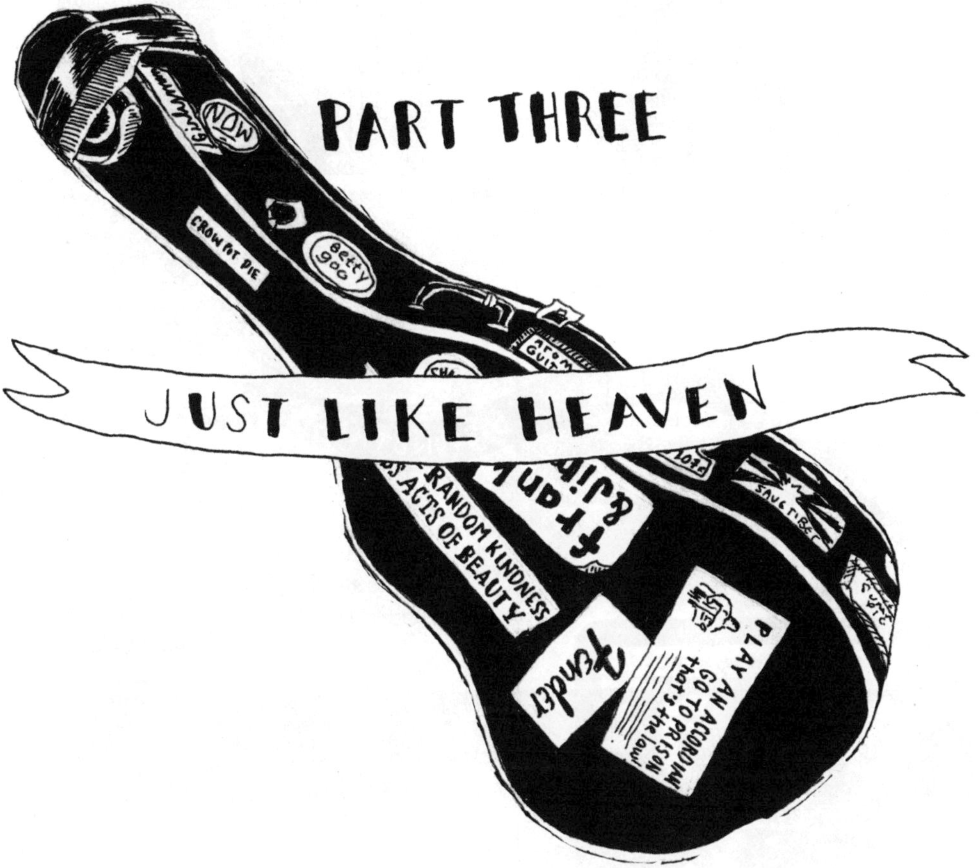
NOW
betty goo
RANDOM KINDNESS
ACTS OF BEAUTY
fender
PLAY AN ACCORDIAN
GO TO PRISON
that's the law!

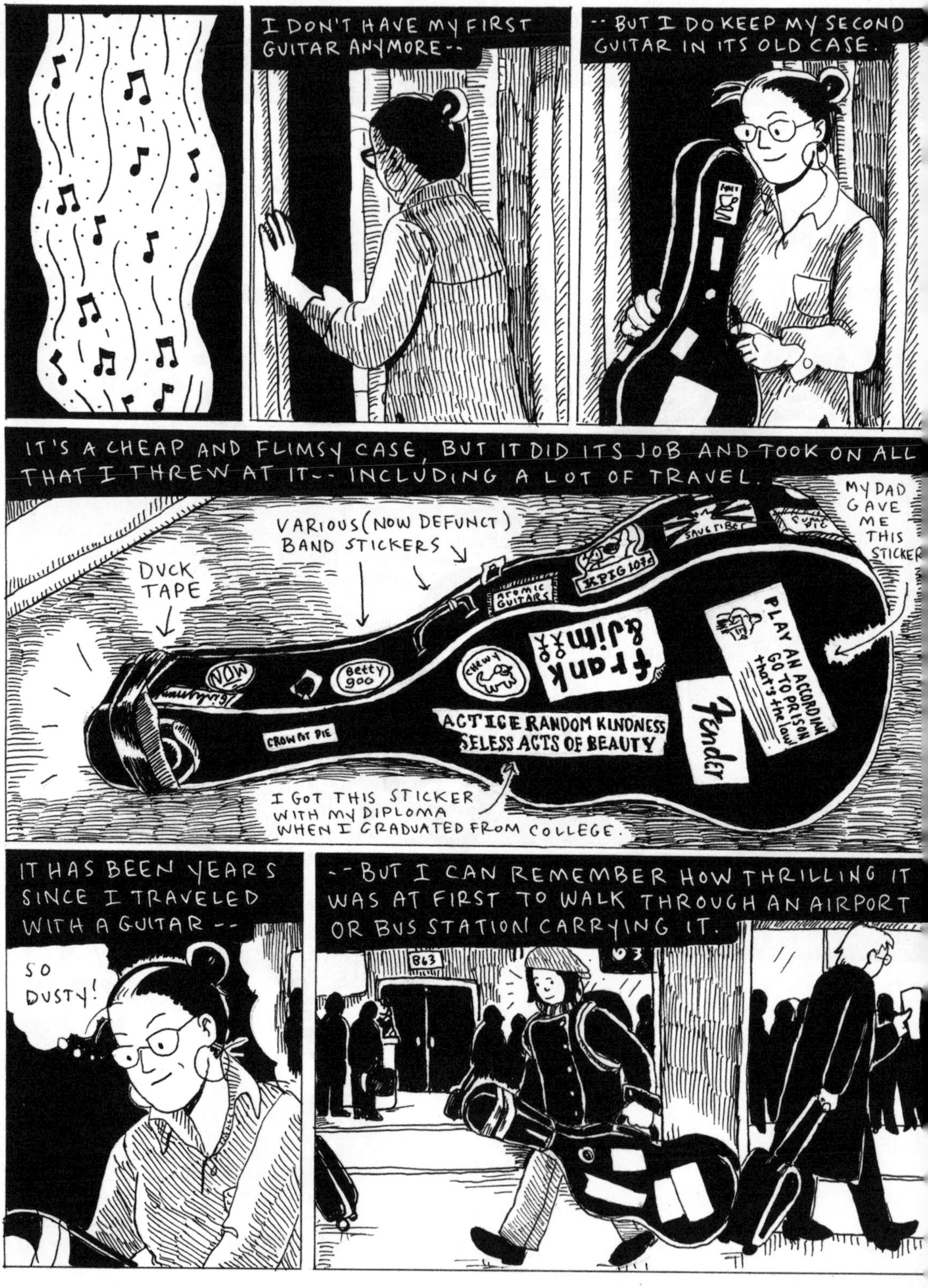
I DON'T HAVE MY FIRST GUITAR ANYMORE--
--BUT I DO KEEP MY SECOND GUITAR IN ITS OLD CASE.
IT'S A CHEAP AND FLIMSY CASE, BUT IT DID ITS JOB AND TOOK ON ALL THAT I THREW AT IT-- INCLUDING A LOT OF TRAVEL.
DUCK TAPE
VARIOUS (NOW DEFUNCT) BAND STICKERS
MY DAD GAVE ME THIS STICKER
NOW
betty goo
CHEWY
CROW POT PIE
ATOMIC GUITARS
KPIG 107.5
frank & jim
ACT ICE RANDOM KINDNESS
SELESS ACTS OF BEAUTY
Fender
PLAY AN ACCORDIAN GO TO PRISON that's the law
I GOT THIS STICKER WITH MY DIPLOMA WHEN I GRADUATED FROM COLLEGE.
IT HAS BEEN YEARS SINCE I TRAVELED WITH A GUITAR--
SO DUSTY!
--BUT I CAN REMEMBER HOW THRILLING IT WAS AT FIRST TO WALK THROUGH AN AIRPORT OR BUS STATION CARRYING IT.
B63

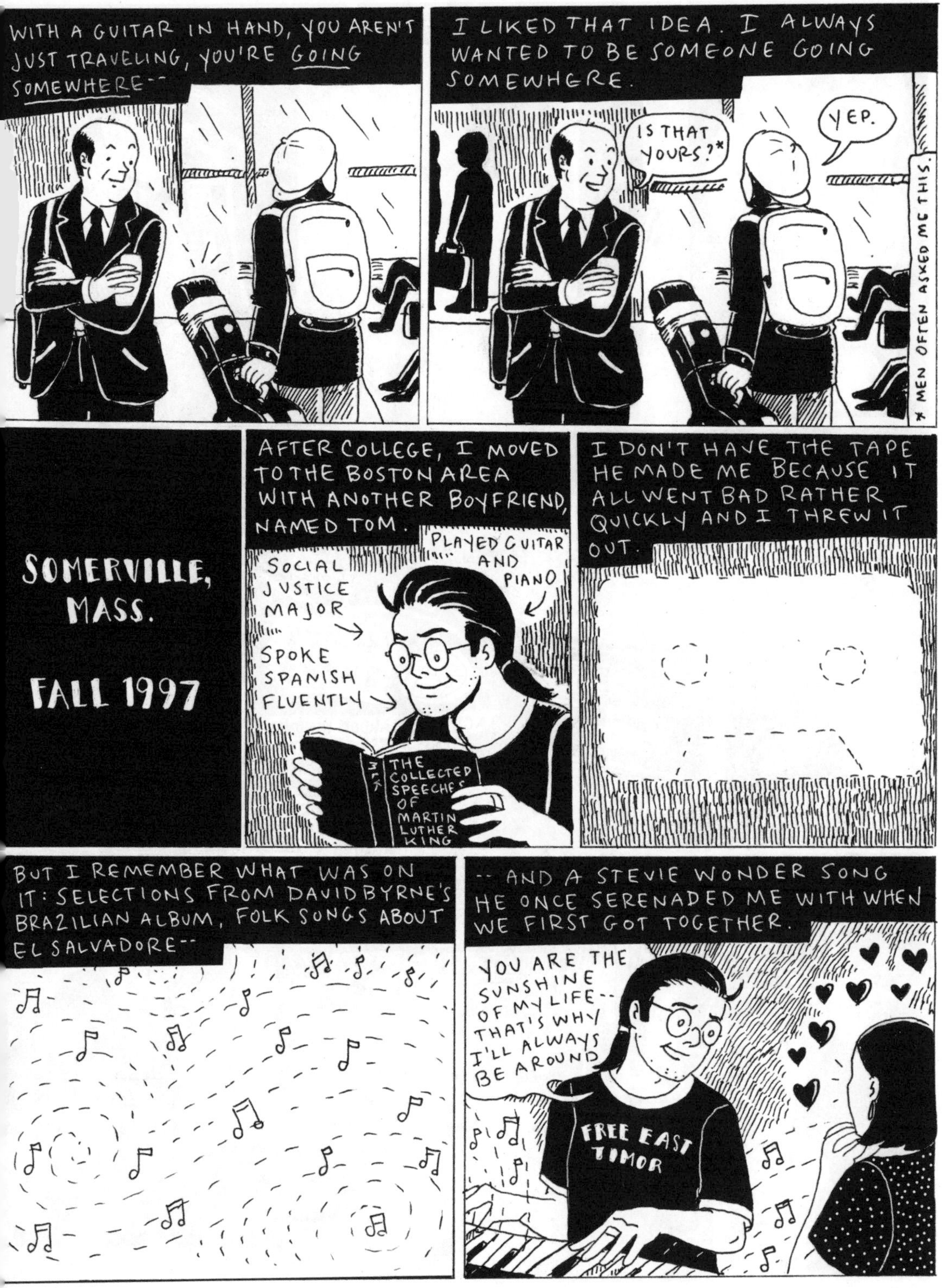
WITH A GUITAR IN HAND, YOU AREN'T JUST TRAVELING, YOU'RE GOING SOMEWHERE--
I LIKED THAT IDEA. I ALWAYS WANTED TO BE SOMEONE GOING SOMEWHGRE.
IS THAT YOURS?*
YEP.
* MEN OFTEN ASKED ME THIS.
SOMERVILLE, MASS.
FALL 1997
AFTER COLLEGE, I MOVED TO THE BOSTON AREA WITH ANOTHER BOYFRIEND, NAMED TOM.
SOCIAL JUSTICE MAJOR
PLAYED GUITAR AND PIANO
SPOKE SPANISH FLUENTLY
THE COLLECTED SPEECHES OF MARTIN LUTHER KING
I DON'T HAVE THE TAPE HE MADE ME BECAUSE IT ALL WENT BAD RATHER QUICKLY AND I THREW IT OUT.
BUT I REMEMBER WHAT WAS ON IT: SELECTIONS FROM DAVID BYRNE'S BRAZILIAN ALBUM, FOLK SONGS ABOUT EL SALVADORE--
-- AND A STEVIE WONDER SONG HE ONCE SERENADED ME WITH WHEN WE FIRST GOT TOGETHER.
YOU ARE THE SUNSHINE OF MY LIFE-- THAT'S WHY I'LL ALWAYS BE AROUND
FREE EAST TIMOR

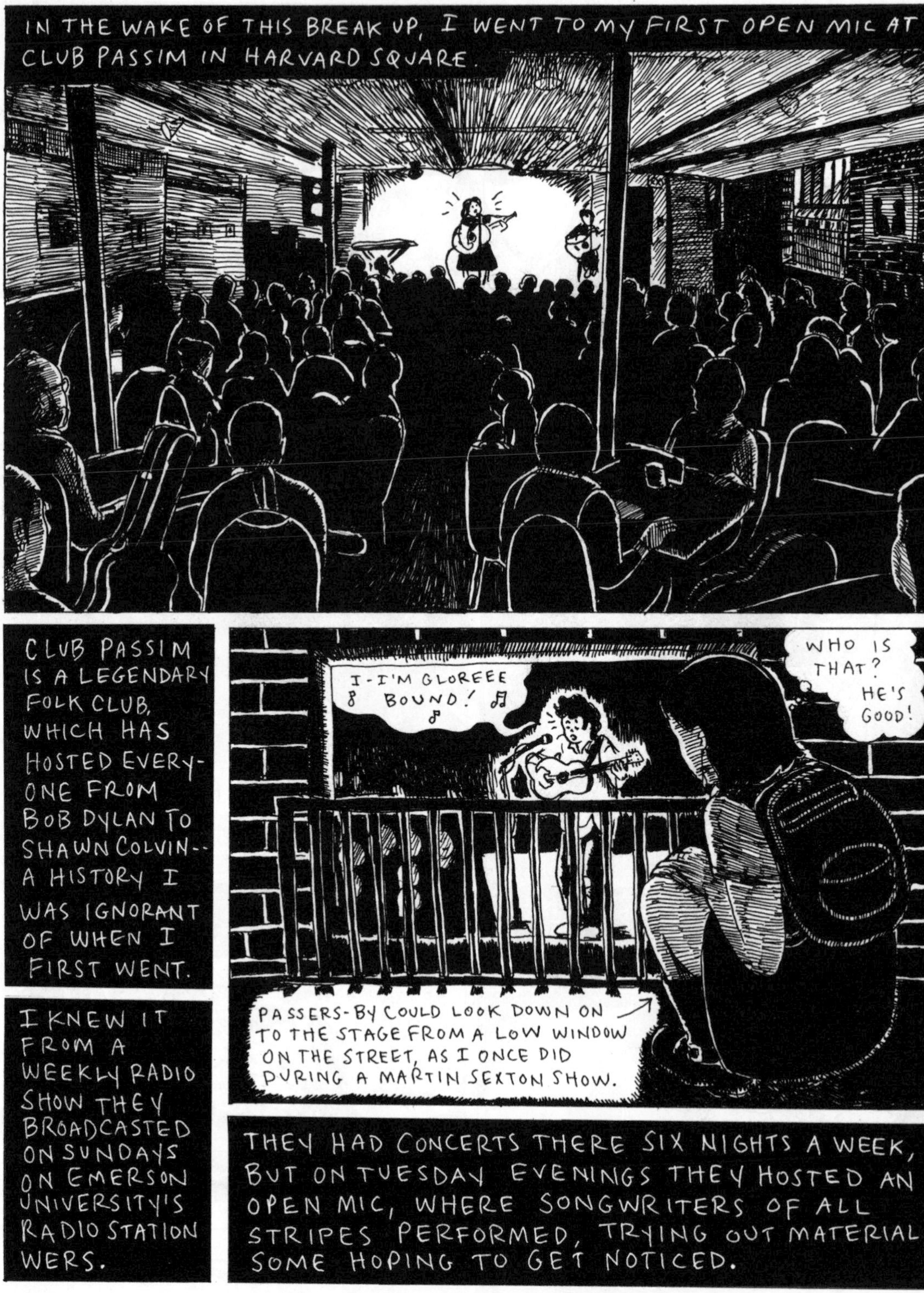
IN THE WAKE OF THIS BREAK UP, I WENT TO MY FIRST OPEN MIC AT CLUB PASSIM IN HARVARD SQUARE.
CLUB PASSIM IS A LEGENDARY FOLK CLUB, WHICH HAS HOSTED EVERYONE FROM BOB DYLAN TO SHAWN COLVIN-- A HISTORY I WAS IGNORANT OF WHEN I FIRST WENT.
I-I'M GLOREEE BOUND!
WHO IS THAT? HE'S GOOD!
PASSERS-BY COULD LOOK DOWN ON TO THE STAGE FROM A LOW WINDOW ON THE STREET, AS I ONCE DID DURING A MARTIN SEXTON SHOW.
I KNEW IT FROM A WEEKLY RADIO SHOW THEY BROADCASTED ON SUNDAYS ON EMERSON UNIVERSITY'S RADIO STATION WERS.
THEY HAD CONCERTS THERE SIX NIGHTS A WEEK, BUT ON TUESDAY EVENINGS THEY HOSTED AN OPEN MIC, WHERE SONGWRITERS OF ALL STRIPES PERFORMED, TRYING OUT MATERIAL, SOME HOPING TO GET NOTICED.

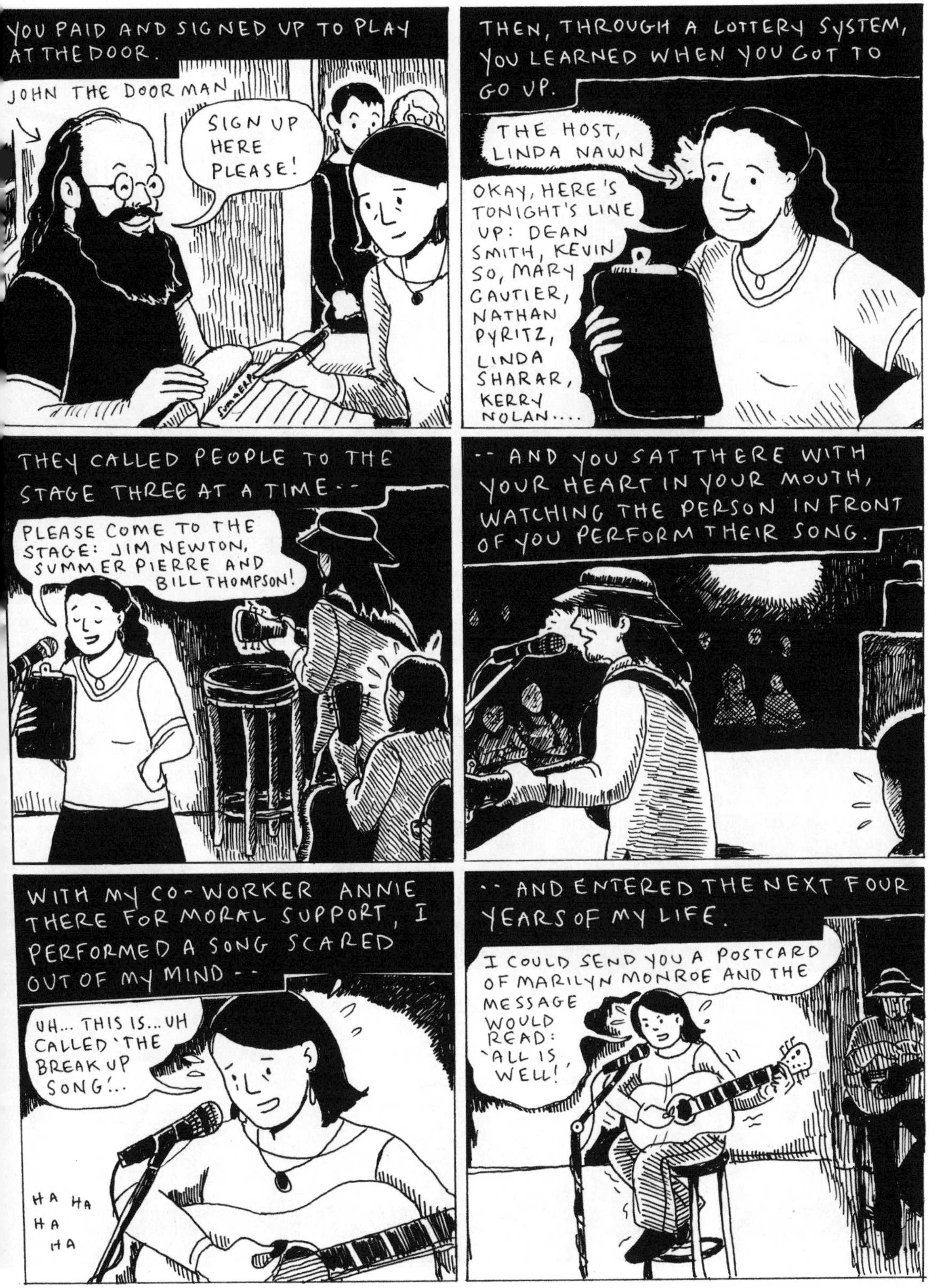
YOU PAID AND SIGNED UP TO PLAY AT THE DOOR.
JOHN THE DOORMAN
SIGN UP HERE PLEASE!
SUMMER P.
THEN, THROUGH A LOTTERY SYSTEM, YOU LEARNED WHEN YOU GOT TO GO UP.
THE HOST, LINDA NAWN
OKAY, HERE'S TONIGHT'S LINE UP: DEAN SMITH, KEVIN SO, MARY GAUTIER, NATHAN PYRITZ, LINDA SHARAR, KERRY NOLAN....
THEY CALLED PEOPLE TO THE STAGE THREE AT A TIME--
PLEASE COME TO THE STAGE: JIM NEWTON, SUMMER PIERRE AND BILL THOMPSON!
-- AND YOU SAT THERE WITH YOUR HEART IN YOUR MOUTH, WATCHING THE PERSON IN FRONT OF YOU PERFORM THEIR SONG.
WITH MY CO-WORKER ANNIE THERE FOR MORAL SUPPORT, I PERFORMED A SONG SCARED OUT OF MY MIND --
UH... THIS IS... UH CALLED 'THE BREAK UP SONG'...
HA HA HA HA
-- AND ENTERED THE NEXT FOUR YEARS OF MY LIFE.
I COULD SEND YOU A POSTCARD OF MARILYN MONROE AND THE MESSAGE WOULD READ: 'ALL IS WELL!'

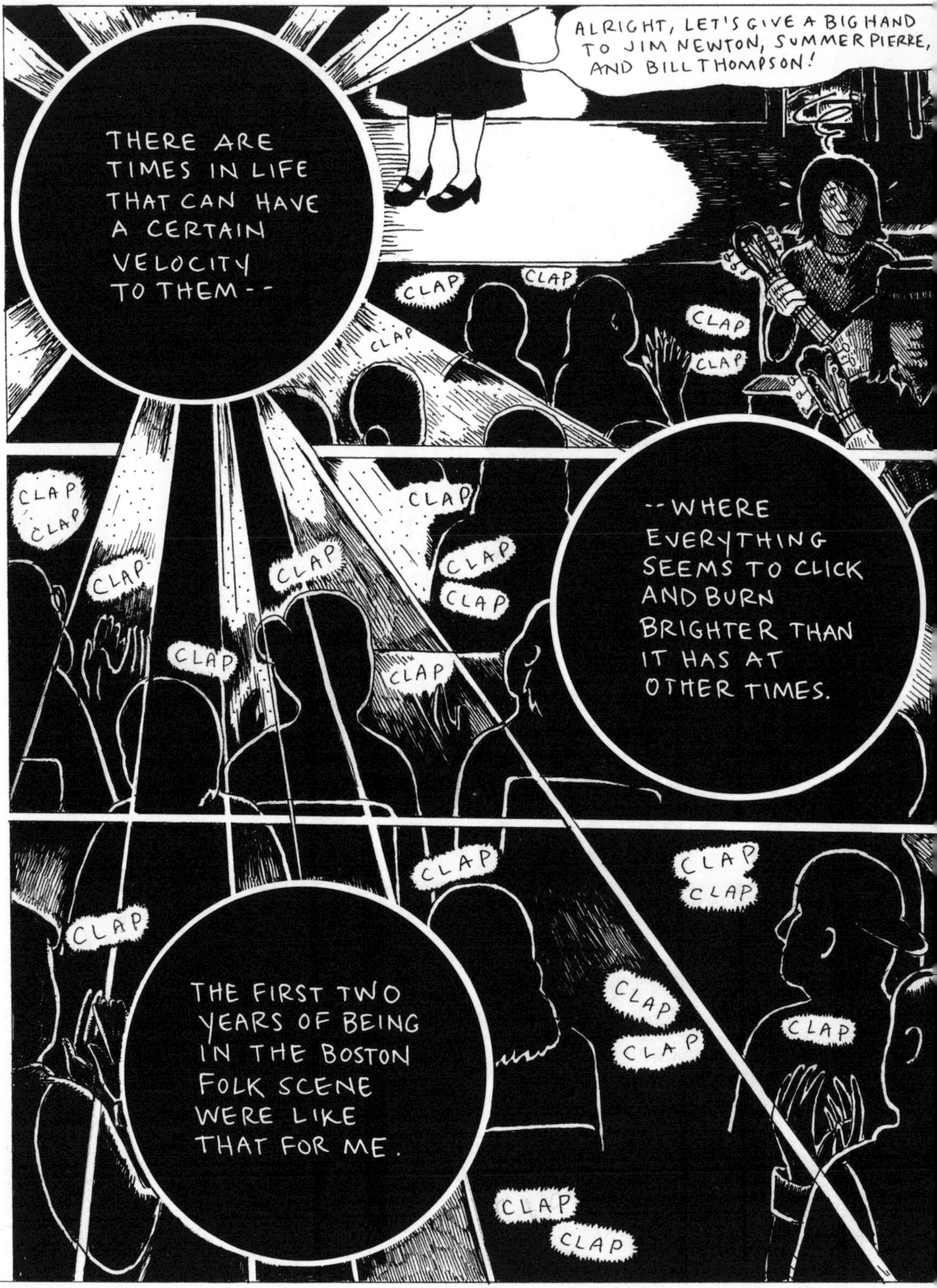
ALRIGHT, LET'S GIVE A BIG HAND TO JIM NEWTON, SUMMER PIERRE, AND BILL THOMPSON!
THERE ARE TIMES IN LIFE THAT CAN HAVE A CERTAIN VELOCITY TO THEM--
CLAP
CLAP
CLAP
CLAP
CLAP
CLAP
CLAP
CLAP
CLAP
CLAP
CLAP
CLAP
CLAP
CLAP
CLAP
--WHERE EVERYTHING SEEMS TO CLICK AND BURN BRIGHTER THAN IT HAS AT OTHER TIMES.
CLAP
CLAP
CLAP
CLAP
THE FIRST TWO YEARS OF BEING IN THE BOSTON FOLK SCENE WERE LIKE THAT FOR ME.
CLAP
CLAP
CLAP
CLAP
CLAP

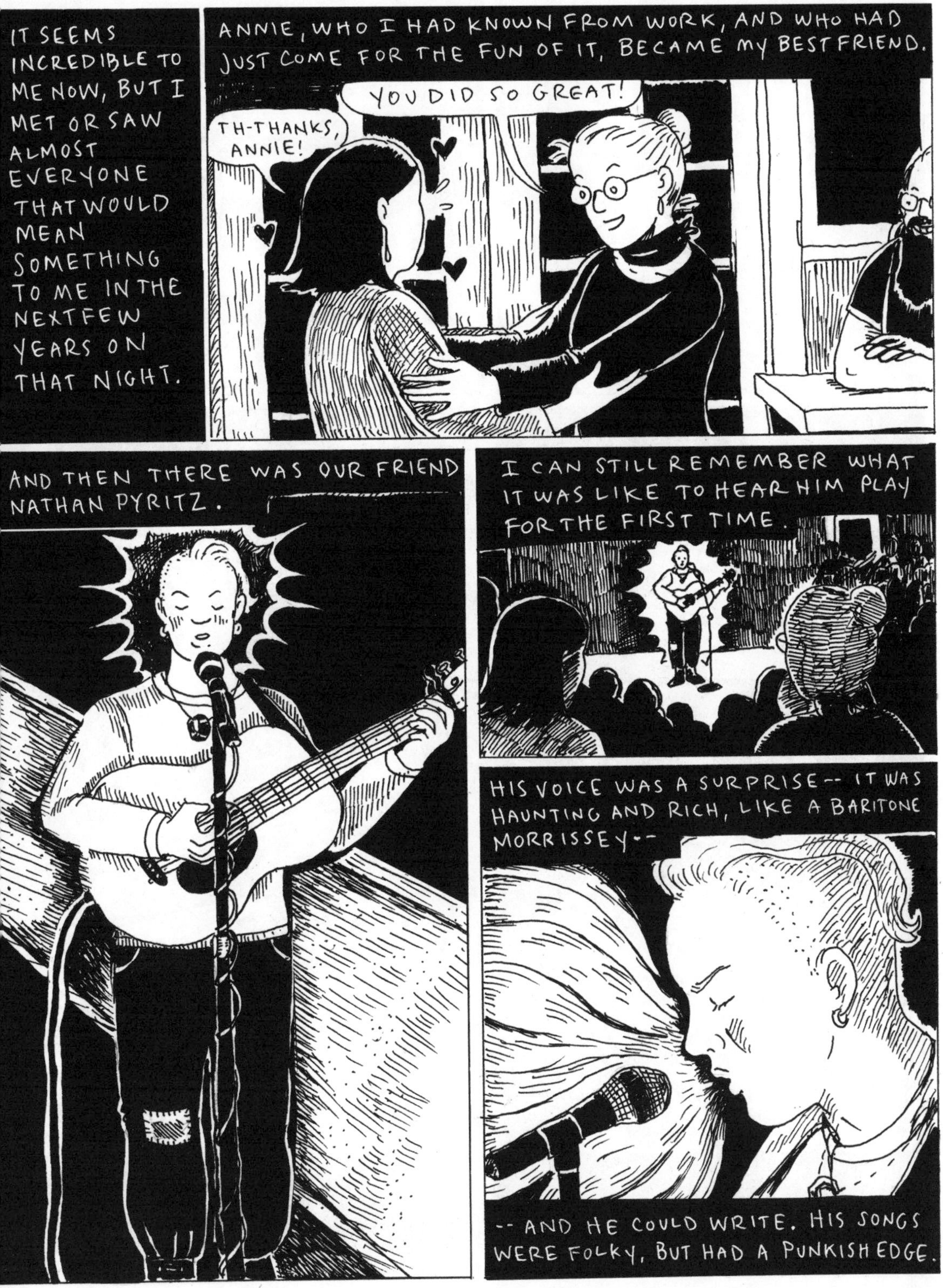
IT SEEMS INCREDIBLE TO ME NOW, BUT I MET OR SAW ALMOST EVERYONE THAT WOULD MEAN SOMETHING TO ME IN THE NEXT FEW YEARS ON THAT NIGHT.
ANNIE, WHO I HAD KNOWN FROM WORK, AND WHO HAD JUST COME FOR THE FUN OF IT, BECAME MY BEST FRIEND.
YOU DID SO GREAT!
TH-THANKS, ANNIE!
AND THEN THERE WAS OUR FRIEND NATHAN PYRITZ.
I CAN STILL REMEMBER WHAT IT WAS LIKE TO HEAR HIM PLAY FOR THE FIRST TIME.
HIS VOICE WAS A SURPRISE -- IT WAS HAUNTING AND RICH, LIKE A BARITONE MORRISSEY --
-- AND HE COULD WRITE. HIS SONGS WERE FOLKY, BUT HAD A PUNKISH EDGE.

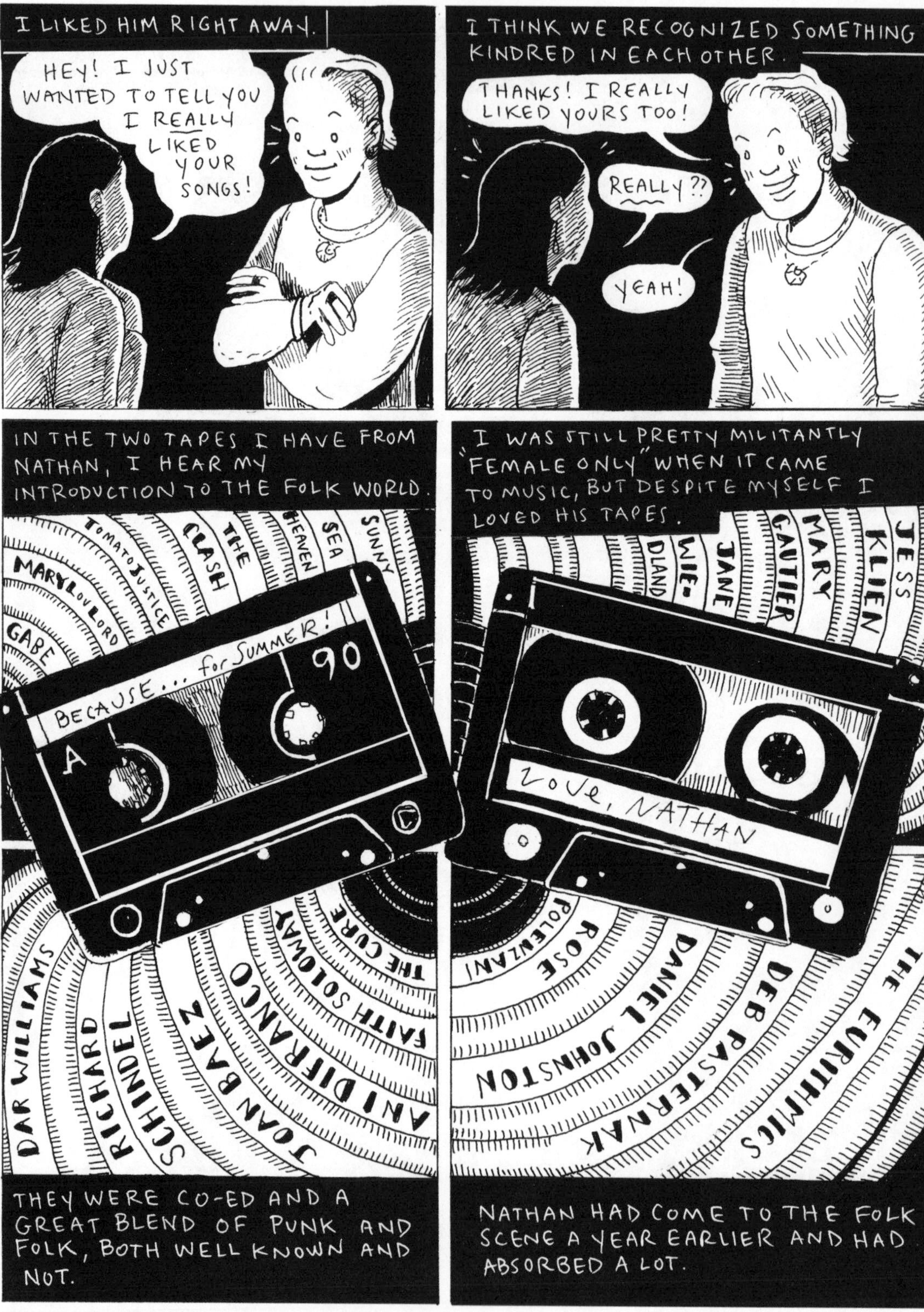
I LIKED HIM RIGHT AWAY.
HEY! I JUST WANTED TO TELL YOU I REALLY LIKED YOUR SONGS!
I THINK WE RECOGNIZED SOMETHING KINDRED IN EACH OTHER.
THANKS! I REALLY LIKED YOURS TOO!
REALLY??
YEAH!
IN THE TWO TAPES I HAVE FROM NATHAN, I HEAR MY INTRODUCTION TO THE FOLK WORLD.
GABE
MARY LOVE LORD
TOMATO JUSTICE
THE CLASH
HEAVEN
SEA
SUNNY
BECAUSE... for SUMMER!
90
A
DAR WILLIAMS
RICHARD SCHINDEL
JOAN BAEZ
ANI DIFRANCO
FAITH SOLOWAY
THE CURE
I WAS STILL PRETTY MILITANTLY "FEMALE ONLY" WHEN IT CAME TO MUSIC, BUT DESPITE MYSELF I LOVED HIS TAPES.
JESS KLIEN
MARY GAUTIER
JANE WIE-DLAND
Love, NATHAN
ROSE POLENZANI
DANIEL JOHNSTON
DEB PASTERNAK
THE EURITHMICS
THEY WERE CO-ED AND A GREAT BLEND OF PUNK AND FOLK, BOTH WELL KNOWN AND NOT.
NATHAN HAD COME TO THE FOLK SCENE A YEAR EARLIER AND HAD ABSORBED A LOT.

I COULD NOT HAVE ASKED FOR A BETTER AMBASSADOR THAN NATHAN TO THE WORLD OF MUSIC I WAS NOW ENTERING --

-- IT WAS A PLACE WHERE WORDS AND FEELINGS WERE SENT ALOFT THROUGH SOUND AND RHYTHM.

A PLACE THAT I FELT AT HOME IN.

I CONTINUED TO MAKE MIXED TAPES FOR PEOPLE, BUT NOT FOR MYSELF. I DIDN'T HAVE TO -- I WAS LIVING IT FIVE NIGHTS A WEEK AT OPEN MICS OR SHOWS I EITHER ATTENDED OR PLAYED.

MY SOUNDTRACK WAS COMPRISED OF THE FRIENDS I PLAYED WITH, THE ARTISTS WHO WERE KNOWN AMONG US, AND THE MUSIC WE SHARED WITH EACH OTHER.

WHATEVER PASSIVE WAY I ONCE LISTENED TO MUSIC WITH WAS GONE. NOW EVERYTHING I LISTENED TO HELD THE POSSABILITY OF A NEW MEANING. I WAS ALL IN.

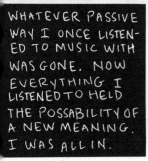

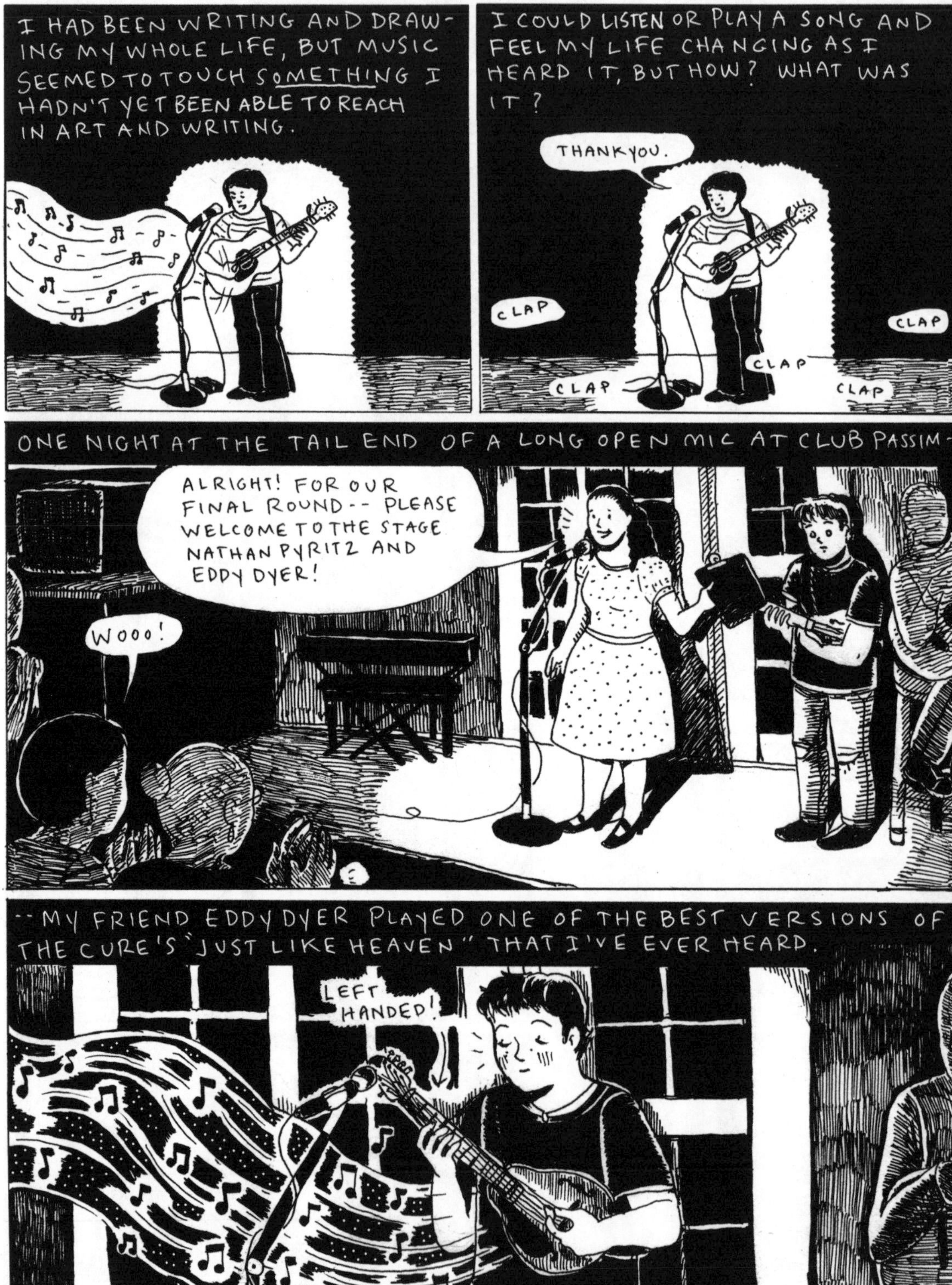
I HAD BEEN WRITING AND DRAWING MY WHOLE LIFE, BUT MUSIC SEEMED TO TOUCH SOMETHING I HADN'T YET BEEN ABLE TO REACH IN ART AND WRITING.
I COULD LISTEN OR PLAY A SONG AND FEEL MY LIFE CHANGING AS I HEARD IT, BUT HOW? WHAT WAS IT?
THANKYOU.
CLAP
CLAP
CLAP
CLAP
CLAP
ONE NIGHT AT THE TAIL END OF A LONG OPEN MIC AT CLUB PASSIM--
ALRIGHT! FOR OUR FINAL ROUND-- PLEASE WELCOME TO THE STAGE NATHAN PYRITZ AND EDDY DYER!
WOOO!
--MY FRIEND EDDY DYER PLAYED ONE OF THE BEST VERSIONS OF THE CURE'S "JUST LIKE HEAVEN" THAT I'VE EVER HEARD.
LEFT HANDED!

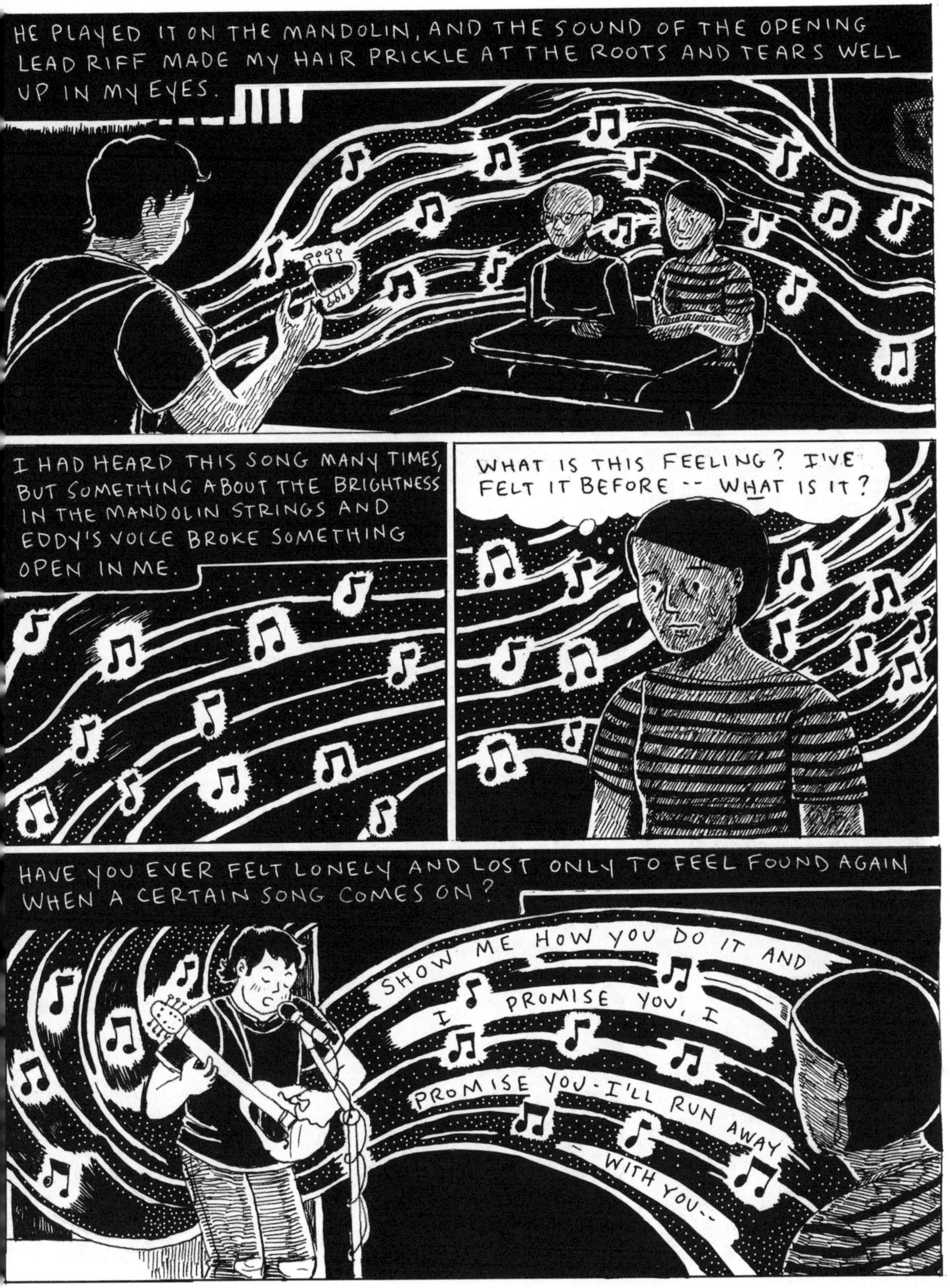
HE PLAYED IT ON THE MANDOLIN, AND THE SOUND OF THE OPENING LEAD RIFF MADE MY HAIR PRICKLE AT THE ROOTS AND TEARS WELL UP IN MY EYES.
I HAD HEARD THIS SONG MANY TIMES, BUT SOMETHING ABOUT THE BRIGHTNESS IN THE MANDOLIN STRINGS AND EDDY'S VOICE BROKE SOMETHING OPEN IN ME.
WHAT IS THIS FEELING? I'VE FELT IT BEFORE -- WHAT IS IT?
HAVE YOU EVER FELT LONELY AND LOST ONLY TO FEEL FOUND AGAIN WHEN A CERTAIN SONG COMES ON?
SHOW ME HOW YOU DO IT AND I PROMISE YOU, I PROMISE YOU - I'LL RUN AWAY WITH YOU--

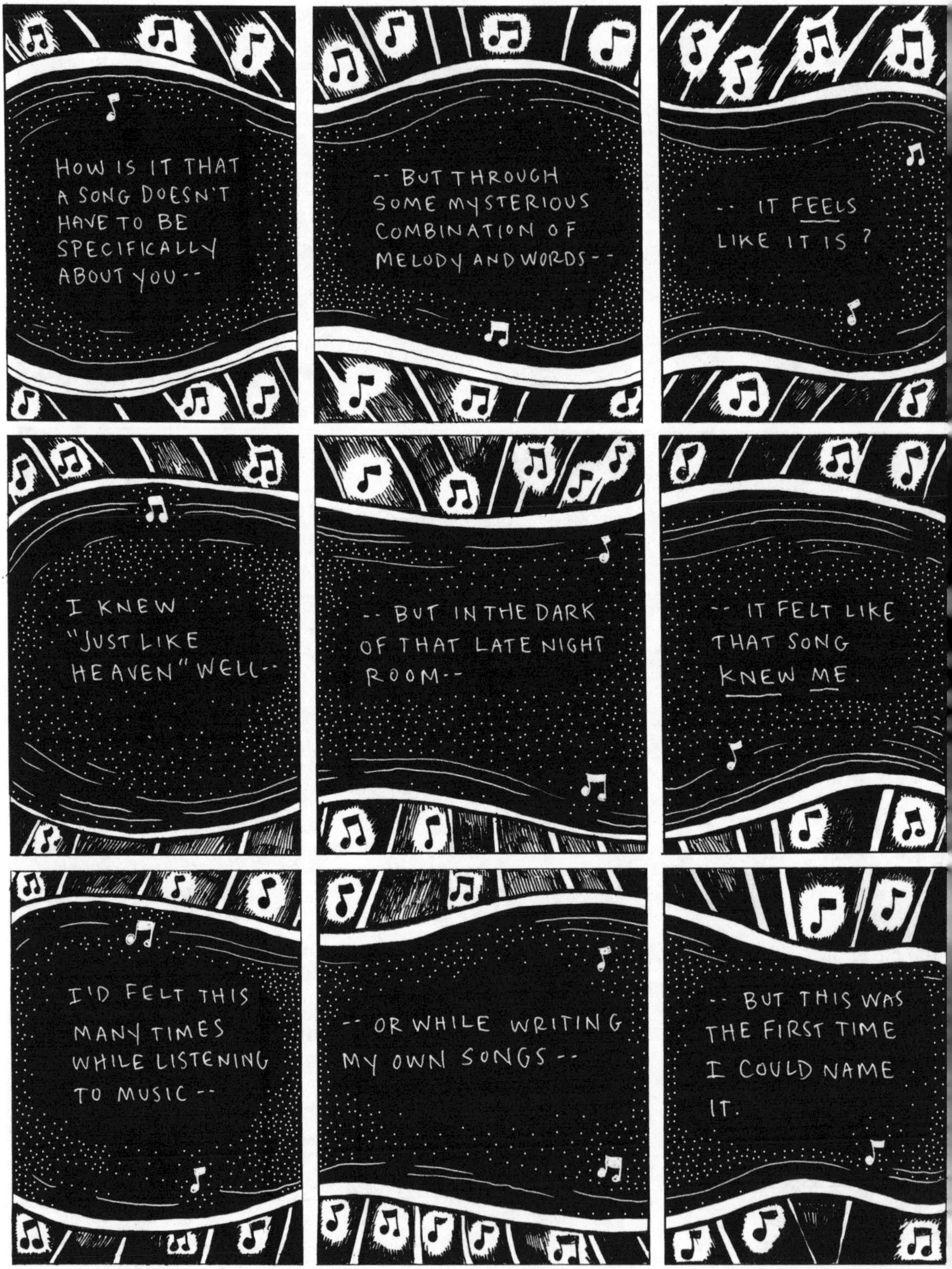
HOW IS IT THAT A SONG DOESN'T HAVE TO BE SPECIFICALLY ABOUT YOU --
-- BUT THROUGH SOME MYSTERIOUS COMBINATION OF MELODY AND WORDS --
-- IT FEELS LIKE IT IS ?
I KNEW "JUST LIKE HEAVEN" WELL --
-- BUT IN THE DARK OF THAT LATE NIGHT ROOM --
-- IT FELT LIKE THAT SONG KNEW ME.
I'D FELT THIS MANY TIMES WHILE LISTENING TO MUSIC --
-- OR WHILE WRITING MY OWN SONGS --
-- BUT THIS WAS THE FIRST TIME I COULD NAME IT.

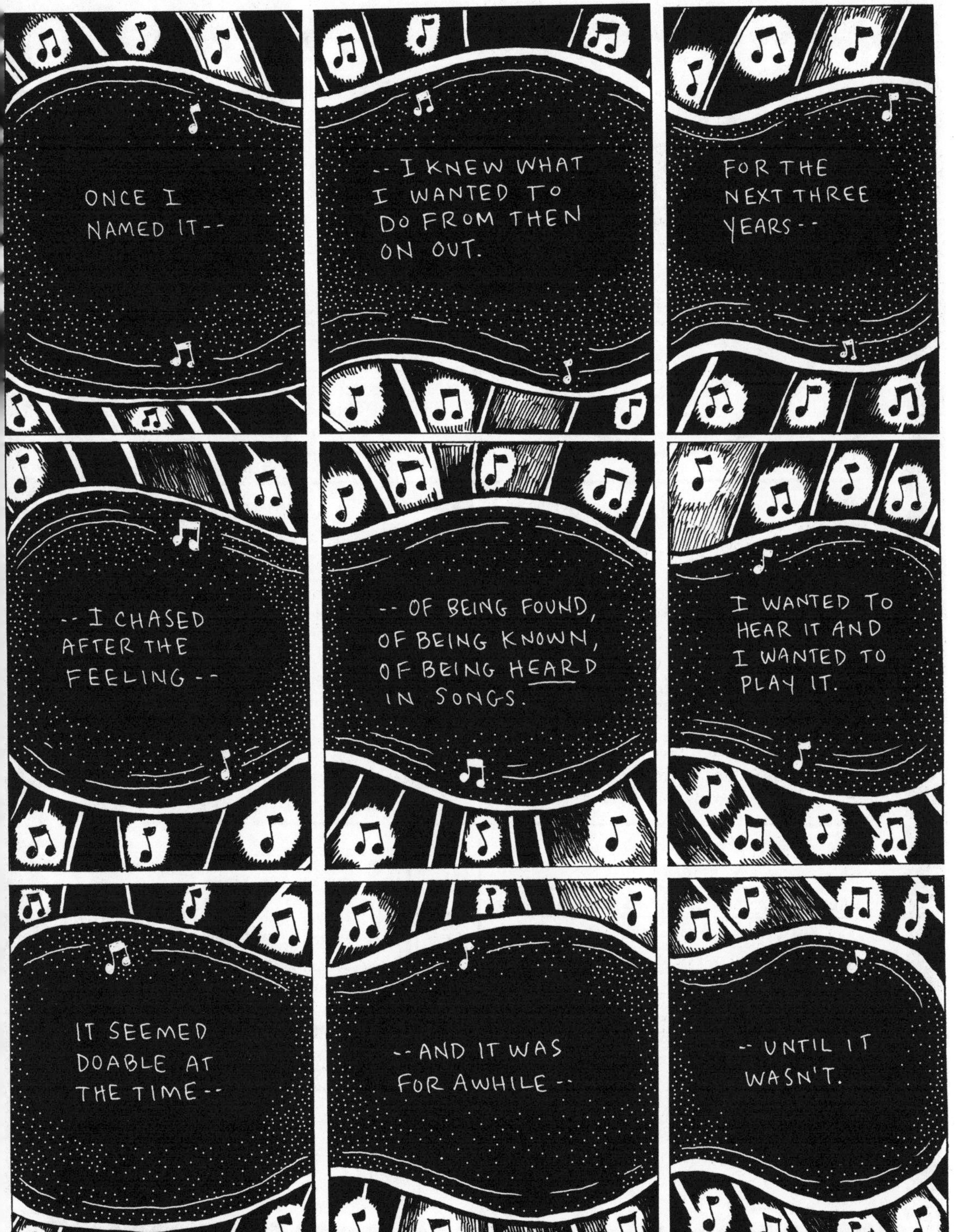
ONCE I NAMED IT--
--I KNEW WHAT I WANTED TO DO FROM THEN ON OUT.
FOR THE NEXT THREE YEARS--
--I CHASED AFTER THE FEELING--
--OF BEING FOUND, OF BEING KNOWN, OF BEING HEARD IN SONGS.
I WANTED TO HEAR IT AND I WANTED TO PLAY IT.
IT SEEMED DOABLE AT THE TIME--
--AND IT WAS FOR AWHILE--
--UNTIL IT WASN'T.

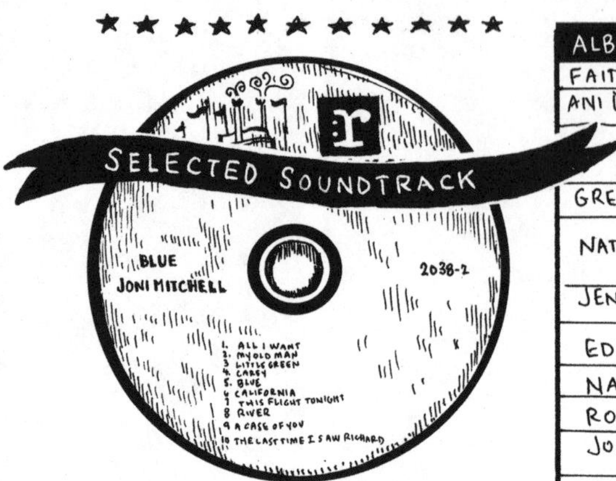
SELECTED SOUNDTRACK
BLUE
JONI MITCHELL
2038-2
1. ALL I WANT
2. MY OLD MAN
3. LITTLE GREEN
4. CAREY
5. BLUE
6. CALIFORNIA
7. THIS FLIGHT TONIGHT
8. RIVER
9. A CASE OF YOU
10. THE LAST TIME I SAW RICHARD

ALBUMS:

- JILL SOBULE – HAPPY TOWN
- FAITH SOLOWAY – TRAINING WHEELS (EP)
- ANI DIFRANCO – NOT A PRETTY GIRL; OUT OF RANGE
- GREG BROWN – THE LIVE ONE
- NATHAN PYRITZ – ROUGH CUTS ALONG THE WAY TO POETRY VOLS. 1 + 2
- JEN TRYNIN – GUNSHY TRIGGER HAPPY
- EDDY DYER – EXPLOSION ALONE
- NATE BOROFSKY – 500 MILES
- ROB LAURENS – SKETCHBOOK (EP)
- JONATHAN POINTER – SCARECROWS BURN
- PJ HARVEY – IS THIS DESIRE?

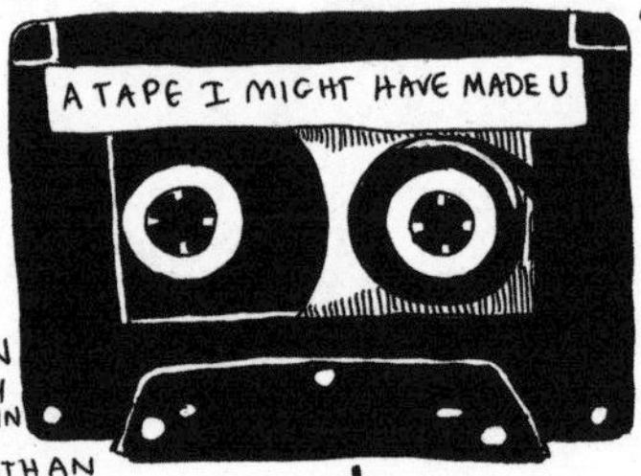
A TAPE I MIGHT HAVE MADE U

A

- I DON'T WANT TO GET BITTER – JILL SOBULE
- THAT'S JUST WHAT YOU ARE – AIMEE MANN
- HAND TO MOUTHVILLE – CASEY CROWLEY
- SWALLOWS ME WHOLE – LORI McKENNA
- JEREUSALEM – DAN BERN
- WESTERN UNION DESPERATE – MARY LOU LORD
- NO MYTH – MICHAEL PENN
- EVERY LITTLE BIT – PATTY GRIFFIN
- ASCENSION DAY – JONATHAN POINTER
- 'TIL YOU'RE DEAD – MELISSA FERRICK
- PERFECT WORLD – LIZ PHAIR

B

- WORLD OF OUR OWN MAKING – MERRIE AMSTERBERG
- ONE REGRET – DEB PASTERNAK
- BETTER THAN NOTHING – JEN TRYNIN
- WAY BELOW THE RADIO – LISA GERMANO
- CHICAGO – FAITH SOLOWAY
- CHELSEA HOTEL – DAN BERN
- 4TH OF JULY – AIMEE MANN
- OLGA'S BIRTHDAY – ROSE POLENZANI
- HAPPY TOWN – JILL SOBULE
- WRITING NOTES – JEN TRYNIN
- HAPPY HOME – PAULA COLE
- PANIC PURE – KRISTIN HERSH

- DAN BERN – DAN BERN; SMARTIEMINE
- MERRIE AMSTERBERG – SEASON OF RAIN
- LIZ PHAIR – WHITE CHOCOLATE SPACE EGG
- LORI McKENNA – PAPERWINGS + HALO
- JAMES O'BRIEN – SPIRIT DAYS
- COUNTING CROWS – AUGUST + EVERYTHING AFTER
- DAVE DERSHAM – EP
- HAMMEL ON TRIAL – BIG AS LIFE
- KRISTEN HERSH – STRANGE ANGELS

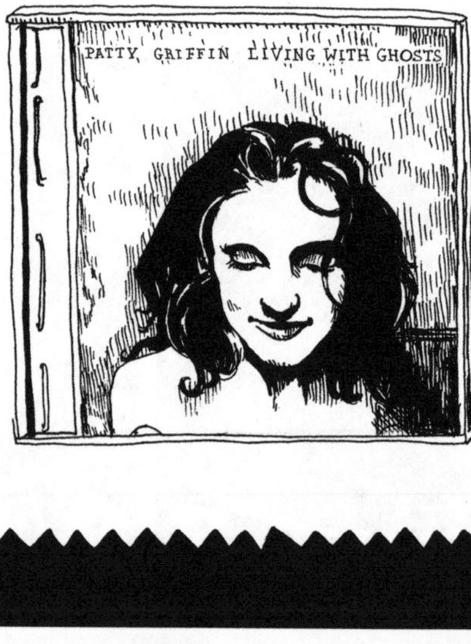
PATTY GRIFFIN LIVING WITH GHOSTS

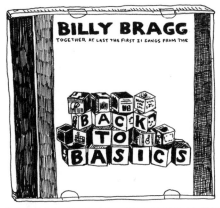

BILLY BRAGG
TOGETHER AT LAST THE FIRST 21 SONGS FROM THE
BACK TO BASICS

VIC CHESNUTT - ABOUT TO CHOKE
MICHAEL TROY - WHISPERS IN THE WIND
ELVIS COSTELLO ⟩ MY AIM IS TRUE
⟩ THIS YEAR'S MODEL
STEVE EARLE - TRANSCENDENTAL BLUES
THE BEATLES ⟩ REVOLVER
⟩ HELP!
⟩ RUBBERSOUL
THE ROLLINGSTONES - SOME GIRLS
BILLY BRAGG + WILCO - MERMAID AVE.
ROSE POLENZANI ⟩ DEMO
⟩ 4 TRACK DEMOS
⟩ DRAEGERSVILLE

★ ★ ★ ★ ★ ★ ★ ★ ★ ★ ★ ★

- BRUCE SPRINGSTEEN ⟩ • GREATEST HITS
  + THE E STREET ⟩ • TRACKS
  BAND ⟩ • LIVE 1975 - 1985
- PATTI SMITH - GONE AGAIN
- MICHELLE SHOCKED - A KIND HEARTED WOMAN
- SUZANNE VEGA - 99.9 F°
- BILLY BRAGG - WORKERS PLAYTIME
- LUCINDA WILLIAMS - CAR WHEELS ON A GRAVEL RD.
- MARY LOU LORD - GOT NO SHADOW
- TOM WAITS - MULE VARIATIONS

★ ★ ★ ★ ★ ★ ★ ★ ★ ★ ★ ★

SWEET RELIEF II: THE SONGS OF VIC CHESNUTT
A
VARIOUS ARTISTS

★ ★ ★ ★ ★ ★ ★ ★ ★ ★ ★ ★

A
GREG BROWN LIVE AT THE FAT FRY (BOOTLEG)

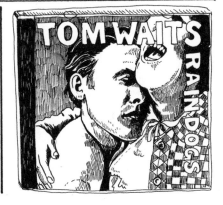

TOM WAITS RAIN DOGS

PART FOUR

THE MISSING TAPE

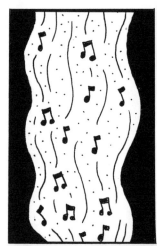

IT'S WEIRD TO ME THAT THERE ARE TAPES I HAVE KEPT FOR 20 YEARS AND YET I DON'T REMEMBER WHAT'S ON THEM--

-- WHILE I'VE HAD A SONG STUCK IN MY HEAD FROM A TAPE I HAVEN'T OWNED IN 20 YEARS.

IT'S FROM THAT MISSING TAPE--

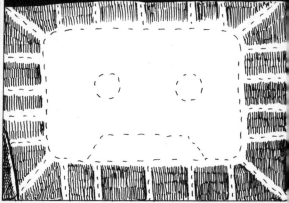

-- THE ONE I THREW OUT, FROM MY EX BOYFRIEND, TOM.

IT'S NOT A BAD SONG IN ITSELF, BUT I CAN'T GET RID OF IT.

YOU ARE THE SUNSHINE OF MY LIFE-- THAT'S WHY I'LL ALWAYS BE AROUND

FREE EAST TIMOR

I GUESS SOME MEMORIES JUST CAN'T BE THROWN OUT.

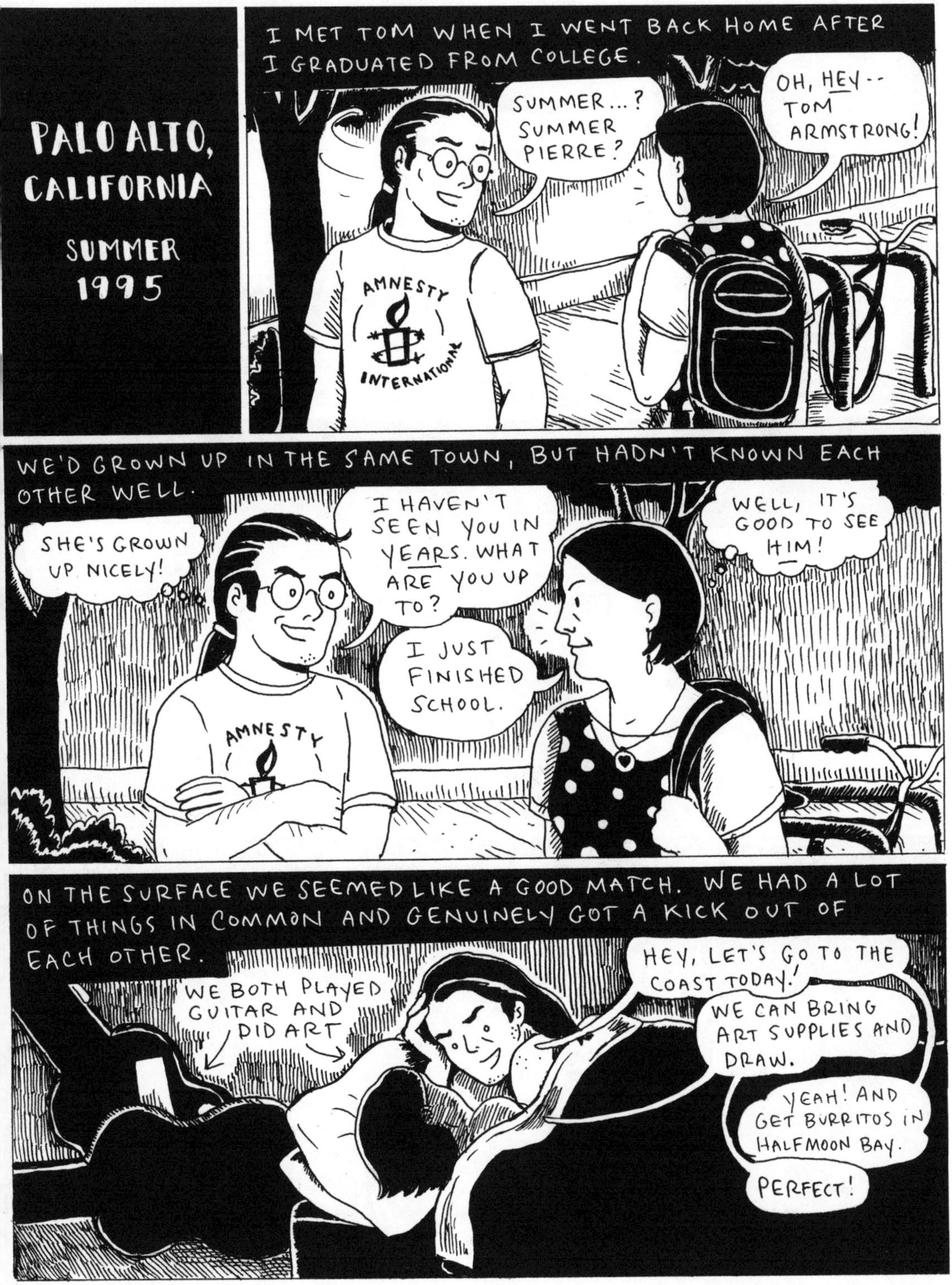
PALO ALTO, CALIFORNIA
SUMMER 1995
I MET TOM WHEN I WENT BACK HOME AFTER I GRADUATED FROM COLLEGE.
SUMMER...? SUMMER PIERRE?
OH, HEY-- TOM ARMSTRONG!
AMNESTY INTERNATIONAL
WE'D GROWN UP IN THE SAME TOWN, BUT HADN'T KNOWN EACH OTHER WELL.
SHE'S GROWN UP NICELY!
I HAVEN'T SEEN YOU IN YEARS. WHAT ARE YOU UP TO?
WELL, IT'S GOOD TO SEE HIM!
I JUST FINISHED SCHOOL.
AMNESTY
ON THE SURFACE WE SEEMED LIKE A GOOD MATCH. WE HAD A LOT OF THINGS IN COMMON AND GENUINELY GOT A KICK OUT OF EACH OTHER.
WE BOTH PLAYED GUITAR AND DID ART
HEY, LET'S GO TO THE COAST TODAY!
WE CAN BRING ART SUPPLIES AND DRAW.
YEAH! AND GET BURRITOS IN HALFMOON BAY.
PERFECT!

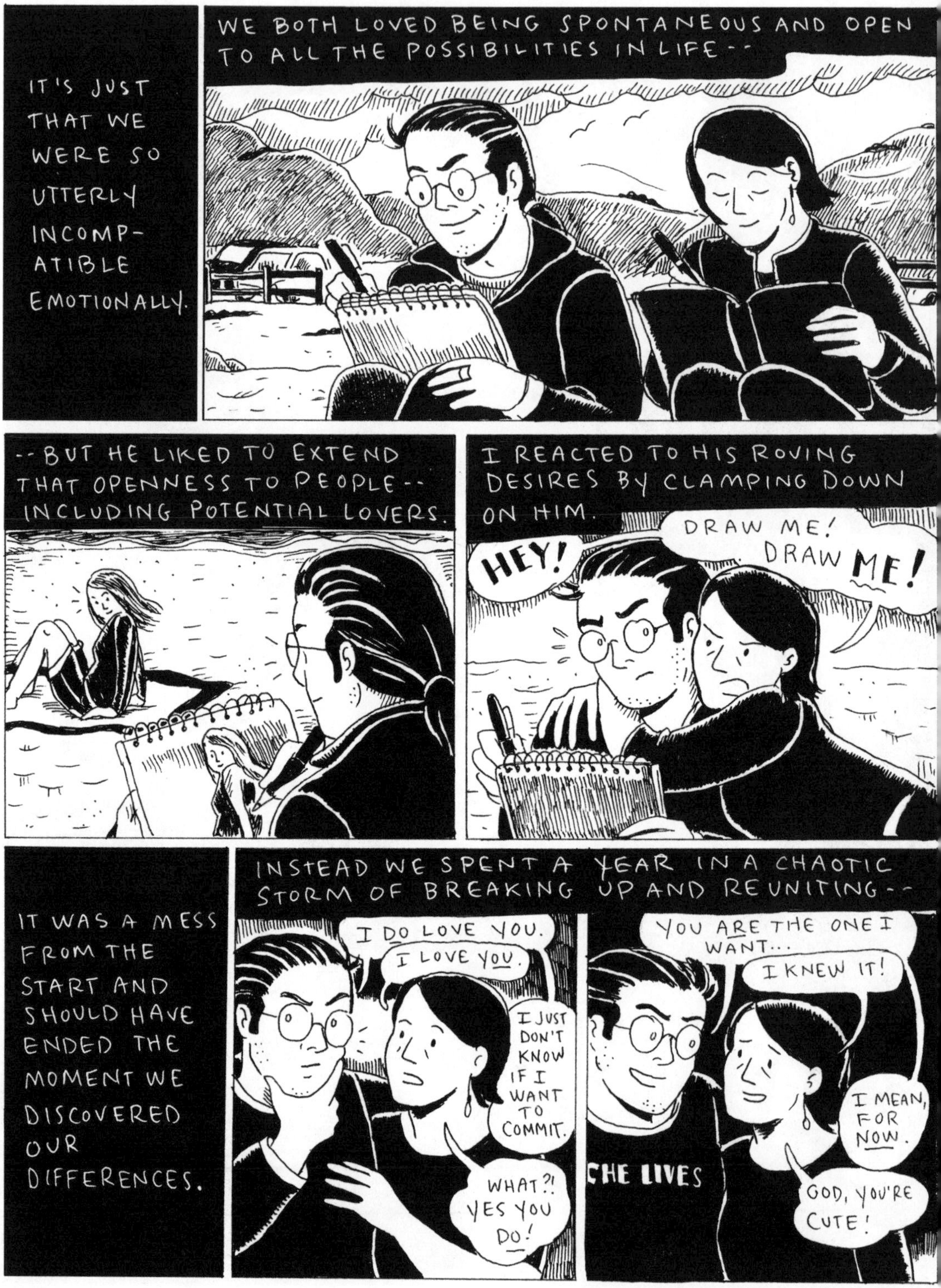
IT'S JUST THAT WE WERE SO UTTERLY INCOMP-ATIBLE EMOTIONALLY.
WE BOTH LOVED BEING SPONTANEOUS AND OPEN TO ALL THE POSSIBILITIES IN LIFE--
--BUT HE LIKED TO EXTEND THAT OPENNESS TO PEOPLE-- INCLUDING POTENTIAL LOVERS.
I REACTED TO HIS ROVING DESIRES BY CLAMPING DOWN ON HIM.
HEY!
DRAW ME! DRAW ME!
IT WAS A MESS FROM THE START AND SHOULD HAVE ENDED THE MOMENT WE DISCOVERED OUR DIFFERENCES.
INSTEAD WE SPENT A YEAR IN A CHAOTIC STORM OF BREAKING UP AND REUNITING--
I DO LOVE YOU.
I LOVE YOU.
I JUST DON'T KNOW IF I WANT TO COMMIT.
WHAT?! YES YOU DO!
YOU ARE THE ONE I WANT...
I KNEW IT!
I MEAN, FOR NOW.
CHE LIVES
GOD, YOU'RE CUTE!

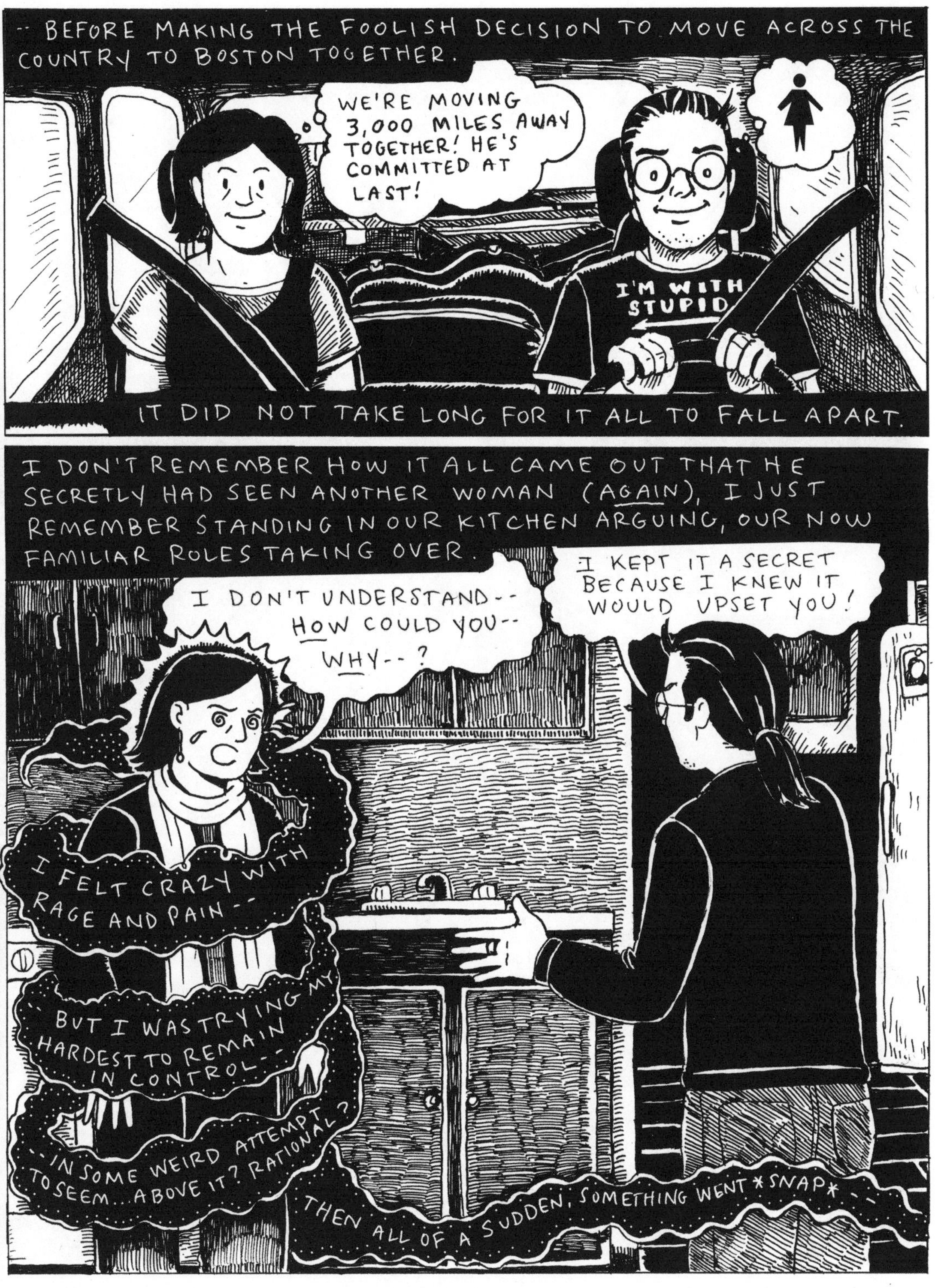
-- BEFORE MAKING THE FOOLISH DECISION TO MOVE ACROSS THE COUNTRY TO BOSTON TOGETHER.
WE'RE MOVING 3,000 MILES AWAY TOGETHER! HE'S COMMITTED AT LAST!
I'M WITH STUPID
IT DID NOT TAKE LONG FOR IT ALL TO FALL APART.
I DON'T REMEMBER HOW IT ALL CAME OUT THAT HE SECRETLY HAD SEEN ANOTHER WOMAN (AGAIN), I JUST REMEMBER STANDING IN OUR KITCHEN ARGUING, OUR NOW FAMILIAR ROLES TAKING OVER.
I DON'T UNDERSTAND-- HOW COULD YOU-- WHY--?
I KEPT IT A SECRET BECAUSE I KNEW IT WOULD UPSET YOU!
I FELT CRAZY WITH RAGE AND PAIN--
--BUT I WAS TRYING MY HARDEST TO REMAIN IN CONTROL--
--IN SOME WEIRD ATTEMPT TO SEEM...ABOVE IT? RATIONAL?
THEN ALL OF A SUDDEN, SOMETHING WENT *SNAP*--

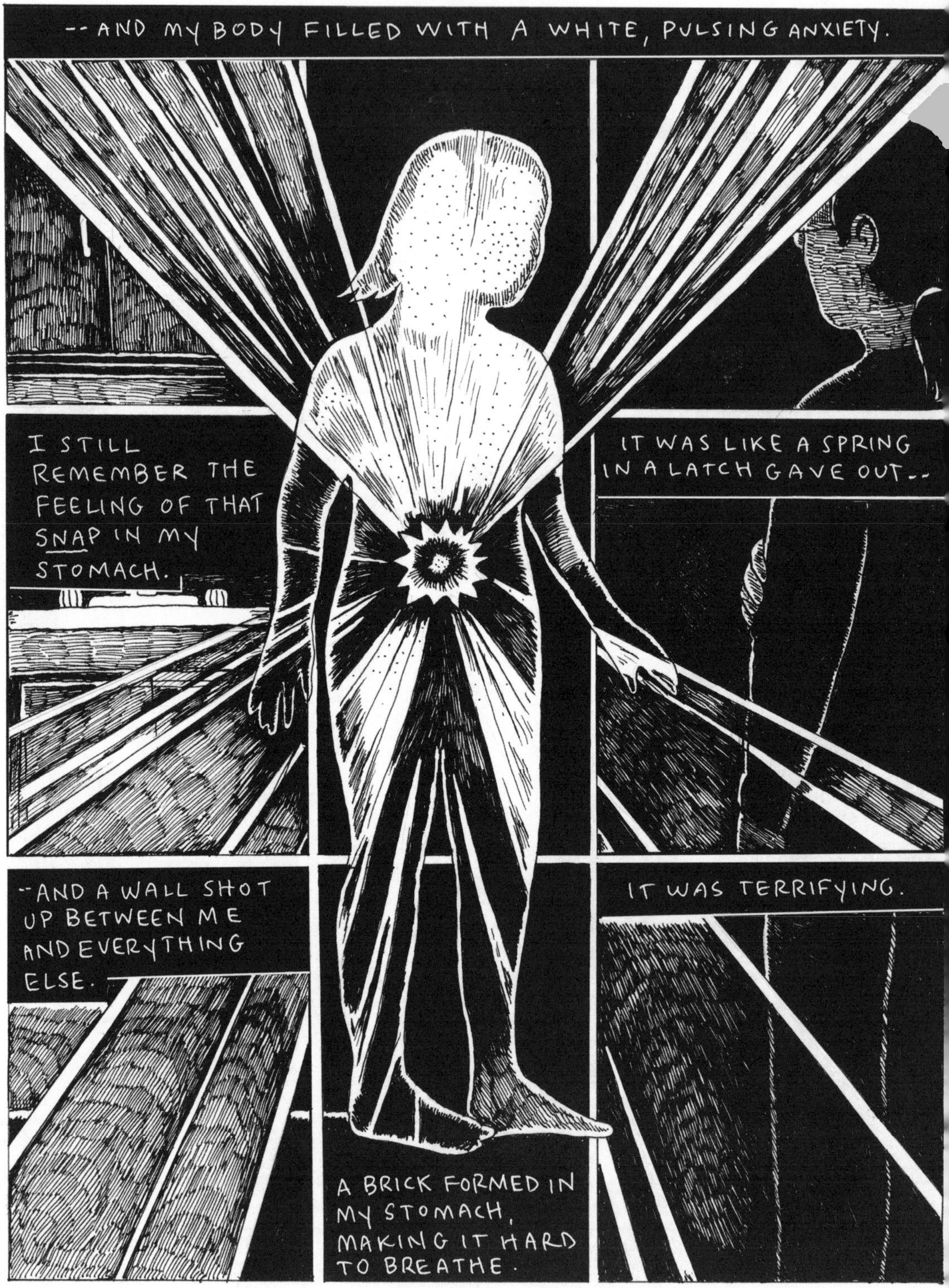
--AND MY BODY FILLED WITH A WHITE, PULSING ANXIETY.
I STILL REMEMBER THE FEELING OF THAT SNAP IN MY STOMACH.
IT WAS LIKE A SPRING IN A LATCH GAVE OUT--
--AND A WALL SHOT UP BETWEEN ME AND EVERYTHING ELSE.
A BRICK FORMED IN MY STOMACH, MAKING IT HARD TO BREATHE.
IT WAS TERRIFYING.

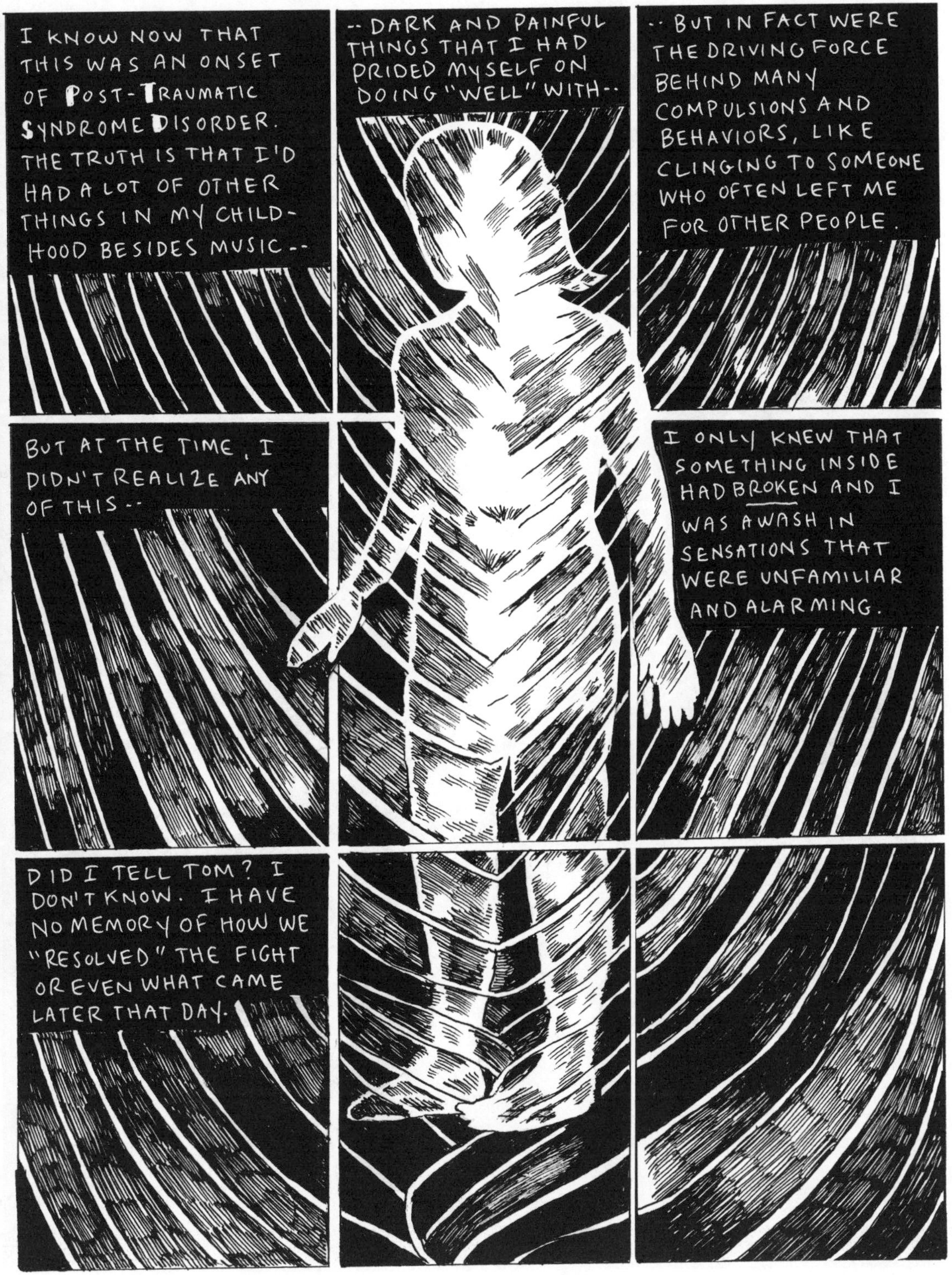
I KNOW NOW THAT THIS WAS AN ONSET OF POST-TRAUMATIC SYNDROME DISORDER. THE TRUTH IS THAT I'D HAD A LOT OF OTHER THINGS IN MY CHILDHOOD BESIDES MUSIC--
--DARK AND PAINFUL THINGS THAT I HAD PRIDED MYSELF ON DOING "WELL" WITH--
--BUT IN FACT WERE THE DRIVING FORCE BEHIND MANY COMPULSIONS AND BEHAVIORS, LIKE CLINGING TO SOMEONE WHO OFTEN LEFT ME FOR OTHER PEOPLE.
BUT AT THE TIME, I DIDN'T REALIZE ANY OF THIS--
I ONLY KNEW THAT SOMETHING INSIDE HAD BROKEN AND I WAS AWASH IN SENSATIONS THAT WERE UNFAMILIAR AND ALARMING.
DID I TELL TOM? I DON'T KNOW. I HAVE NO MEMORY OF HOW WE "RESOLVED" THE FIGHT OR EVEN WHAT CAME LATER THAT DAY.

WHAT I REMEMBER IS WAKING UP THE NEXT DAY EXPECTING THIS "THING" TO HAVE PASSED, LIKE SOME HEADACHE OR WEIRD VIRUS--

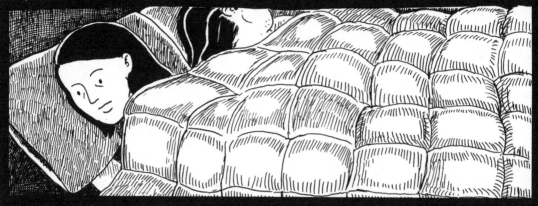

--ONLY TO FEEL THE BRICK IN MY STOMACH REASSURT ITSELF AND A FEELING OF CLAUSTROPHOBIA AND TERROR COME OVER ME.

THAT'S WHEN I KNEW SOMETHING WAS VERY WRONG.

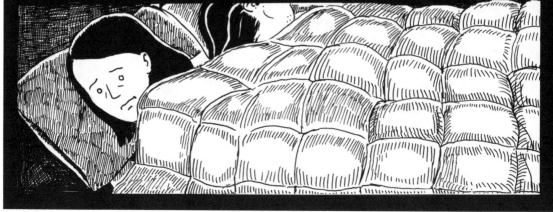

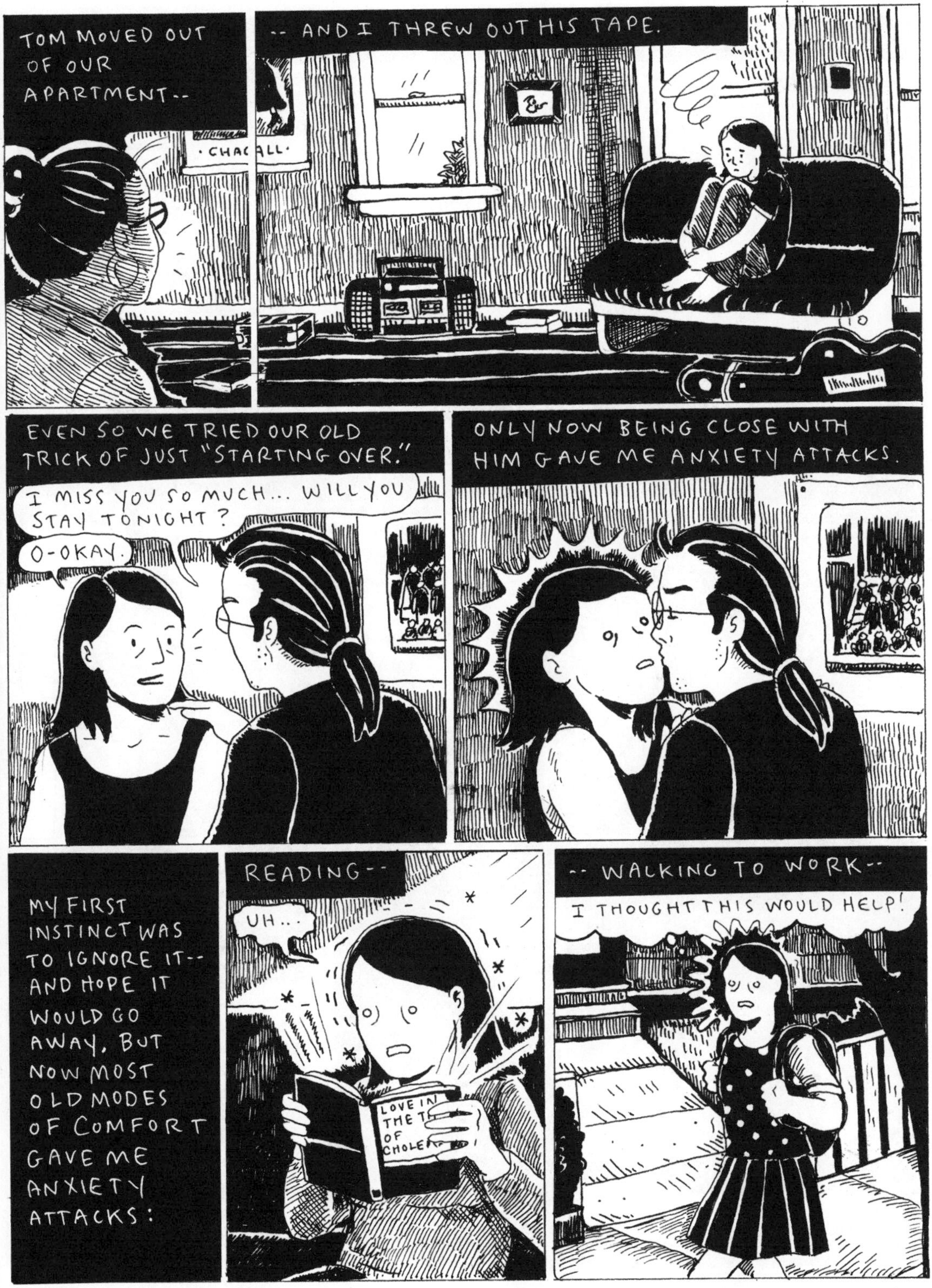
TOM MOVED OUT OF OUR APARTMENT--
CHAGALL
-- AND I THREW OUT HIS TAPE.
EVEN SO WE TRIED OUR OLD TRICK OF JUST "STARTING OVER."
I MISS YOU SO MUCH... WILL YOU STAY TONIGHT?
O-OKAY.
ONLY NOW BEING CLOSE WITH HIM GAVE ME ANXIETY ATTACKS.
MY FIRST INSTINCT WAS TO IGNORE IT-- AND HOPE IT WOULD GO AWAY. BUT NOW MOST OLD MODES OF COMFORT GAVE ME ANXIETY ATTACKS:
READING--
UH...
-- WALKING TO WORK--
I THOUGHT THIS WOULD HELP!

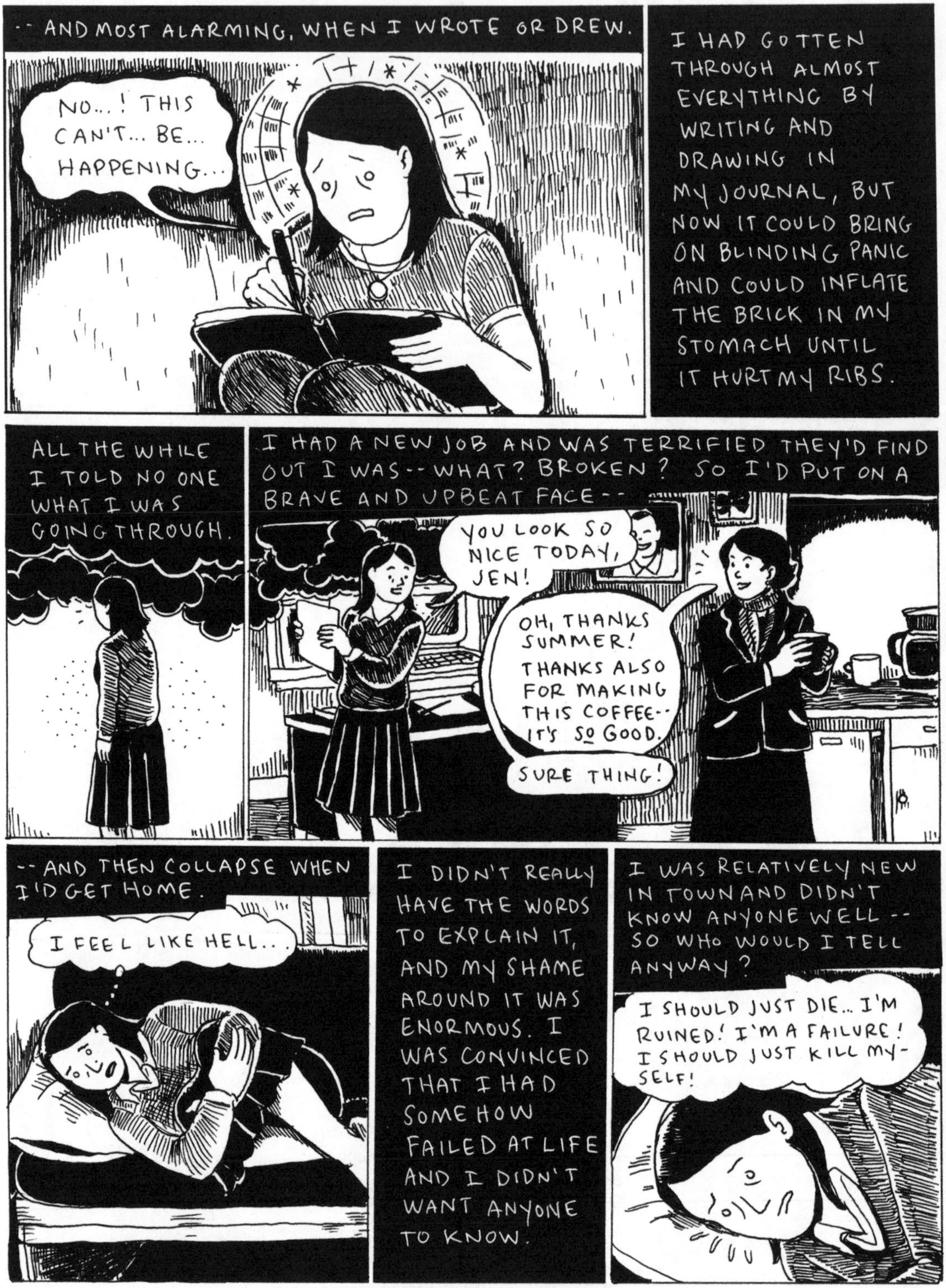
-- AND MOST ALARMING, WHEN I WROTE OR DREW.
NO...! THIS CAN'T... BE... HAPPENING...
I HAD GOTTEN THROUGH ALMOST EVERYTHING BY WRITING AND DRAWING IN MY JOURNAL, BUT NOW IT COULD BRING ON BLINDING PANIC AND COULD INFLATE THE BRICK IN MY STOMACH UNTIL IT HURT MY RIBS.
ALL THE WHILE I TOLD NO ONE WHAT I WAS GOING THROUGH.
I HAD A NEW JOB AND WAS TERRIFIED THEY'D FIND OUT I WAS -- WHAT? BROKEN? SO I'D PUT ON A BRAVE AND UPBEAT FACE --
YOU LOOK SO NICE TODAY, JEN!
OH, THANKS SUMMER! THANKS ALSO FOR MAKING THIS COFFEE -- IT'S SO GOOD.
SURE THING!
-- AND THEN COLLAPSE WHEN I'D GET HOME.
I FEEL LIKE HELL...
I DIDN'T REALLY HAVE THE WORDS TO EXPLAIN IT, AND MY SHAME AROUND IT WAS ENORMOUS. I WAS CONVINCED THAT I HAD SOMEHOW FAILED AT LIFE AND I DIDN'T WANT ANYONE TO KNOW.
I WAS RELATIVELY NEW IN TOWN AND DIDN'T KNOW ANYONE WELL -- SO WHO WOULD I TELL ANYWAY?
I SHOULD JUST DIE... I'M RUINED! I'M A FAILURE! I SHOULD JUST KILL MY-SELF!

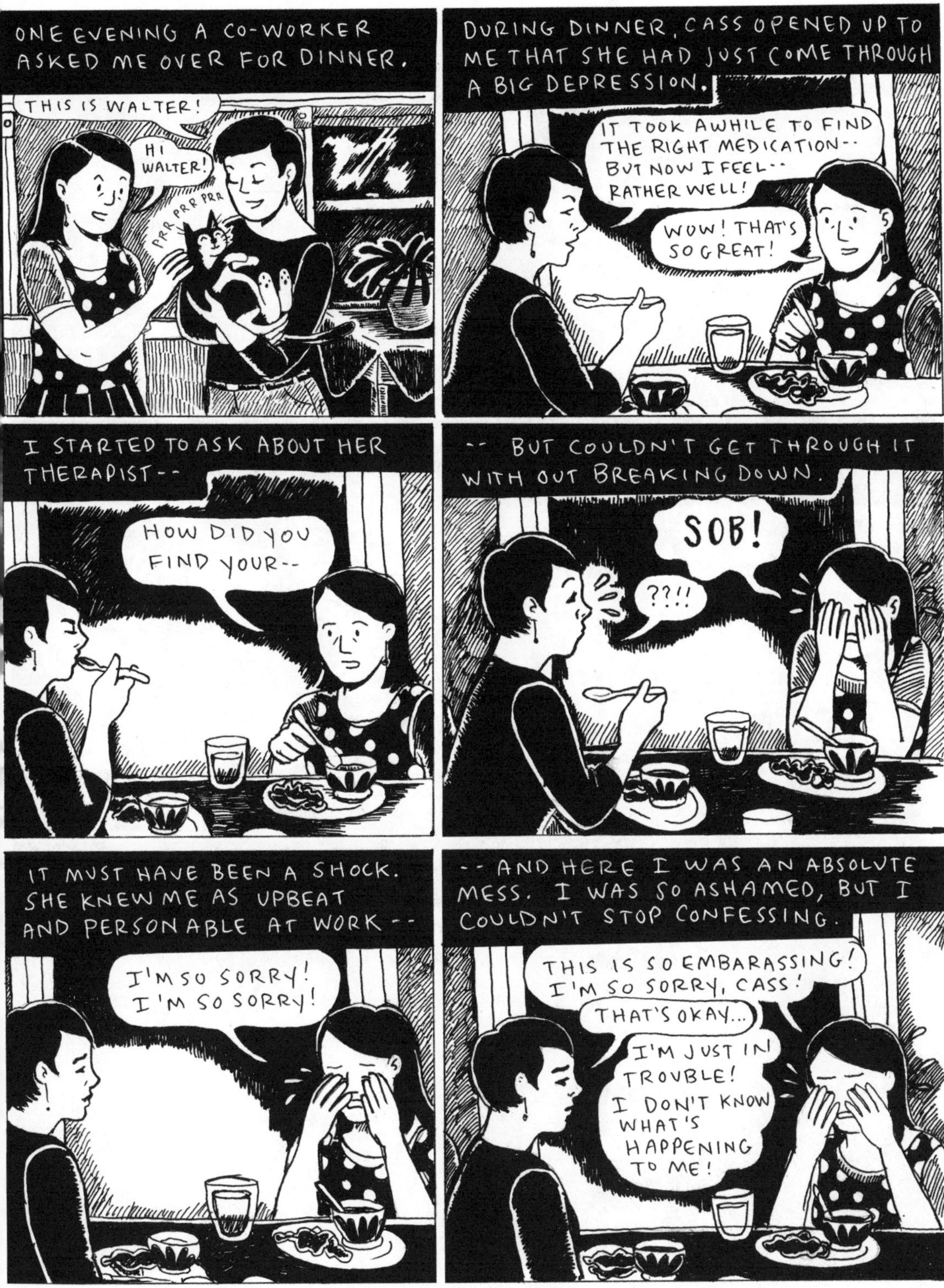
ONE EVENING A CO-WORKER ASKED ME OVER FOR DINNER.
THIS IS WALTER!
HI WALTER!
PRR PRR PRR
DURING DINNER, CASS OPENED UP TO ME THAT SHE HAD JUST COME THROUGH A BIG DEPRESSION.
IT TOOK AWHILE TO FIND THE RIGHT MEDICATION-- BUT NOW I FEEL-- RATHER WELL!
WOW! THAT'S SO GREAT!
I STARTED TO ASK ABOUT HER THERAPIST--
HOW DID YOU FIND YOUR--
-- BUT COULDN'T GET THROUGH IT WITH OUT BREAKING DOWN.
SOB!
??!!
IT MUST HAVE BEEN A SHOCK. SHE KNEW ME AS UPBEAT AND PERSONABLE AT WORK--
I'M SO SORRY! I'M SO SORRY!
-- AND HERE I WAS AN ABSOLUTE MESS. I WAS SO ASHAMED, BUT I COULDN'T STOP CONFESSING.
THIS IS SO EMBARASSING! I'M SO SORRY, CASS!
THAT'S OKAY...
I'M JUST IN TROUBLE! I DON'T KNOW WHAT'S HAPPENING TO ME!

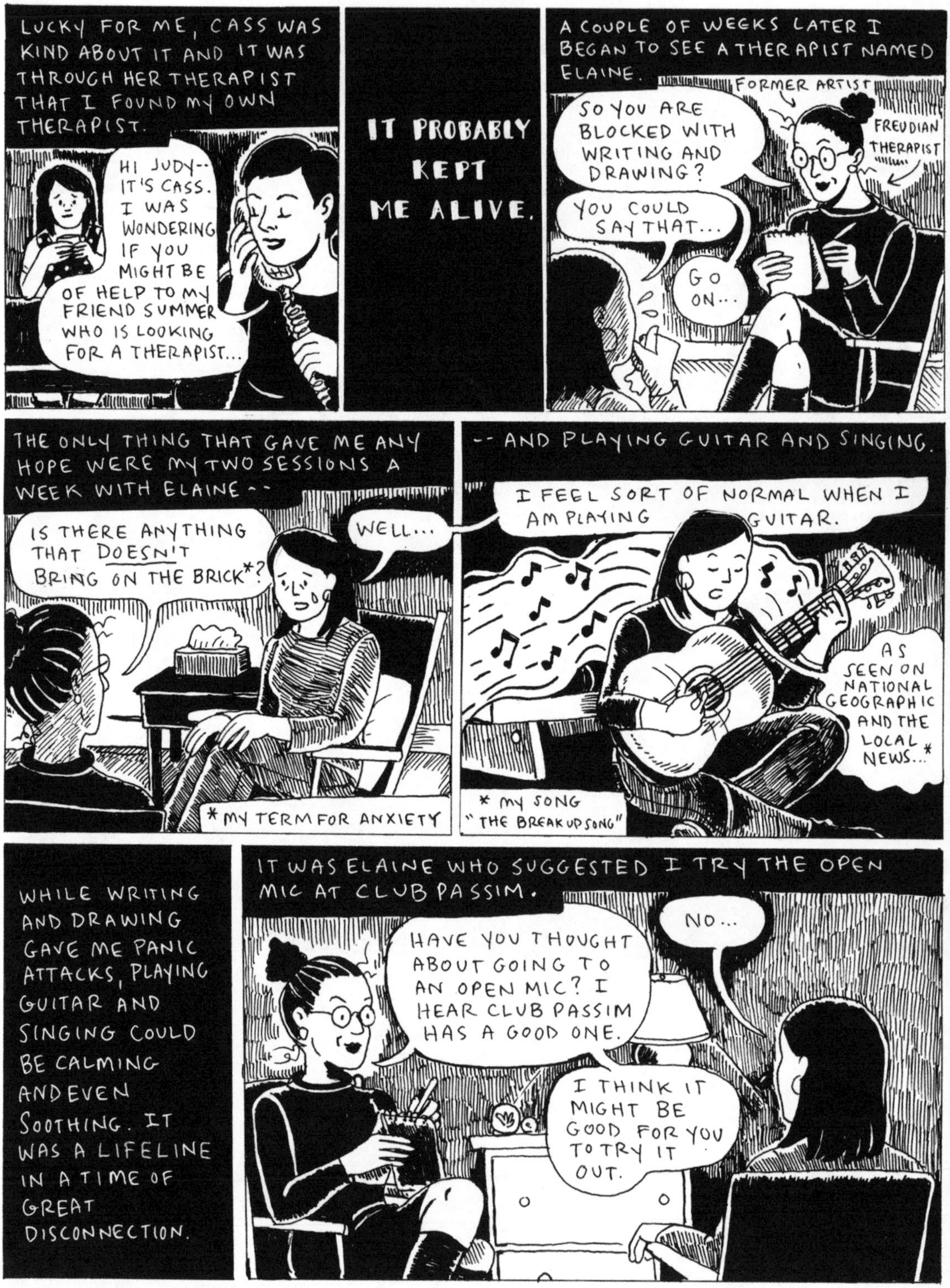
LUCKY FOR ME, CASS WAS KIND ABOUT IT AND IT WAS THROUGH HER THERAPIST THAT I FOUND MY OWN THERAPIST.
HI JUDY-- IT'S CASS. I WAS WONDERING IF YOU MIGHT BE OF HELP TO MY FRIEND SUMMER WHO IS LOOKING FOR A THERAPIST...
IT PROBABLY KEPT ME ALIVE.
A COUPLE OF WEEKS LATER I BEGAN TO SEE A THERAPIST NAMED ELAINE.
FORMER ARTIST
FREUDIAN THERAPIST
SO YOU ARE BLOCKED WITH WRITING AND DRAWING?
YOU COULD SAY THAT...
GO ON...
THE ONLY THING THAT GAVE ME ANY HOPE WERE MY TWO SESSIONS A WEEK WITH ELAINE--
IS THERE ANYTHING THAT DOESN'T BRING ON THE BRICK*?
WELL...
* MY TERM FOR ANXIETY
--AND PLAYING GUITAR AND SINGING.
I FEEL SORT OF NORMAL WHEN I AM PLAYING GUITAR.
AS SEEN ON NATIONAL GEOGRAPHIC AND THE LOCAL NEWS...*
* MY SONG "THE BREAKUP SONG"
WHILE WRITING AND DRAWING GAVE ME PANIC ATTACKS, PLAYING GUITAR AND SINGING COULD BE CALMING AND EVEN SOOTHING. IT WAS A LIFELINE IN A TIME OF GREAT DISCONNECTION.
IT WAS ELAINE WHO SUGGESTED I TRY THE OPEN MIC AT CLUB PASSIM.
HAVE YOU THOUGHT ABOUT GOING TO AN OPEN MIC? I HEAR CLUB PASSIM HAS A GOOD ONE.
NO...
I THINK IT MIGHT BE GOOD FOR YOU TO TRY IT OUT.

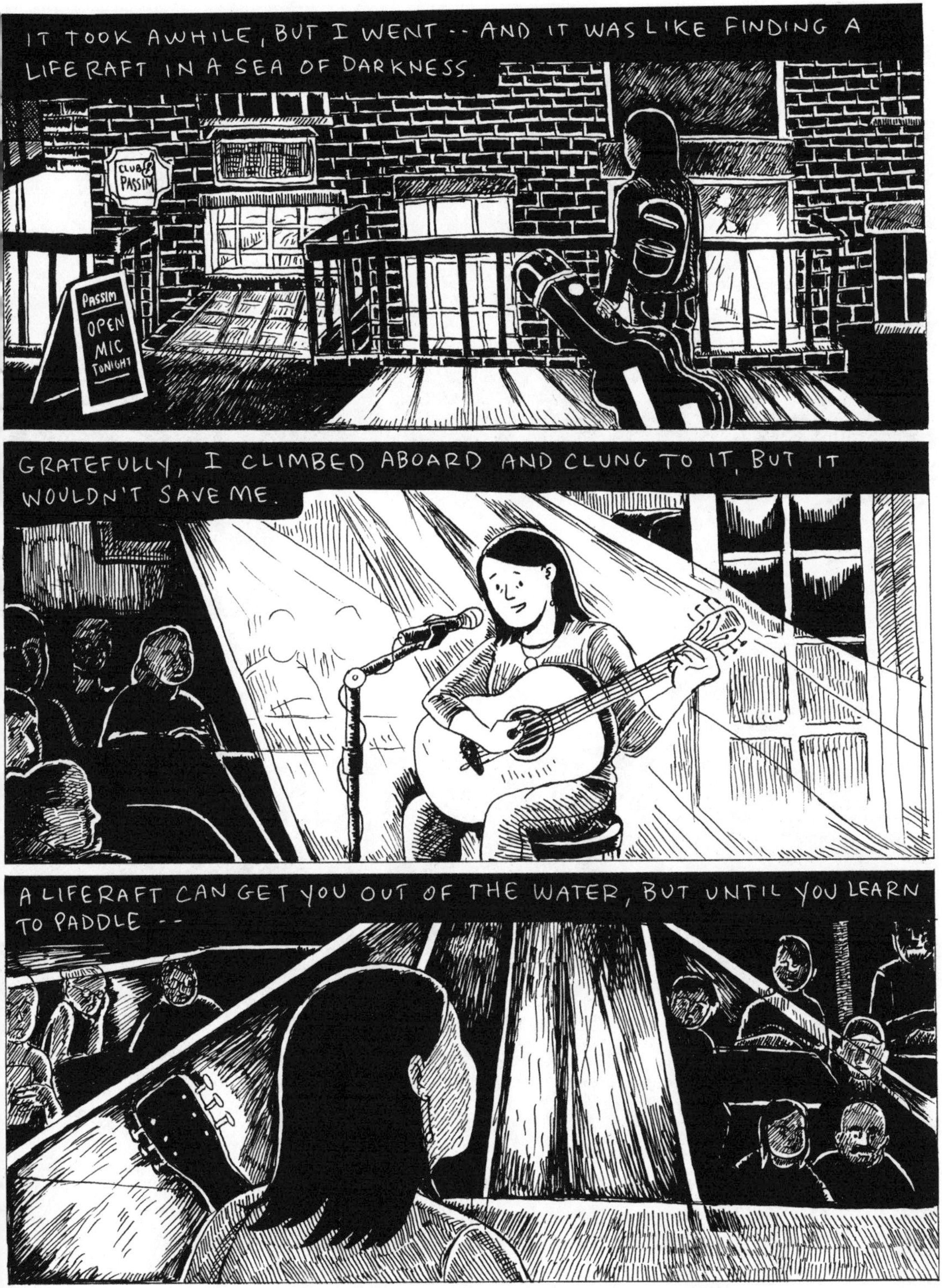
IT TOOK AWHILE, BUT I WENT -- AND IT WAS LIKE FINDING A LIFERAFT IN A SEA OF DARKNESS.
CLUB PASSIM
PASSIM
OPEN MIC TONIGHT
GRATEFULLY, I CLIMBED ABOARD AND CLUNG TO IT, BUT IT WOULDN'T SAVE ME.
A LIFERAFT CAN GET YOU OUT OF THE WATER, BUT UNTIL YOU LEARN TO PADDLE --

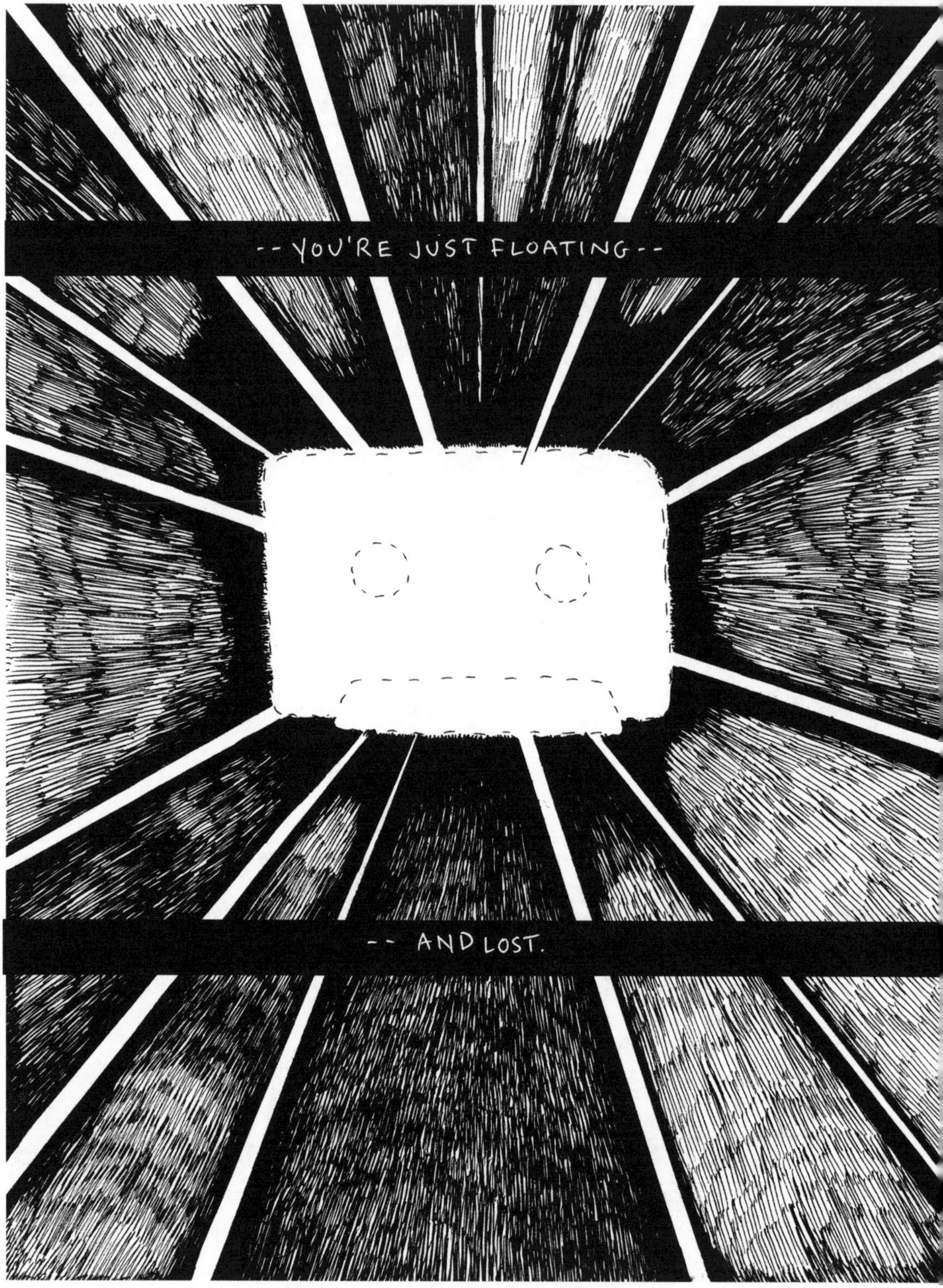
--YOU'RE JUST FLOATING--
-- AND LOST.

PART FIVE

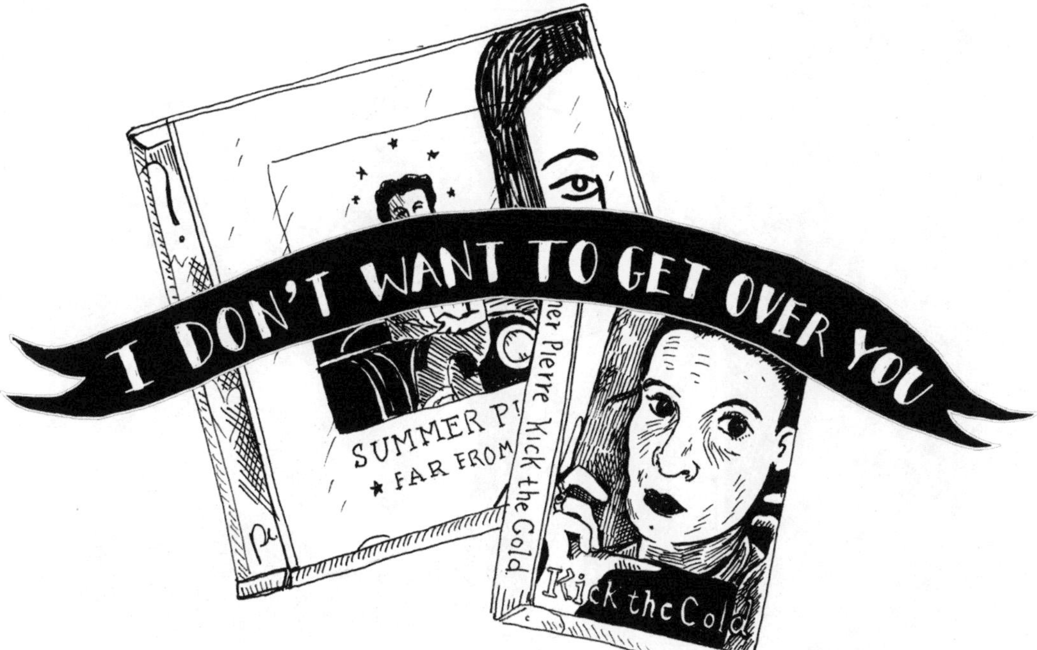
I DON'T WANT TO GET OVER YOU
SUMMER P
FAR FROM
ner Pierre Kick the Cold
Kick the Cold

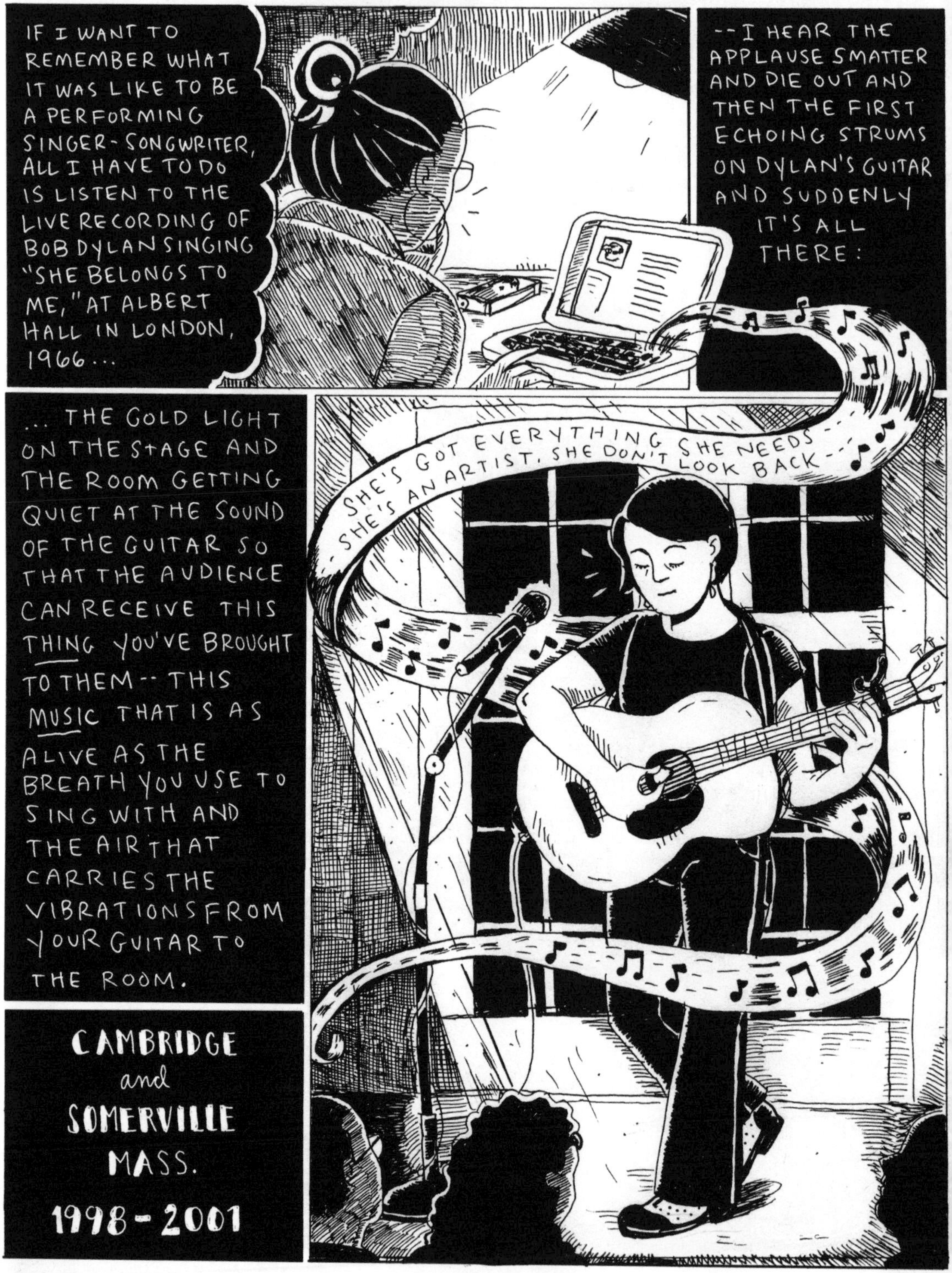
IF I WANT TO REMEMBER WHAT IT WAS LIKE TO BE A PERFORMING SINGER-SONGWRITER, ALL I HAVE TO DO IS LISTEN TO THE LIVE RECORDING OF BOB DYLAN SINGING "SHE BELONGS TO ME," AT ALBERT HALL IN LONDON, 1966...
--I HEAR THE APPLAUSE SMATTER AND DIE OUT AND THEN THE FIRST ECHOING STRUMS ON DYLAN'S GUITAR AND SUDDENLY IT'S ALL THERE:
... THE GOLD LIGHT ON THE STAGE AND THE ROOM GETTING QUIET AT THE SOUND OF THE GUITAR SO THAT THE AUDIENCE CAN RECEIVE THIS THING YOU'VE BROUGHT TO THEM -- THIS MUSIC THAT IS AS ALIVE AS THE BREATH YOU USE TO SING WITH AND THE AIR THAT CARRIES THE VIBRATIONS FROM YOUR GUITAR TO THE ROOM.
SHE'S GOT EVERYTHING SHE NEEDS
SHE'S AN ARTIST, SHE DON'T LOOK BACK
CAMBRIDGE and SOMERVILLE MASS. 1998-2001

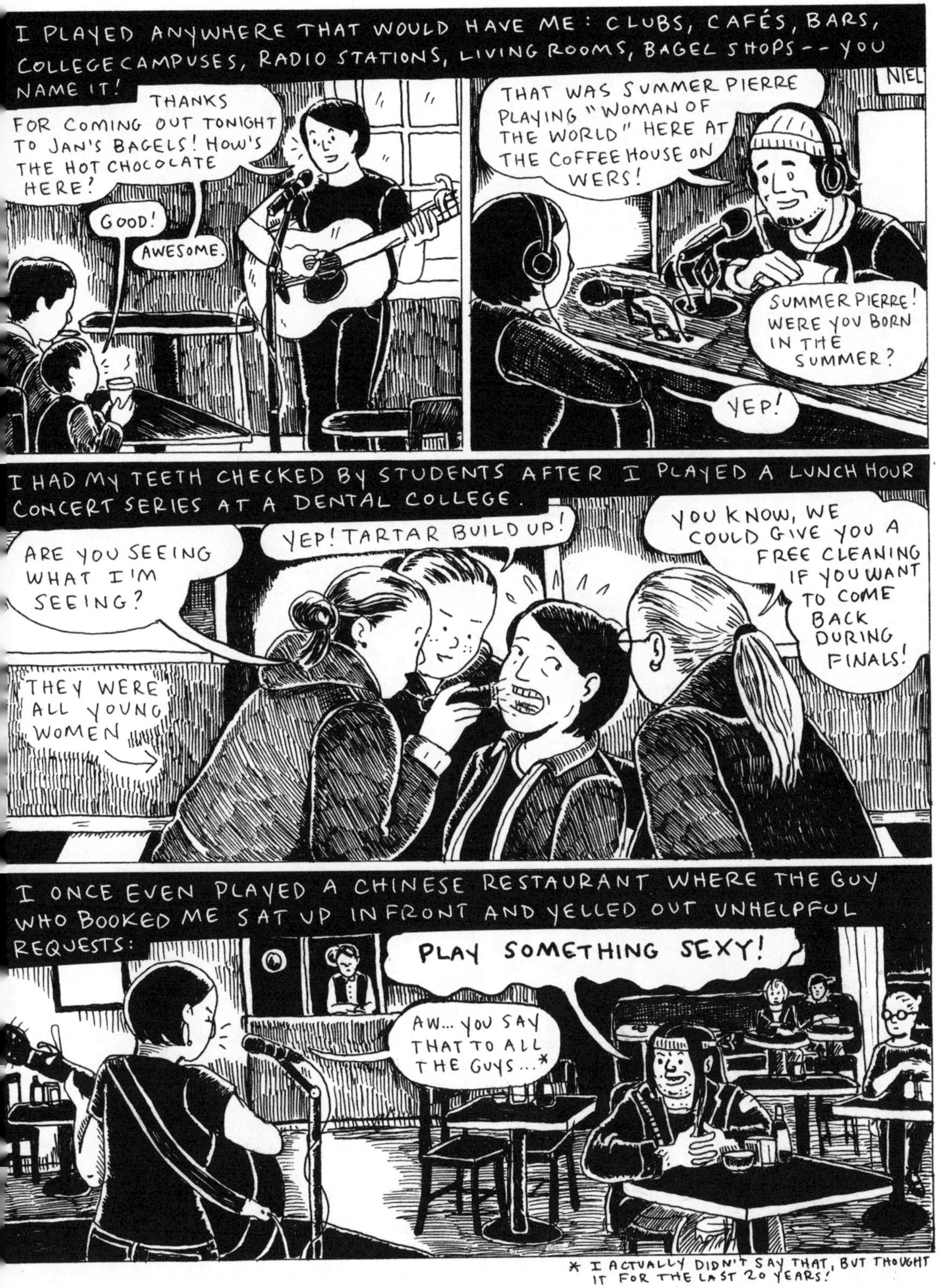
I PLAYED ANYWHERE THAT WOULD HAVE ME: CLUBS, CAFÉS, BARS, COLLEGE CAMPUSES, RADIO STATIONS, LIVING ROOMS, BAGEL SHOPS -- YOU NAME IT!
THANKS FOR COMING OUT TONIGHT TO JAN'S BAGELS! HOW'S THE HOT CHOCOLATE HERE?
GOOD!
AWESOME.
THAT WAS SUMMER PIERRE PLAYING "WOMAN OF THE WORLD" HERE AT THE COFFEE HOUSE ON WERS!
SUMMER PIERRE! WERE YOU BORN IN THE SUMMER?
YEP!
I HAD MY TEETH CHECKED BY STUDENTS AFTER I PLAYED A LUNCH HOUR CONCERT SERIES AT A DENTAL COLLEGE.
ARE YOU SEEING WHAT I'M SEEING?
YEP! TARTAR BUILD UP!
YOU KNOW, WE COULD GIVE YOU A FREE CLEANING IF YOU WANT TO COME BACK DURING FINALS!
THEY WERE ALL YOUNG WOMEN
I ONCE EVEN PLAYED A CHINESE RESTAURANT WHERE THE GUY WHO BOOKED ME SAT UP IN FRONT AND YELLED OUT UNHELPFUL REQUESTS:
PLAY SOMETHING SEXY!
AW... YOU SAY THAT TO ALL THE GUYS...*
* I ACTUALLY DIDN'T SAY THAT, BUT THOUGHT IT FOR THE LAST 20 YEARS!

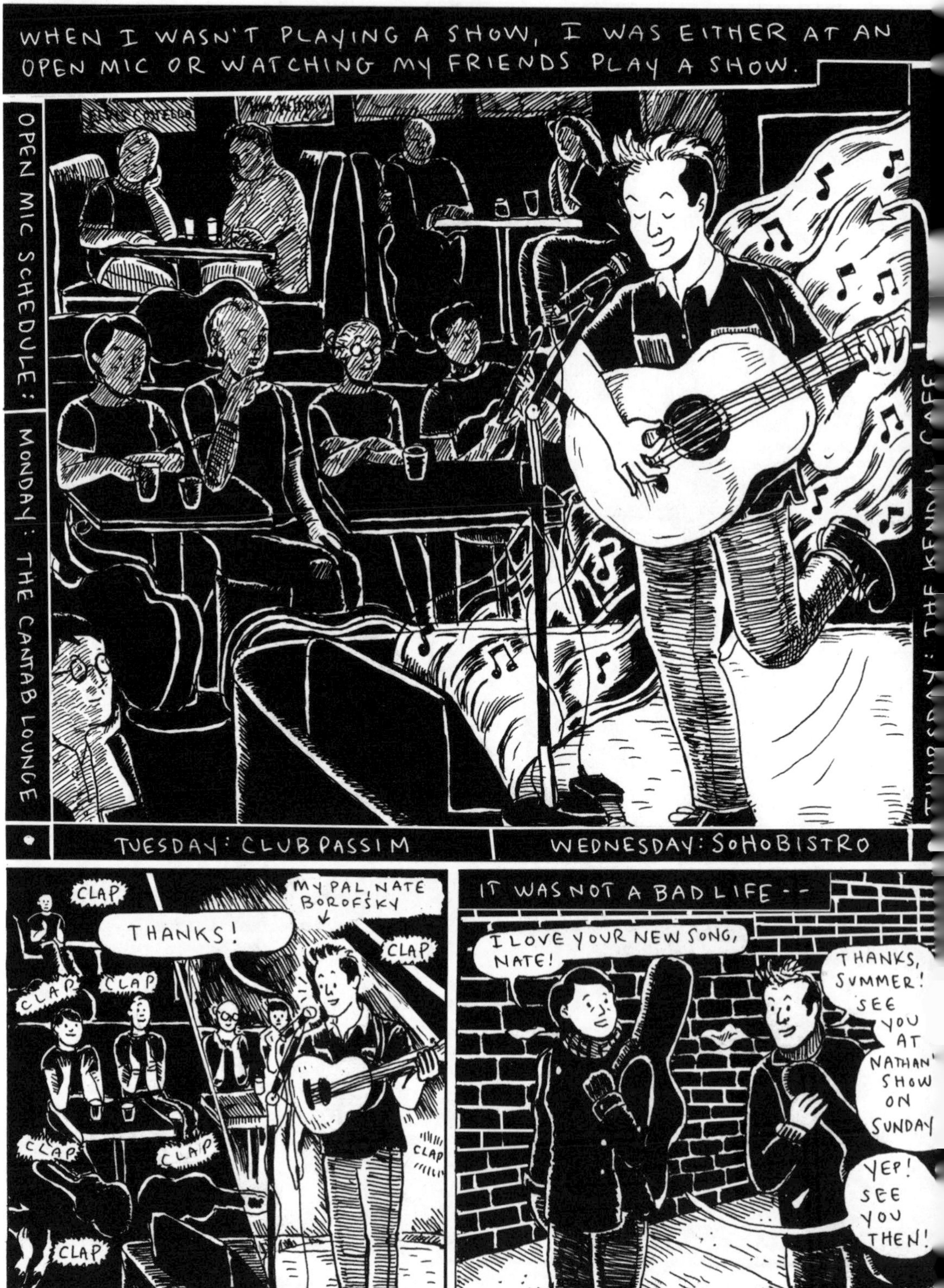

WHEN I WASN'T PLAYING A SHOW, I WAS EITHER AT AN OPEN MIC OR WATCHING MY FRIENDS PLAY A SHOW.
OPEN MIC SCHEDULE:
MONDAY: THE CANTAB LOUNGE
TUESDAY: CLUB PASSIM
WEDNESDAY: SOHOBISTRO
CLAP
MY PAL, NATE BOROFSKY
THANKS!
CLAP
CLAP
CLAP
CLAP
CLAP
CLAP
CLAP
IT WAS NOT A BAD LIFE --
I LOVE YOUR NEW SONG, NATE!
THANKS, SUMMER! SEE YOU AT NATHAN' SHOW ON SUNDAY
YEP! SEE YOU THEN!

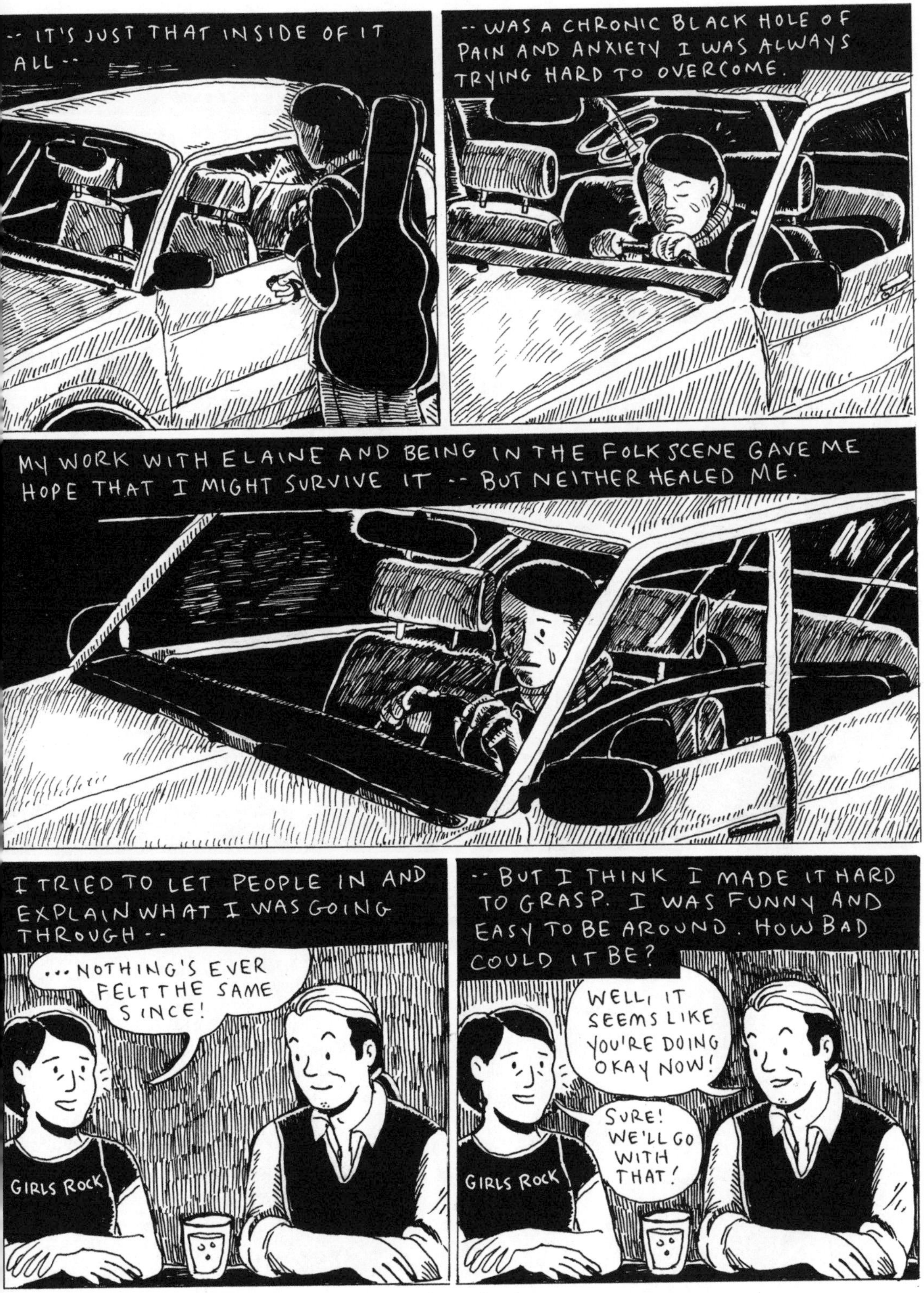
-- IT'S JUST THAT INSIDE OF IT ALL --
-- WAS A CHRONIC BLACK HOLE OF PAIN AND ANXIETY I WAS ALWAYS TRYING HARD TO OVERCOME.
MY WORK WITH ELAINE AND BEING IN THE FOLK SCENE GAVE ME HOPE THAT I MIGHT SURVIVE IT -- BUT NEITHER HEALED ME.
I TRIED TO LET PEOPLE IN AND EXPLAIN WHAT I WAS GOING THROUGH --
... NOTHING'S EVER FELT THE SAME SINCE!
GIRLS ROCK
-- BUT I THINK I MADE IT HARD TO GRASP. I WAS FUNNY AND EASY TO BE AROUND. HOW BAD COULD IT BE?
WELL, IT SEEMS LIKE YOU'RE DOING OKAY NOW!
SURE! WE'LL GO WITH THAT!
GIRLS ROCK

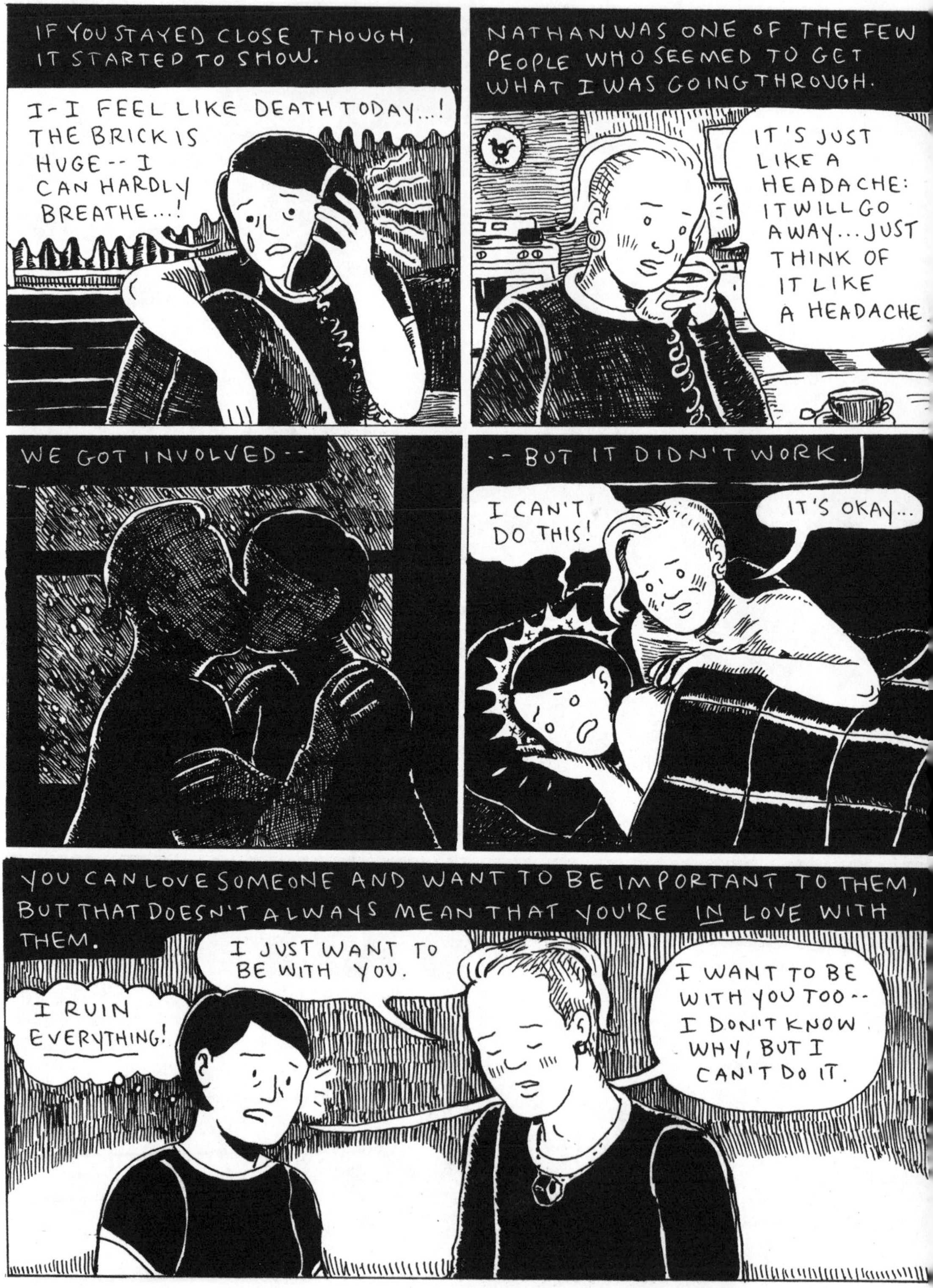
IF YOU STAYED CLOSE THOUGH, IT STARTED TO SHOW.
I-I FEEL LIKE DEATH TODAY...! THE BRICK IS HUGE-- I CAN HARDLY BREATHE...!
NATHAN WAS ONE OF THE FEW PEOPLE WHO SEEMED TO GET WHAT I WAS GOING THROUGH.
IT'S JUST LIKE A HEADACHE: IT WILL GO AWAY... JUST THINK OF IT LIKE A HEADACHE
WE GOT INVOLVED--
--BUT IT DIDN'T WORK.
I CAN'T DO THIS!
IT'S OKAY...
YOU CAN LOVE SOMEONE AND WANT TO BE IMPORTANT TO THEM, BUT THAT DOESN'T ALWAYS MEAN THAT YOU'RE IN LOVE WITH THEM.
I JUST WANT TO BE WITH YOU.
I RUIN EVERYTHING!
I WANT TO BE WITH YOU TOO-- I DON'T KNOW WHY, BUT I CAN'T DO IT.

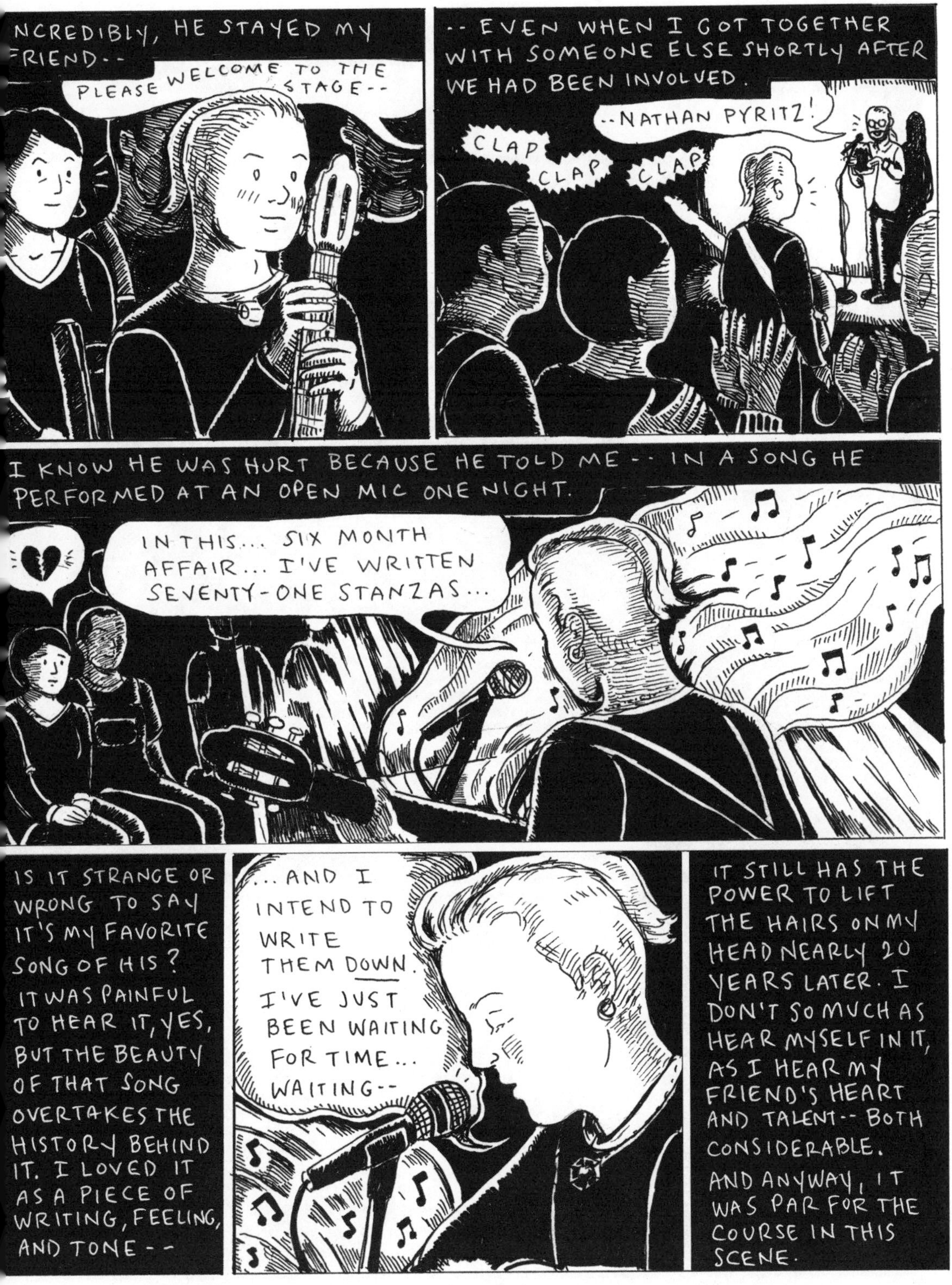
NCREDIBLY, HE STAYED MY FRIEND--
PLEASE WELCOME TO THE STAGE--
--EVEN WHEN I GOT TOGETHER WITH SOMEONE ELSE SHORTLY AFTER WE HAD BEEN INVOLVED.
--NATHAN PYRITZ!
CLAP
CLAP
CLAP
I KNOW HE WAS HURT BECAUSE HE TOLD ME-- IN A SONG HE PERFORMED AT AN OPEN MIC ONE NIGHT.
IN THIS... SIX MONTH AFFAIR... I'VE WRITTEN SEVENTY-ONE STANZAS...
IS IT STRANGE OR WRONG TO SAY IT'S MY FAVORITE SONG OF HIS? IT WAS PAINFUL TO HEAR IT, YES, BUT THE BEAUTY OF THAT SONG OVERTAKES THE HISTORY BEHIND IT. I LOVED IT AS A PIECE OF WRITING, FEELING, AND TONE--
...AND I INTEND TO WRITE THEM DOWN. I'VE JUST BEEN WAITING FOR TIME... WAITING--
IT STILL HAS THE POWER TO LIFT THE HAIRS ON MY HEAD NEARLY 20 YEARS LATER. I DON'T SO MUCH AS HEAR MYSELF IN IT, AS I HEAR MY FRIEND'S HEART AND TALENT-- BOTH CONSIDERABLE.
AND ANYWAY, IT WAS PAR FOR THE COURSE IN THIS SCENE.

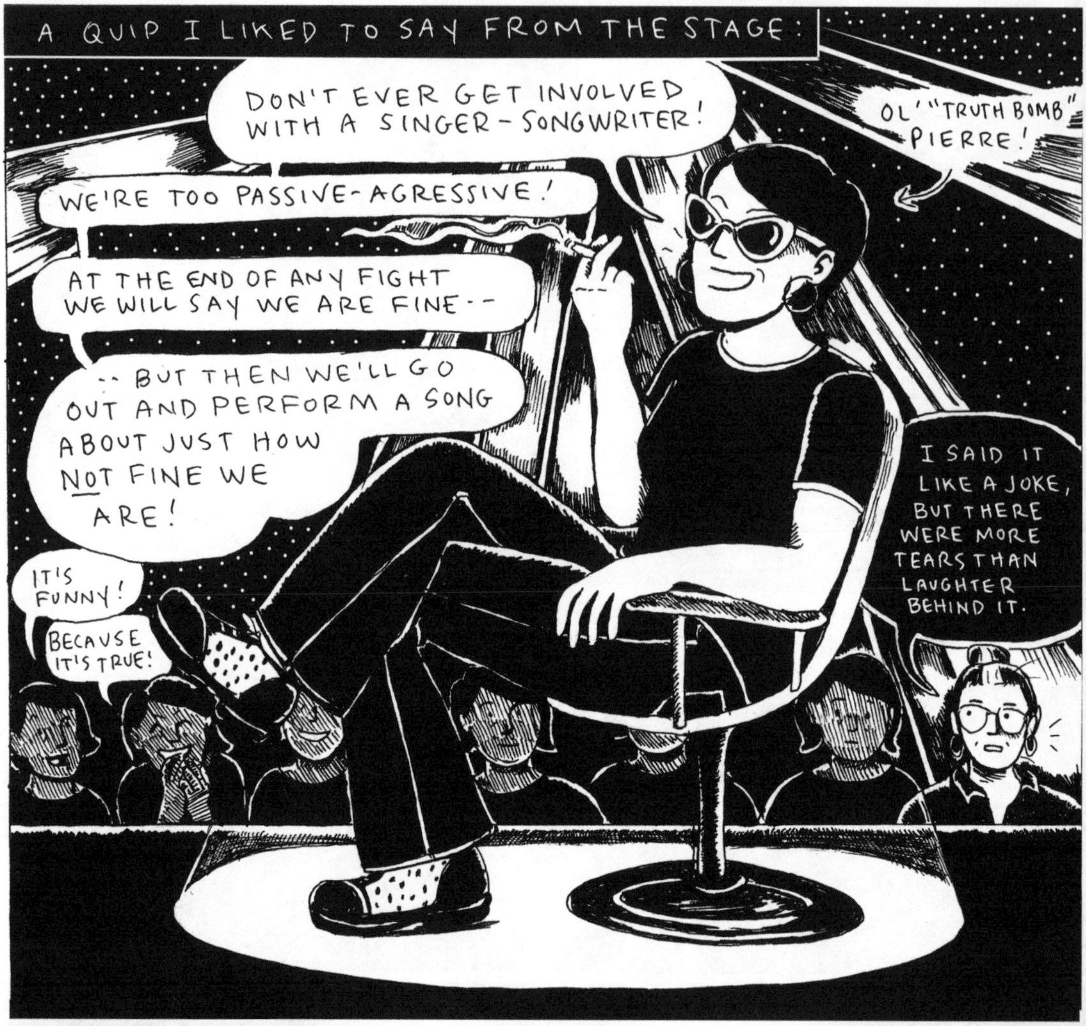
A QUIP I LIKED TO SAY FROM THE STAGE:
DON'T EVER GET INVOLVED WITH A SINGER-SONGWRITER!
OL' "TRUTH BOMB" PIERRE!
WE'RE TOO PASSIVE-AGRESSIVE!
AT THE END OF ANY FIGHT WE WILL SAY WE ARE FINE--
--BUT THEN WE'LL GO OUT AND PERFORM A SONG ABOUT JUST HOW NOT FINE WE ARE!
I SAID IT LIKE A JOKE, BUT THERE WERE MORE TEARS THAN LAUGHTER BEHIND IT.
IT'S FUNNY!
BECAUSE IT'S TRUE!

HEARTBREAK WAS A FAMILIAR THEME IN SONGS PERFORMED AT OPEN MICS AND SHOWS. YOU ALWAYS KNEW WHO WAS GOING THROUGH A BREAK-UP SIMPLY BY THE SONGS THEY PERFORMED.

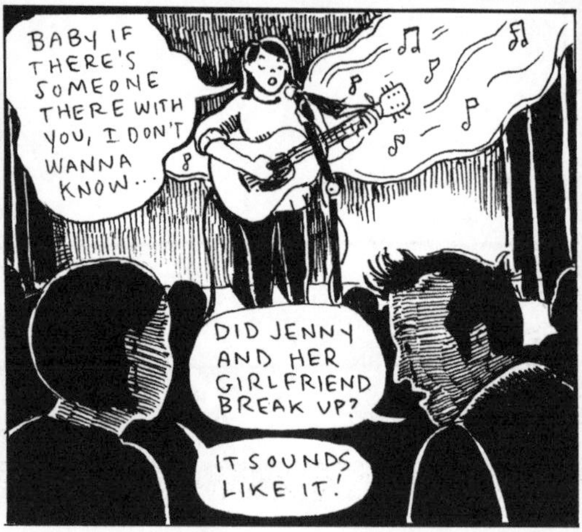
BABY IF THERE'S SOMEONE THERE WITH YOU, I DON'T WANNA KNOW...
DID JENNY AND HER GIRLFRIEND BREAK UP?
IT SOUNDS LIKE IT!

IN SOME CASES, THE ARTISTS WERE NEVER BETTER THAN WHEN THEY WERE IN THE THROES OF SOME PAINFUL RELATIONSHIP ISSUES--PRESENT COMPANY INCLUDED!

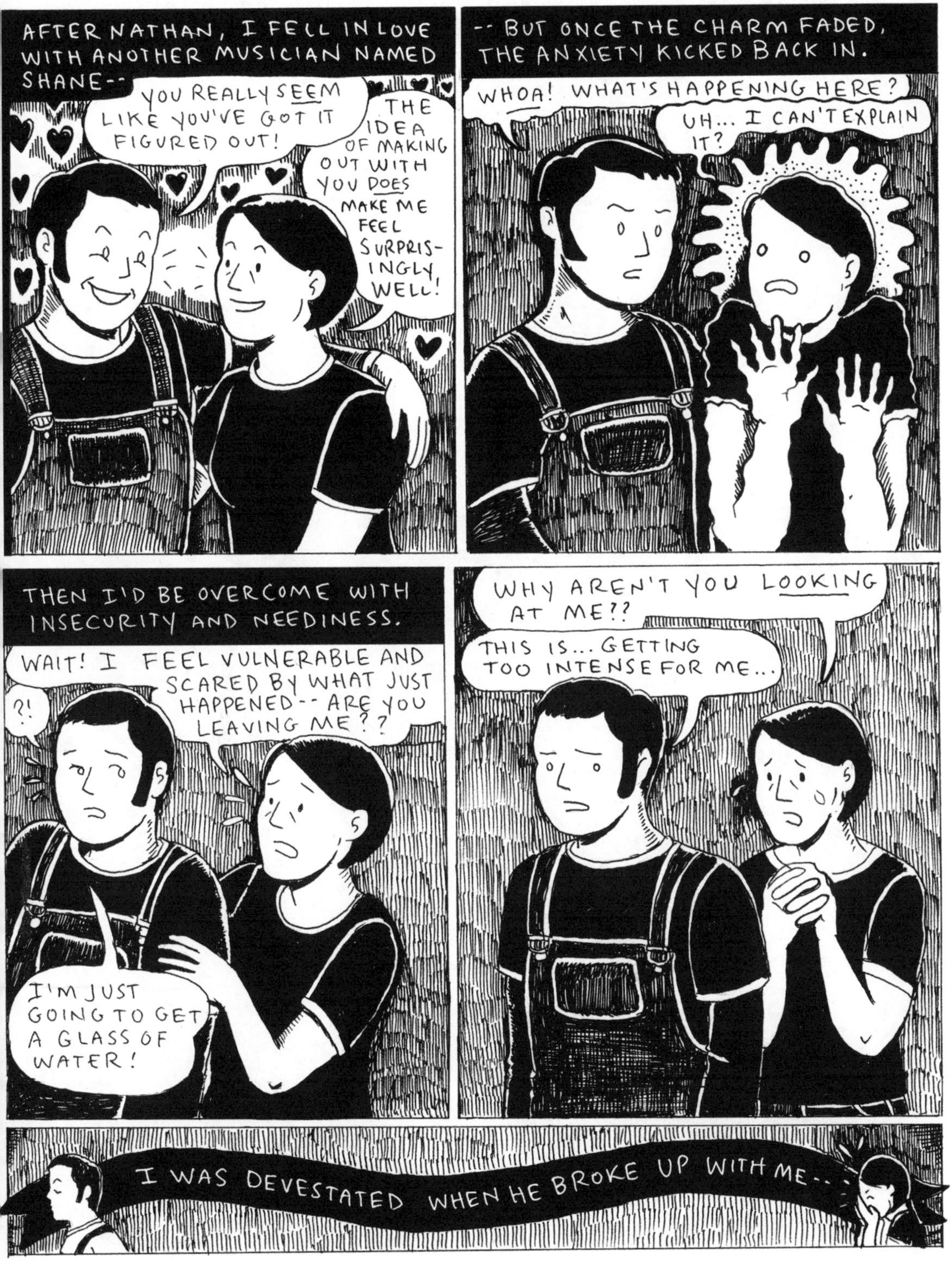
AFTER NATHAN, I FELL IN LOVE WITH ANOTHER MUSICIAN NAMED SHANE--
YOU REALLY SEEM LIKE YOU'VE GOT IT FIGURED OUT!
THE IDEA OF MAKING OUT WITH YOU DOES MAKE ME FEEL SURPRISINGLY WELL!
-- BUT ONCE THE CHARM FADED, THE ANXIETY KICKED BACK IN.
WHOA! WHAT'S HAPPENING HERE?
UH... I CAN'T EXPLAIN IT?
THEN I'D BE OVERCOME WITH INSECURITY AND NEEDINESS.
WAIT! I FEEL VULNERABLE AND SCARED BY WHAT JUST HAPPENED-- ARE YOU LEAVING ME??
?!
I'M JUST GOING TO GET A GLASS OF WATER!
WHY AREN'T YOU LOOKING AT ME??
THIS IS... GETTING TOO INTENSE FOR ME...
I WAS DEVESTATED WHEN HE BROKE UP WITH ME...

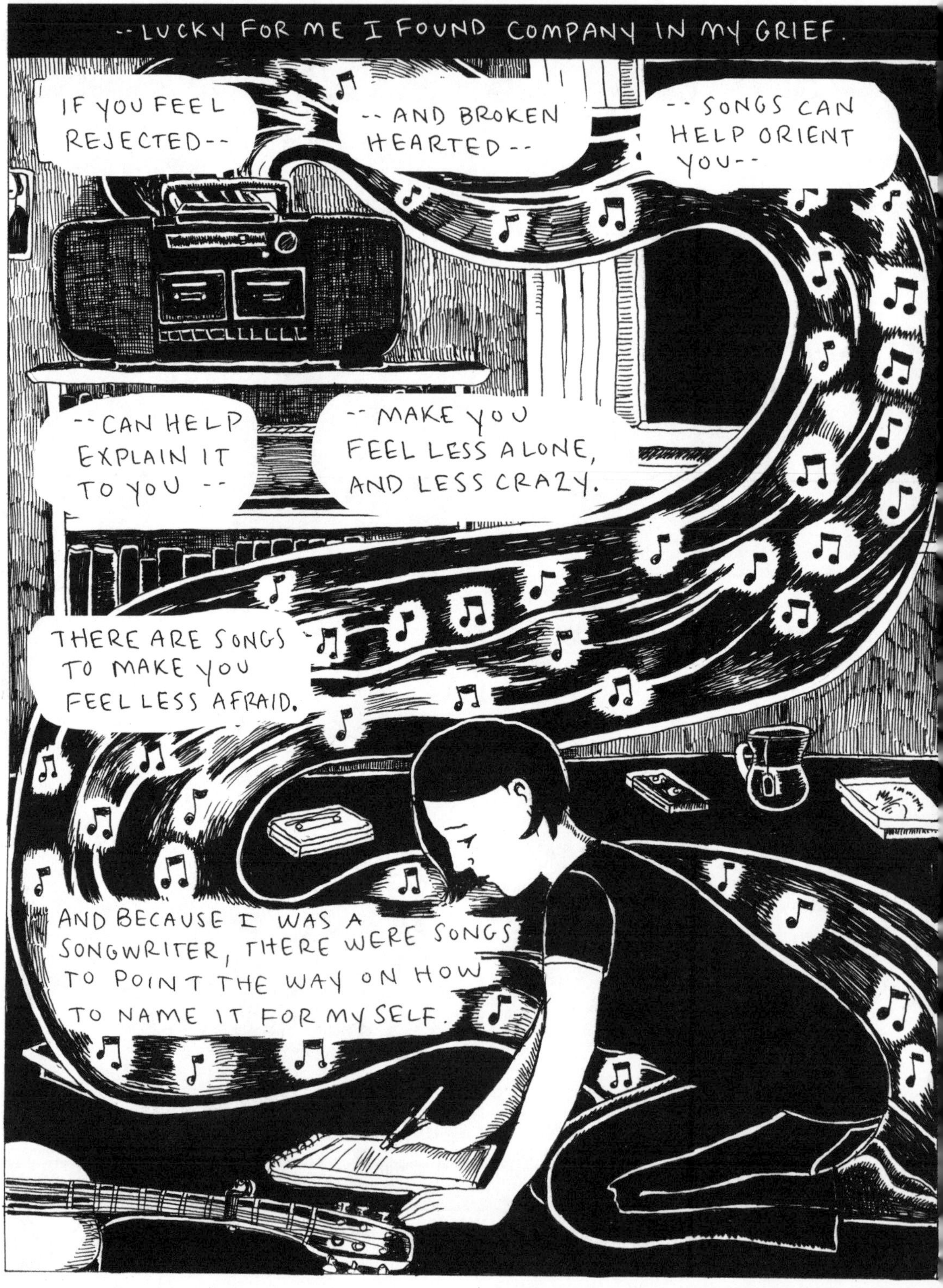
--LUCKY FOR ME I FOUND COMPANY IN MY GRIEF.
IF YOU FEEL REJECTED--
--AND BROKEN HEARTED--
--SONGS CAN HELP ORIENT YOU--
--CAN HELP EXPLAIN IT TO YOU --
--MAKE YOU FEEL LESS ALONE, AND LESS CRAZY.
THERE ARE SONGS TO MAKE YOU FEEL LESS AFRAID.
AND BECAUSE I WAS A SONGWRITER, THERE WERE SONGS TO POINT THE WAY ON HOW TO NAME IT FOR MYSELF.

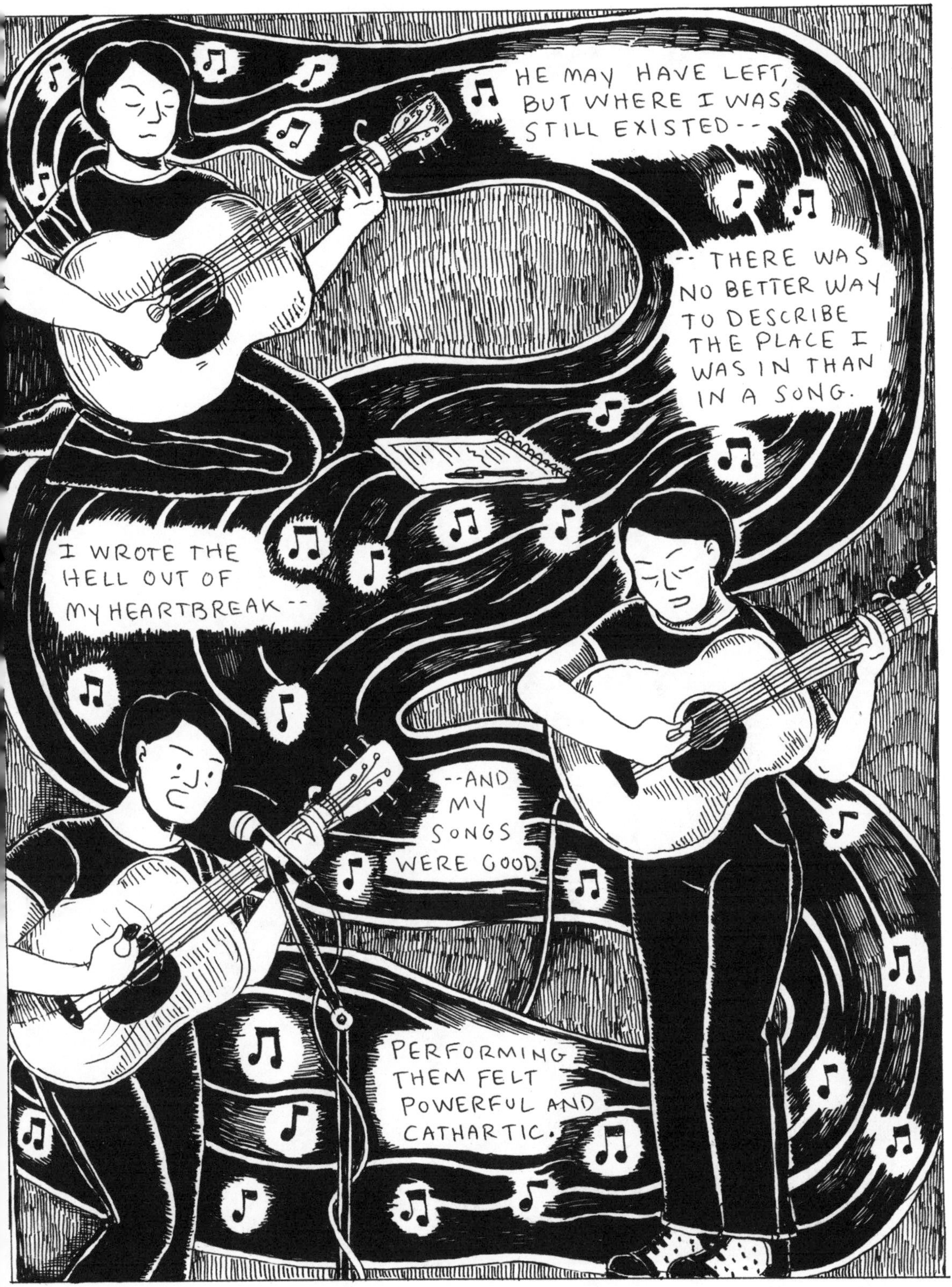
HE MAY HAVE LEFT, BUT WHERE I WAS STILL EXISTED--
--THERE WAS NO BETTER WAY TO DESCRIBE THE PLACE I WAS IN THAN IN A SONG.
I WROTE THE HELL OUT OF MY HEARTBREAK--
--AND MY SONGS WERE GOOD.
PERFORMING THEM FELT POWERFUL AND CATHARTIC.

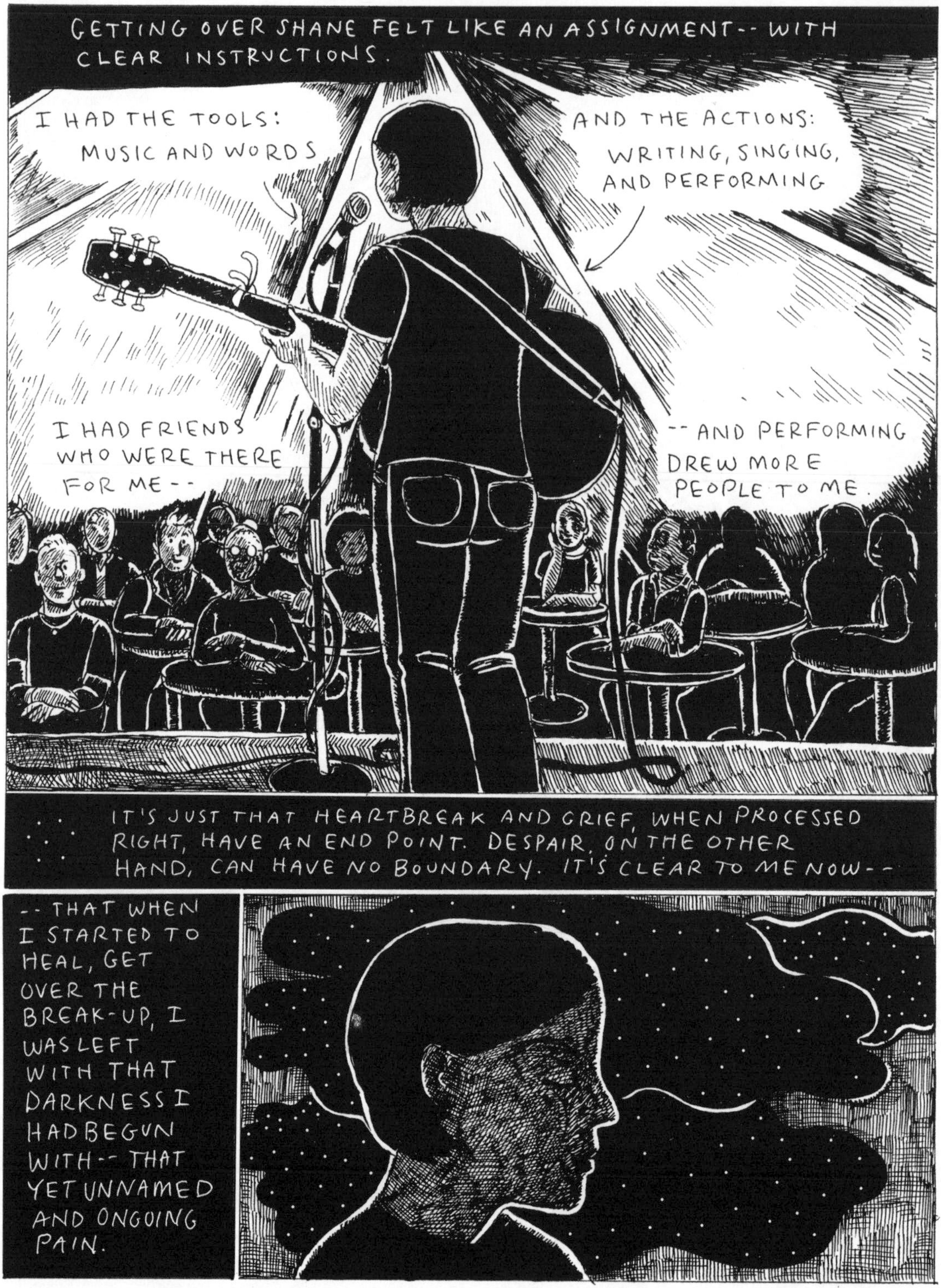
GETTING OVER SHANE FELT LIKE AN ASSIGNMENT-- WITH CLEAR INSTRUCTIONS.
I HAD THE TOOLS: MUSIC AND WORDS
AND THE ACTIONS: WRITING, SINGING, AND PERFORMING
I HAD FRIENDS WHO WERE THERE FOR ME--
--AND PERFORMING DREW MORE PEOPLE TO ME.
... IT'S JUST THAT HEARTBREAK AND GRIEF, WHEN PROCESSED RIGHT, HAVE AN END POINT. DESPAIR, ON THE OTHER HAND, CAN HAVE NO BOUNDARY. IT'S CLEAR TO ME NOW--
--THAT WHEN I STARTED TO HEAL, GET OVER THE BREAK-UP, I WAS LEFT WITH THAT DARKNESS I HAD BEGUN WITH-- THAT YET UNNAMED AND ONGOING PAIN.

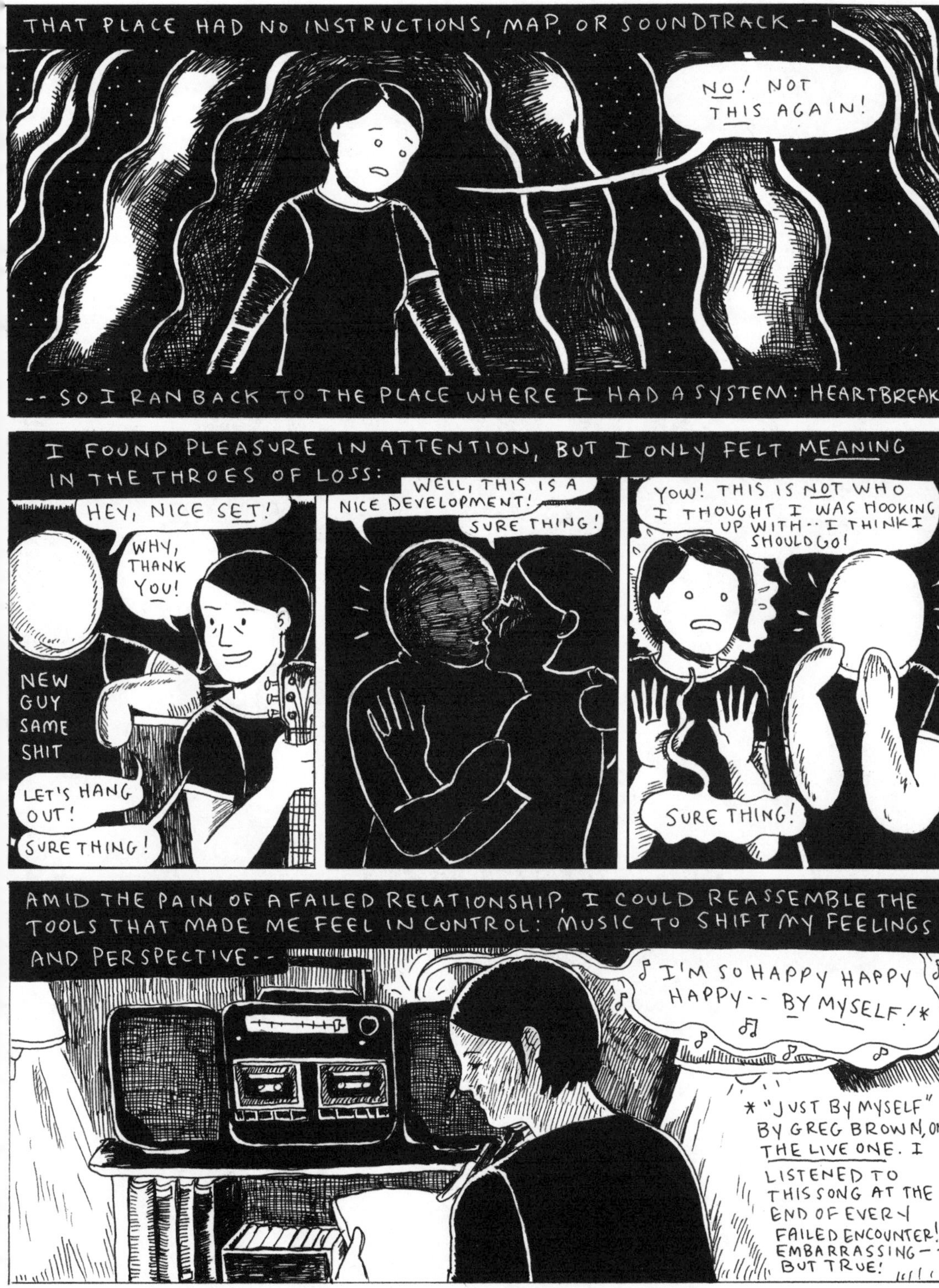
THAT PLACE HAD NO INSTRUCTIONS, MAP, OR SOUNDTRACK--
NO! NOT THIS AGAIN!
--SO I RAN BACK TO THE PLACE WHERE I HAD A SYSTEM: HEARTBREAK.
I FOUND PLEASURE IN ATTENTION, BUT I ONLY FELT MEANING IN THE THROES OF LOSS:
HEY, NICE SET!
WHY, THANK YOU!
NEW GUY SAME SHIT
LET'S HANG OUT!
SURE THING!
WELL, THIS IS A NICE DEVELOPMENT!
SURE THING!
YOW! THIS IS NOT WHO I THOUGHT I WAS HOOKING UP WITH.. I THINK I SHOULD GO!
SURE THING!
AMID THE PAIN OF A FAILED RELATIONSHIP, I COULD REASSEMBLE THE TOOLS THAT MADE ME FEEL IN CONTROL: MUSIC TO SHIFT MY FEELINGS AND PERSPECTIVE--
I'M SO HAPPY HAPPY HAPPY-- BY MYSELF!*
* "JUST BY MYSELF" BY GREG BROWN, ON THE LIVE ONE. I LISTENED TO THIS SONG AT THE END OF EVERY FAILED ENCOUNTER! EMBARRASSING-- BUT TRUE!

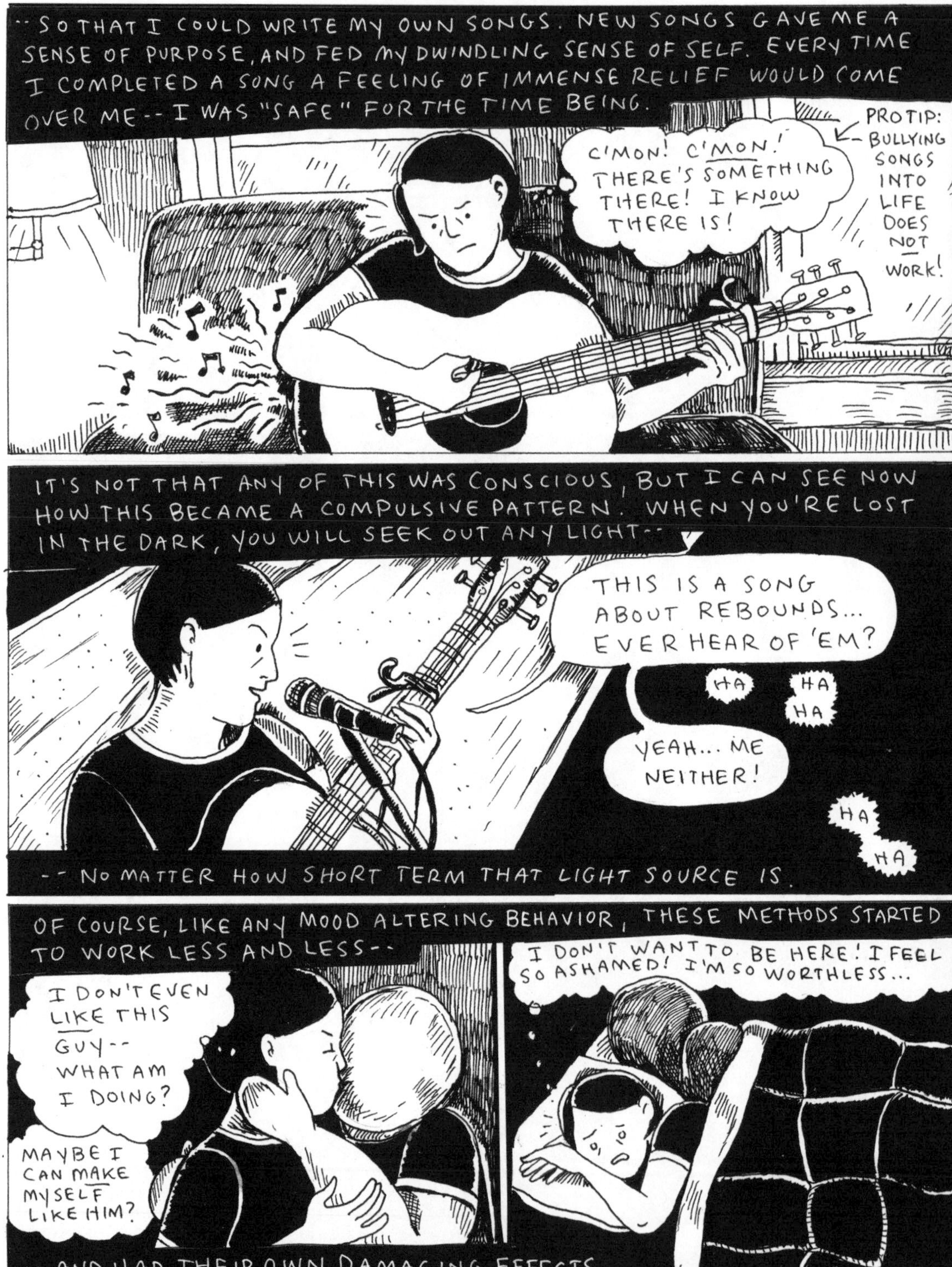
--SO THAT I COULD WRITE MY OWN SONGS. NEW SONGS GAVE ME A SENSE OF PURPOSE, AND FED MY DWINDLING SENSE OF SELF. EVERY TIME I COMPLETED A SONG A FEELING OF IMMENSE RELIEF WOULD COME OVER ME-- I WAS "SAFE" FOR THE TIME BEING.
C'MON! C'MON! THERE'S SOMETHING THERE! I KNOW THERE IS!
PROTIP: BULLYING SONGS INTO LIFE DOES NOT WORK!
IT'S NOT THAT ANY OF THIS WAS CONSCIOUS, BUT I CAN SEE NOW HOW THIS BECAME A COMPULSIVE PATTERN. WHEN YOU'RE LOST IN THE DARK, YOU WILL SEEK OUT ANY LIGHT--
THIS IS A SONG ABOUT REBOUNDS... EVER HEAR OF 'EM?
HA
HA HA
YEAH... ME NEITHER!
HA HA
-- NO MATTER HOW SHORT TERM THAT LIGHT SOURCE IS.
OF COURSE, LIKE ANY MOOD ALTERING BEHAVIOR, THESE METHODS STARTED TO WORK LESS AND LESS--
I DON'T EVEN LIKE THIS GUY-- WHAT AM I DOING?
MAYBE I CAN MAKE MYSELF LIKE HIM?
I DON'T WANT TO BE HERE! I FEEL SO ASHAMED! I'M SO WORTHLESS...
-- AND HAD THEIR OWN DAMAGING EFFECTS.

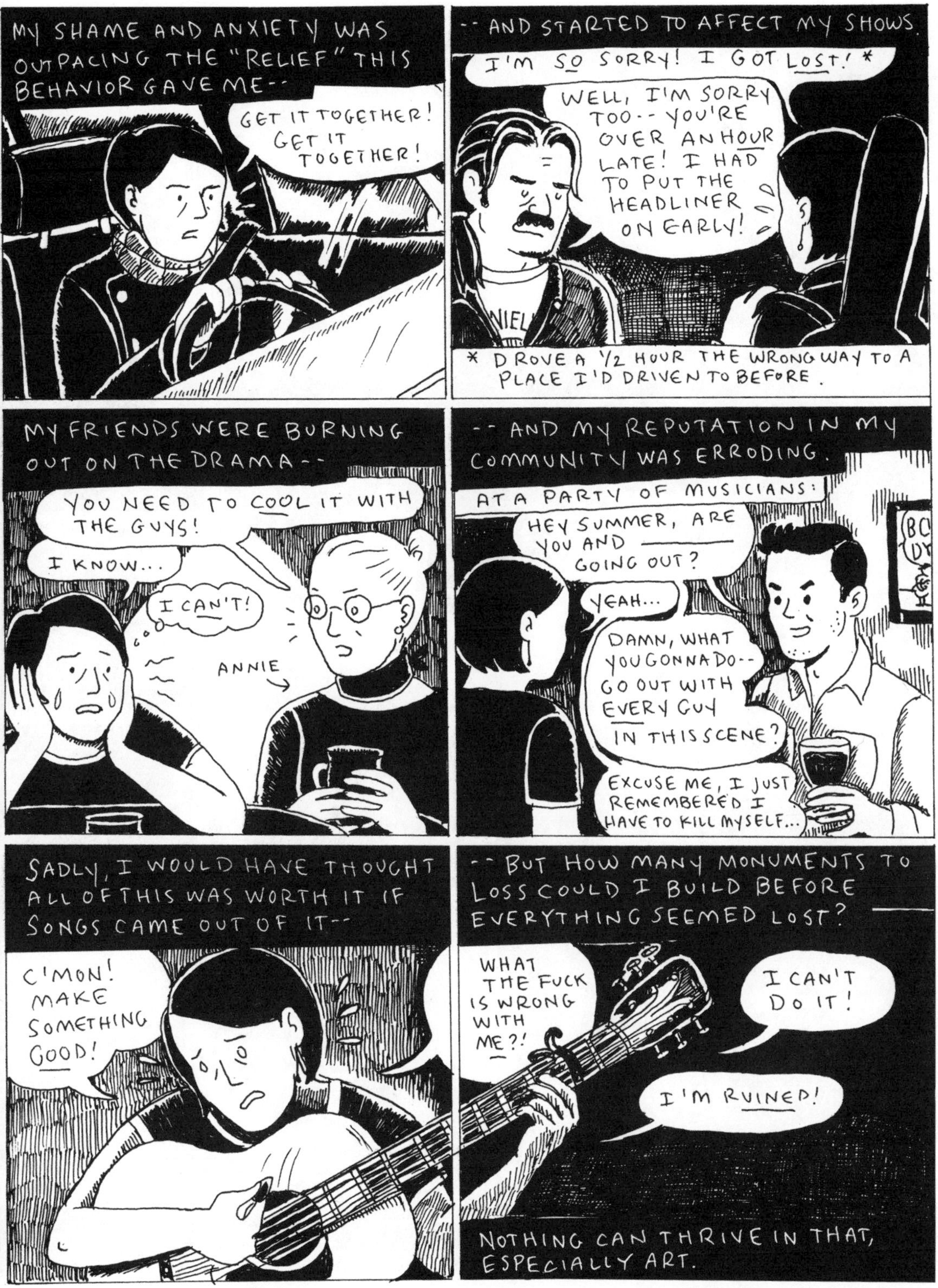
MY SHAME AND ANXIETY WAS OUTPACING THE "RELIEF" THIS BEHAVIOR GAVE ME--
GET IT TOGETHER! GET IT TOGETHER!
-- AND STARTED TO AFFECT MY SHOWS.
I'M SO SORRY! I GOT LOST! *
WELL, I'M SORRY TOO -- YOU'RE OVER AN HOUR LATE! I HAD TO PUT THE HEADLINER ON EARLY!
* DROVE A 1/2 HOUR THE WRONG WAY TO A PLACE I'D DRIVEN TO BEFORE.
MY FRIENDS WERE BURNING OUT ON THE DRAMA--
YOU NEED TO COOL IT WITH THE GUYS!
I KNOW...
I CAN'T!
ANNIE
-- AND MY REPUTATION IN MY COMMUNITY WAS ERRODING.
AT A PARTY OF MUSICIANS:
HEY SUMMER, ARE YOU AND ______ GOING OUT?
YEAH...
DAMN, WHAT YOU GONNA DO -- GO OUT WITH EVERY GUY IN THIS SCENE?
EXCUSE ME, I JUST REMEMBERED I HAVE TO KILL MYSELF...
SADLY, I WOULD HAVE THOUGHT ALL OF THIS WAS WORTH IT IF SONGS CAME OUT OF IT--
C'MON! MAKE SOMETHING GOOD!
-- BUT HOW MANY MONUMENTS TO LOSS COULD I BUILD BEFORE EVERYTHING SEEMED LOST?
WHAT THE FUCK IS WRONG WITH ME?!
I CAN'T DO IT!
I'M RUINED!
NOTHING CAN THRIVE IN THAT, ESPECIALLY ART.

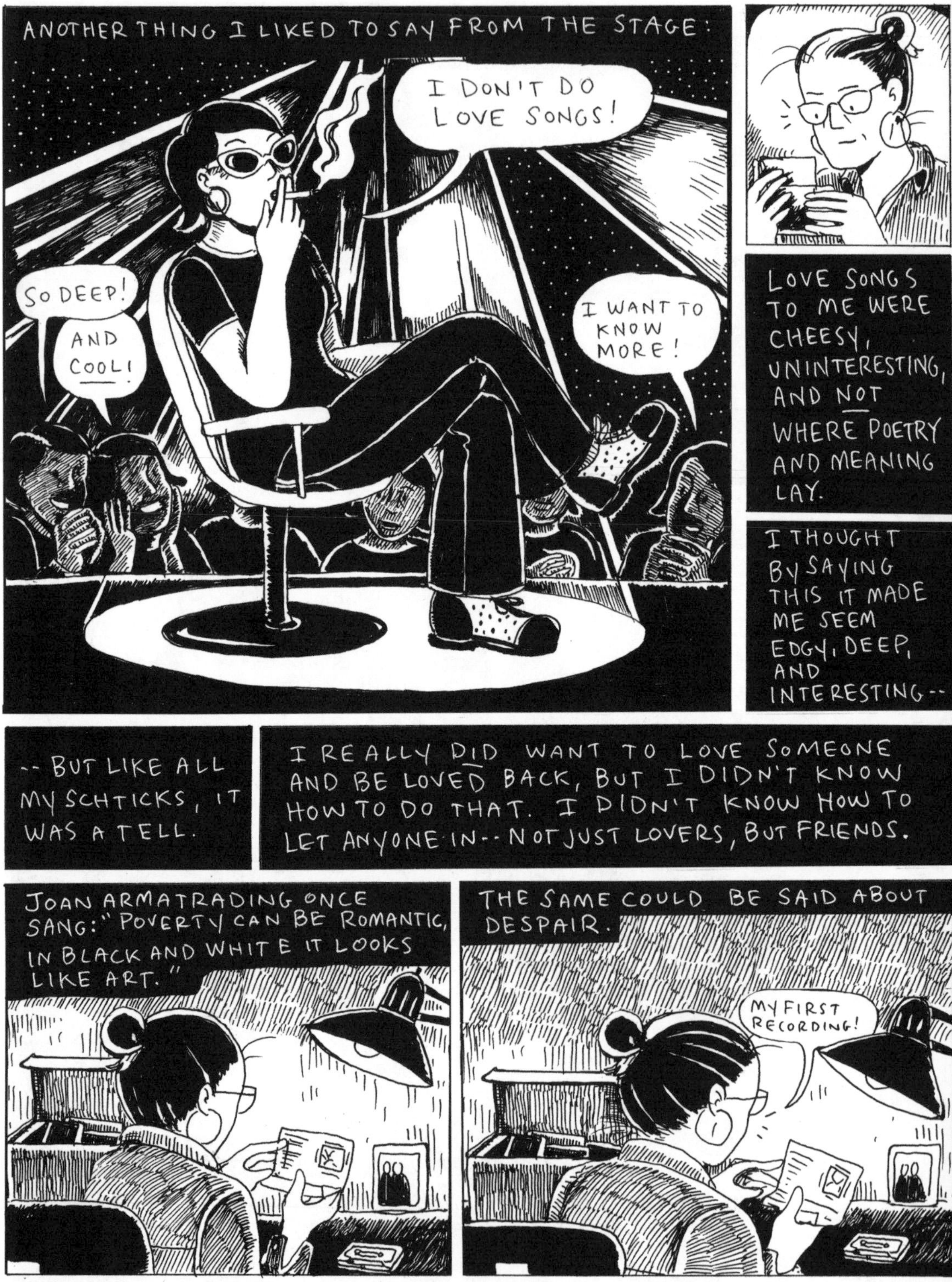
ANOTHER THING I LIKED TO SAY FROM THE STAGE:
I DON'T DO LOVE SONGS!
SO DEEP!
AND COOL!
I WANT TO KNOW MORE!
LOVE SONGS TO ME WERE CHEESY, UNINTERESTING, AND NOT WHERE POETRY AND MEANING LAY.
I THOUGHT BY SAYING THIS IT MADE ME SEEM EDGY, DEEP, AND INTERESTING--
-- BUT LIKE ALL MY SCHTICKS, IT WAS A TELL.
I REALLY DID WANT TO LOVE SOMEONE AND BE LOVED BACK, BUT I DIDN'T KNOW HOW TO DO THAT. I DIDN'T KNOW HOW TO LET ANYONE IN -- NOT JUST LOVERS, BUT FRIENDS.
JOAN ARMATRADING ONCE SANG: "POVERTY CAN BE ROMANTIC, IN BLACK AND WHITE IT LOOKS LIKE ART."
THE SAME COULD BE SAID ABOUT DESPAIR.
MY FIRST RECORDING!

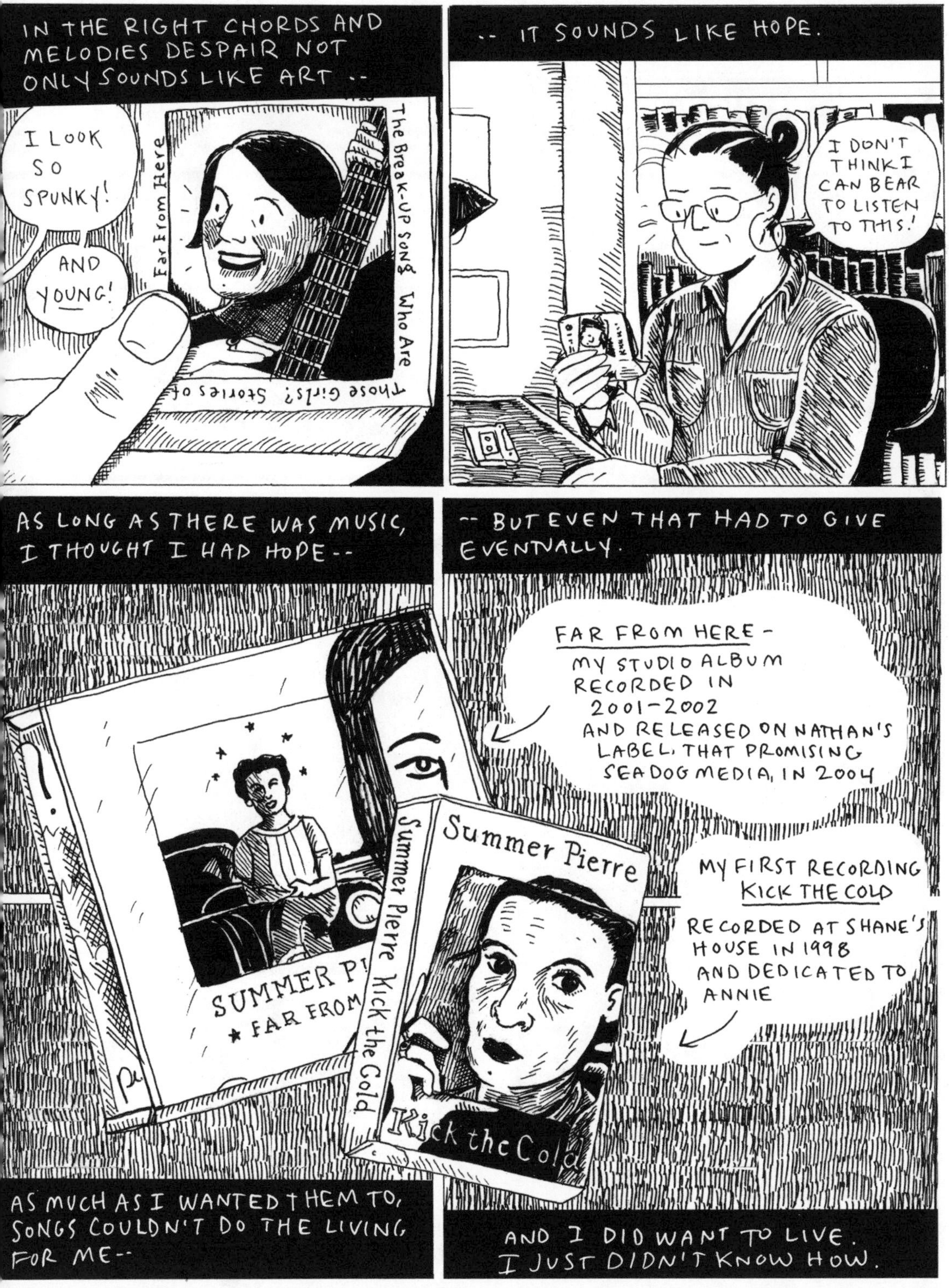
IN THE RIGHT CHORDS AND MELODIES DESPAIR NOT ONLY SOUNDS LIKE ART --
I LOOK SO SPUNKY!
AND YOUNG!
Far From Here
The Break-Up Song Who Are Those Girls? Stories of
-- IT SOUNDS LIKE HOPE.
I DON'T THINK I CAN BEAR TO LISTEN TO THIS!
AS LONG AS THERE WAS MUSIC, I THOUGHT I HAD HOPE --
-- BUT EVEN THAT HAD TO GIVE EVENTUALLY.
FAR FROM HERE - MY STUDIO ALBUM RECORDED IN 2001-2002 AND RELEASED ON NATHAN'S LABEL, THAT PROMISING SEADOG MEDIA, IN 2004
SUMMER P
FAR FROM
Summer Pierre
Summer Pierre Kick the Cold
Kick the Cold
MY FIRST RECORDING KICK THE COLD RECORDED AT SHANE'S HOUSE IN 1998 AND DEDICATED TO ANNIE
AS MUCH AS I WANTED THEM TO, SONGS COULDN'T DO THE LIVING FOR ME --
AND I DID WANT TO LIVE. I JUST DIDN'T KNOW HOW.

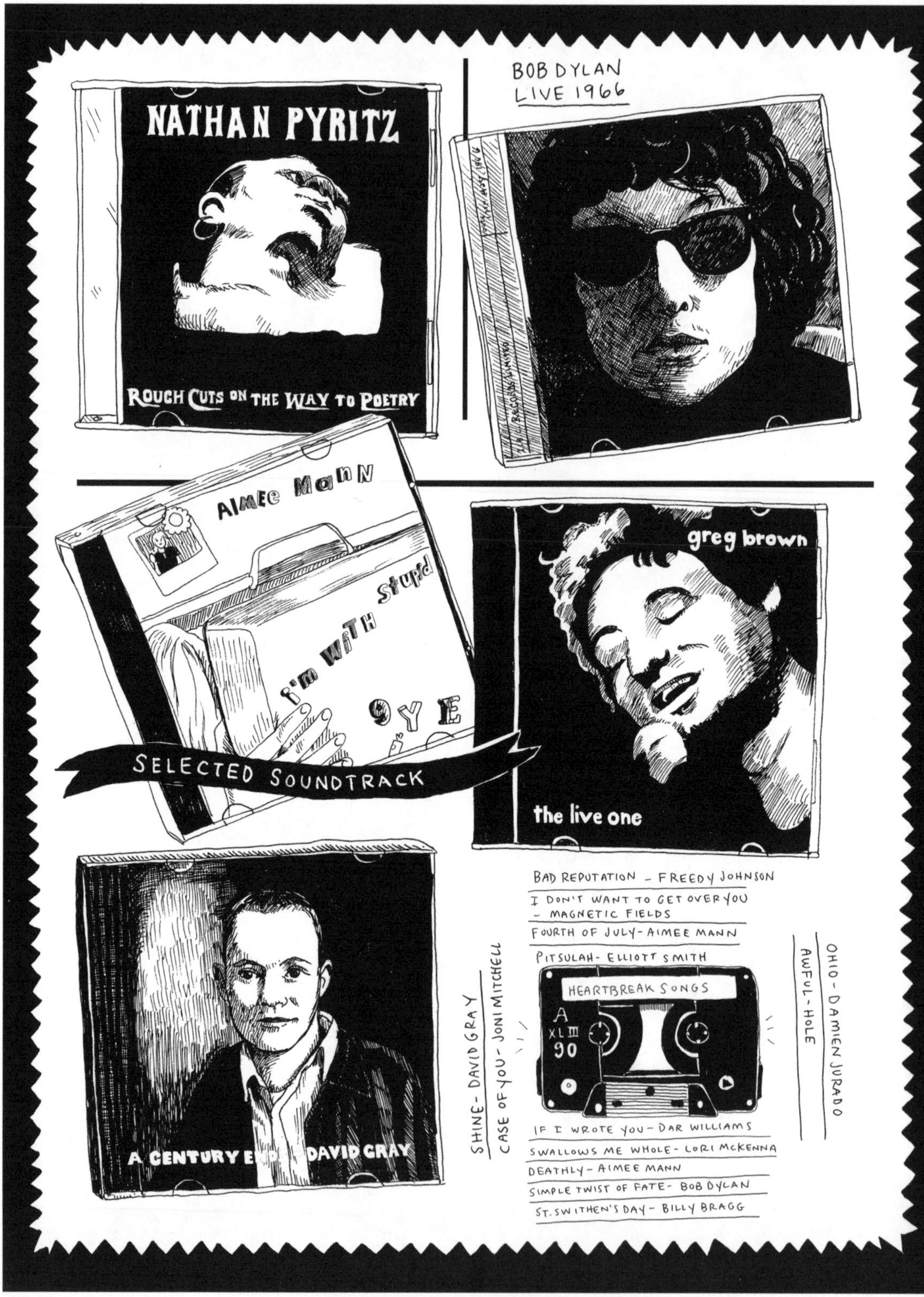

NATHAN PYRITZ
ROUGH CUTS ON THE WAY TO POETRY
BOB DYLAN
LIVE 1966
AIMEE MANN
I'M WITH STUPID
greg brown
the live one
SELECTED SOUNDTRACK
A CENTURY E
DAVID GRAY
BAD REPUTATION - FREEDY JOHNSON
I DON'T WANT TO GET OVER YOU - MAGNETIC FIELDS
FOURTH OF JULY - AIMEE MANN
PITSULAH - ELLIOTT SMITH
SHINE - DAVID GRAY
CASE OF YOU - JONI MITCHELL
HEARTBREAK SONGS
A
XLII
90
OHIO - DAMIEN JURADO
AWFUL - HOLE
IF I WROTE YOU - DAR WILLIAMS
SWALLOWS ME WHOLE - LORI MCKENNA
DEATHLY - AIMEE MANN
SIMPLE TWIST OF FATE - BOB DYLAN
ST. SWITHEN'S DAY - BILLY BRAGG

PART SIX

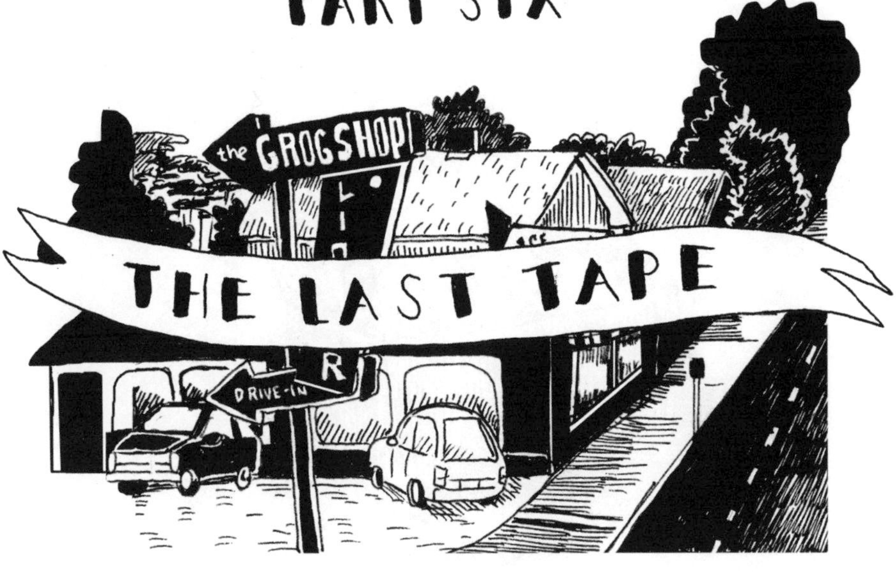
the GROGSHOP
THE LAST TAPE
DRIVE-IN
R

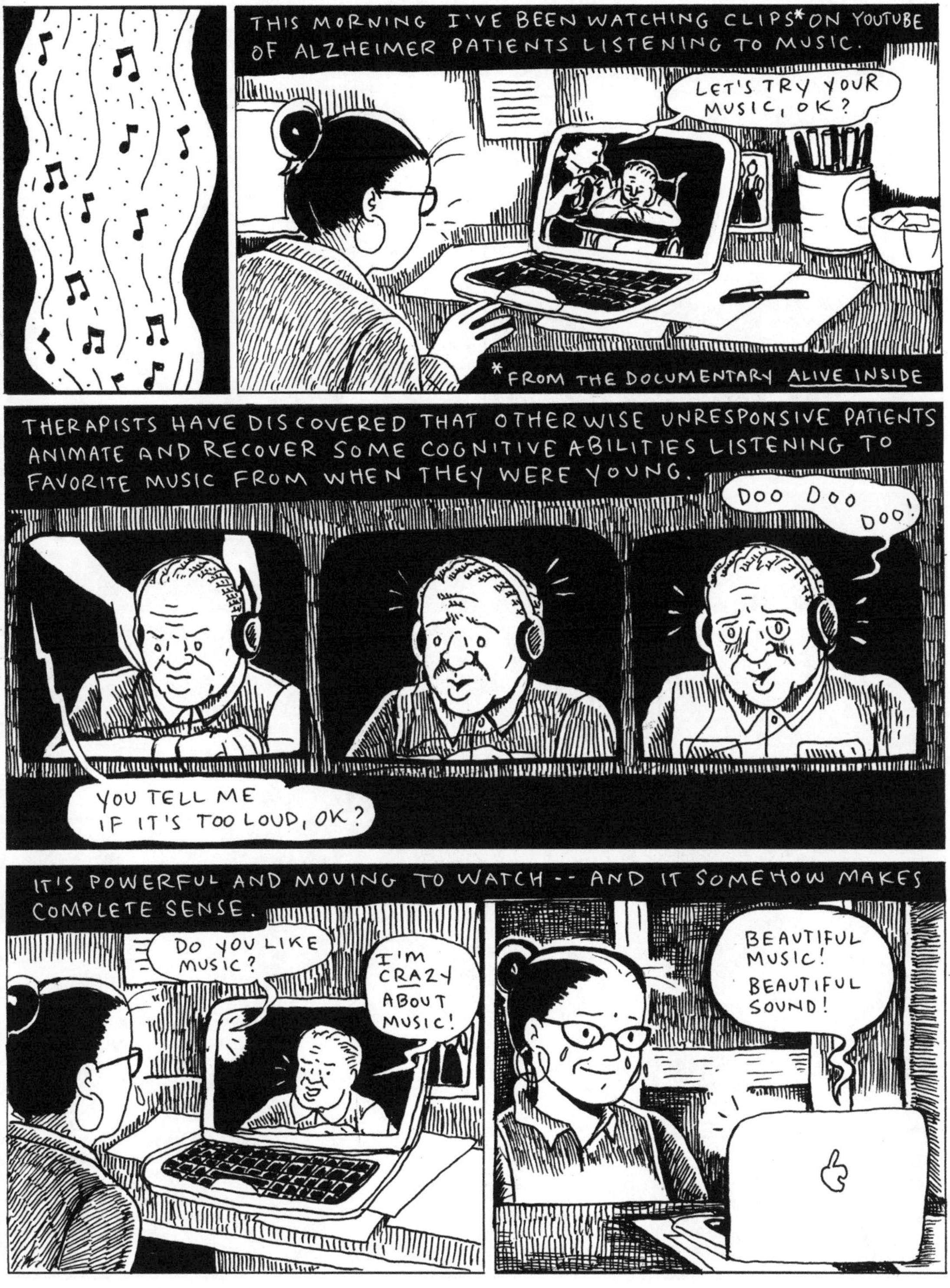

THIS MORNING I'VE BEEN WATCHING CLIPS* ON YOUTUBE OF ALZHEIMER PATIENTS LISTENING TO MUSIC.
LET'S TRY YOUR MUSIC, OK?
*FROM THE DOCUMENTARY ALIVE INSIDE
THERAPISTS HAVE DISCOVERED THAT OTHERWISE UNRESPONSIVE PATIENTS ANIMATE AND RECOVER SOME COGNITIVE ABILITIES LISTENING TO FAVORITE MUSIC FROM WHEN THEY WERE YOUNG.
YOU TELL ME IF IT'S TOO LOUD, OK?
DOO DOO DOO DOO!
IT'S POWERFUL AND MOVING TO WATCH -- AND IT SOMEHOW MAKES COMPLETE SENSE.
DO YOU LIKE MUSIC?
I'M CRAZY ABOUT MUSIC!
BEAUTIFUL MUSIC!
BEAUTIFUL SOUND!

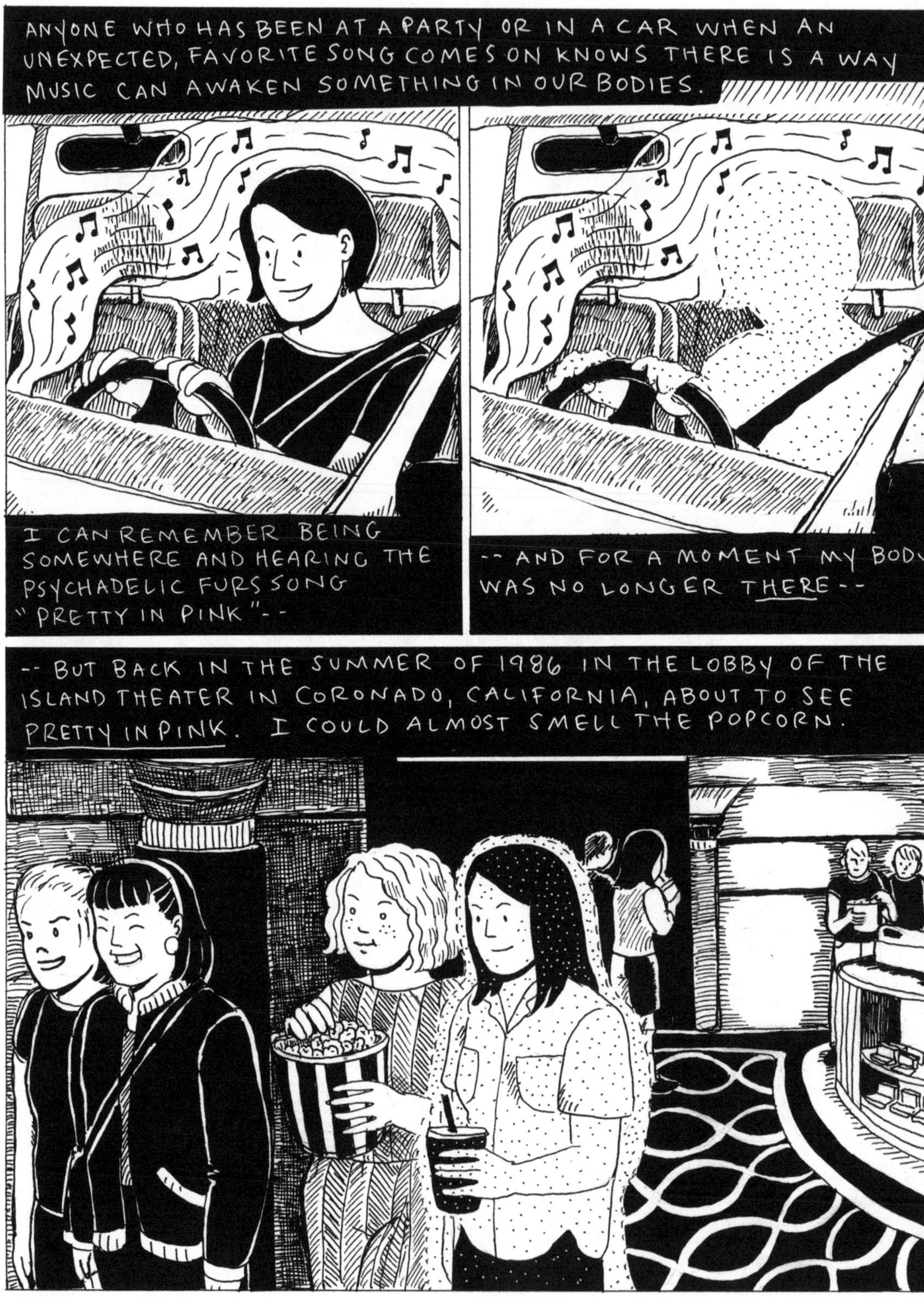
ANYONE WHO HAS BEEN AT A PARTY OR IN A CAR WHEN AN UNEXPECTED, FAVORITE SONG COMES ON KNOWS THERE IS A WAY MUSIC CAN AWAKEN SOMETHING IN OUR BODIES.
I CAN REMEMBER BEING SOMEWHERE AND HEARING THE PSYCHADELIC FURS SONG "PRETTY IN PINK"--
-- AND FOR A MOMENT MY BODY WAS NO LONGER THERE--
-- BUT BACK IN THE SUMMER OF 1986 IN THE LOBBY OF THE ISLAND THEATER IN CORONADO, CALIFORNIA, ABOUT TO SEE PRETTY IN PINK. I COULD ALMOST SMELL THE POPCORN.

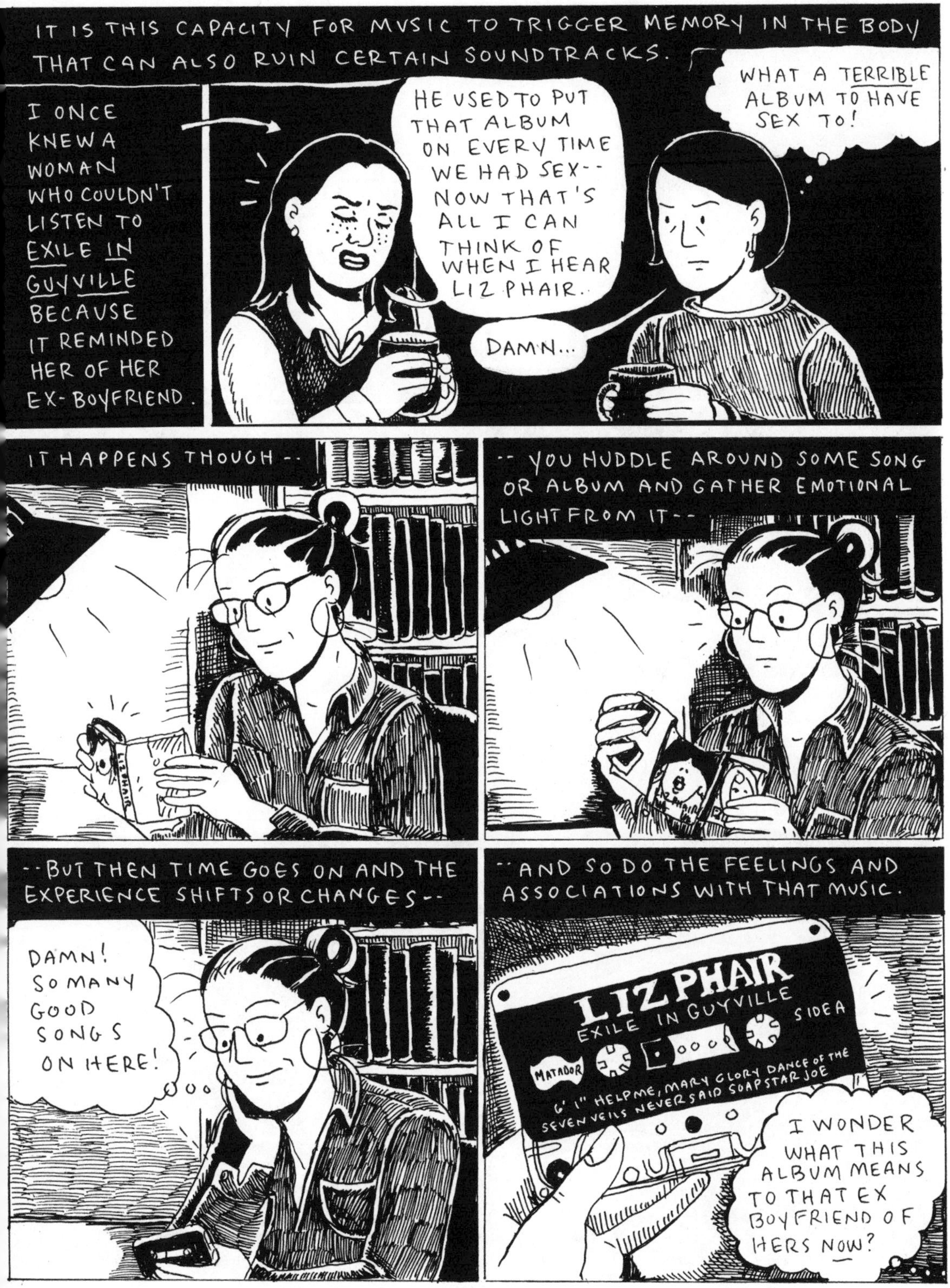
IT IS THIS CAPACITY FOR MUSIC TO TRIGGER MEMORY IN THE BODY THAT CAN ALSO RUIN CERTAIN SOUNDTRACKS.
I ONCE KNEW A WOMAN WHO COULDN'T LISTEN TO EXILE IN GUYVILLE BECAUSE IT REMINDED HER OF HER EX-BOYFRIEND.
HE USED TO PUT THAT ALBUM ON EVERY TIME WE HAD SEX-- NOW THAT'S ALL I CAN THINK OF WHEN I HEAR LIZ PHAIR.
DAMN...
WHAT A TERRIBLE ALBUM TO HAVE SEX TO!
IT HAPPENS THOUGH--
LIZ PHAIR
-- YOU HUDDLE AROUND SOME SONG OR ALBUM AND GATHER EMOTIONAL LIGHT FROM IT--
--BUT THEN TIME GOES ON AND THE EXPERIENCE SHIFTS OR CHANGES--
DAMN! SO MANY GOOD SONGS ON HERE!
--AND SO DO THE FEELINGS AND ASSOCIATIONS WITH THAT MUSIC.
LIZ PHAIR
EXILE IN GUYVILLE
SIDE A
MATADOR
6' 1" HELP ME, MARY GLORY DANCE OF THE SEVEN VEILS NEVER SAID SOAPSTAR JOE
I WONDER WHAT THIS ALBUM MEANS TO THAT EX BOYFRIEND OF HERS NOW?

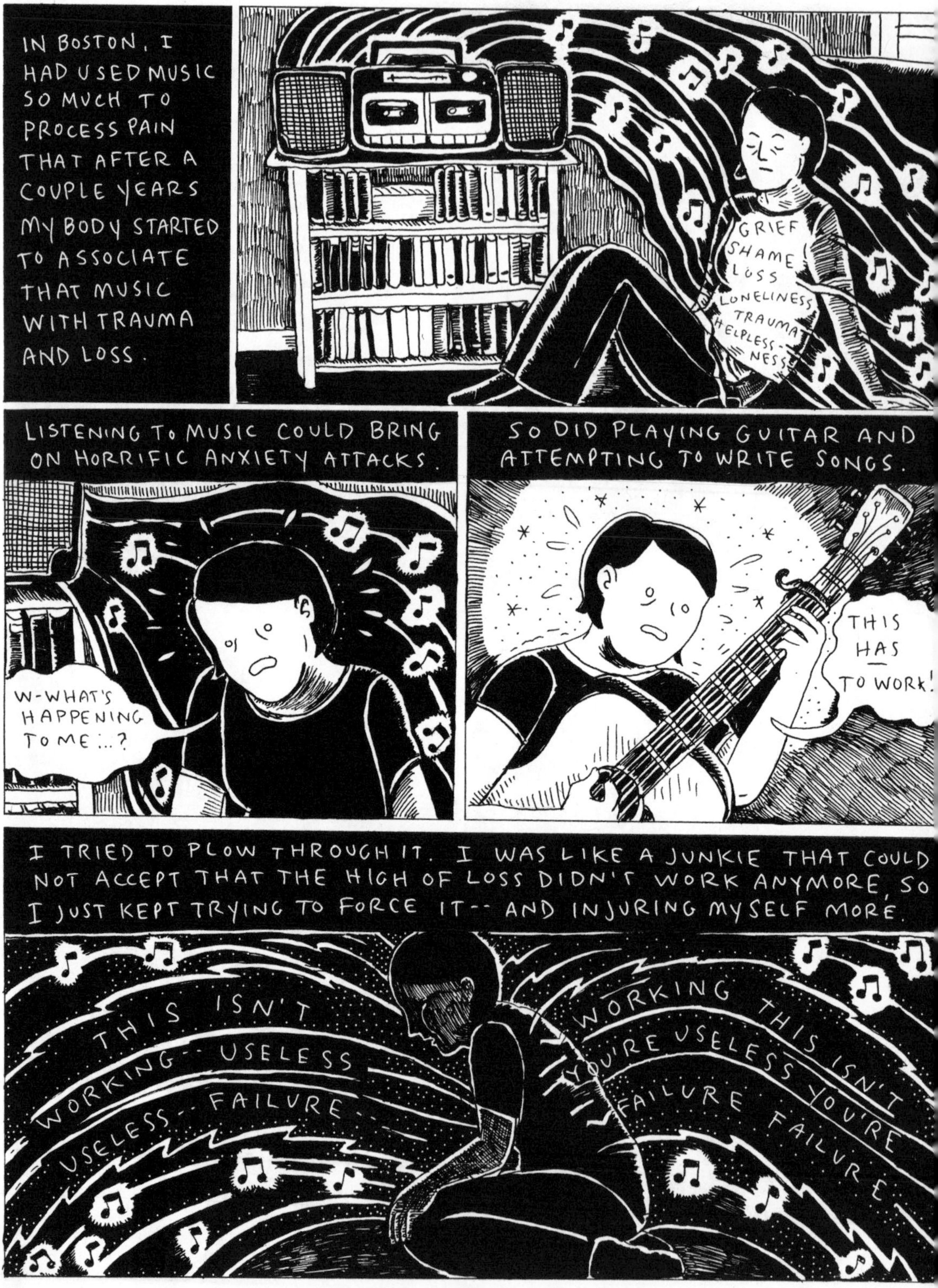
IN BOSTON, I HAD USED MUSIC SO MUCH TO PROCESS PAIN THAT AFTER A COUPLE YEARS MY BODY STARTED TO ASSOCIATE THAT MUSIC WITH TRAUMA AND LOSS.
GRIEF
SHAME
LOSS
LONELINESS
TRAUMA
HELPLESS-NESS
LISTENING TO MUSIC COULD BRING ON HORRIFIC ANXIETY ATTACKS.
W-WHAT'S HAPPENING TO ME...?
SO DID PLAYING GUITAR AND ATTEMPTING TO WRITE SONGS.
THIS HAS TO WORK!
I TRIED TO PLOW THROUGH IT. I WAS LIKE A JUNKIE THAT COULD NOT ACCEPT THAT THE HIGH OF LOSS DIDN'T WORK ANYMORE, SO I JUST KEPT TRYING TO FORCE IT-- AND INJURING MYSELF MORE.
THIS ISN'T WORKING-- USELESS
USELESS-- FAILURE--
WORKING THIS ISN'T
YOU'RE USELESS YOU'RE
FAILURE FAILURE

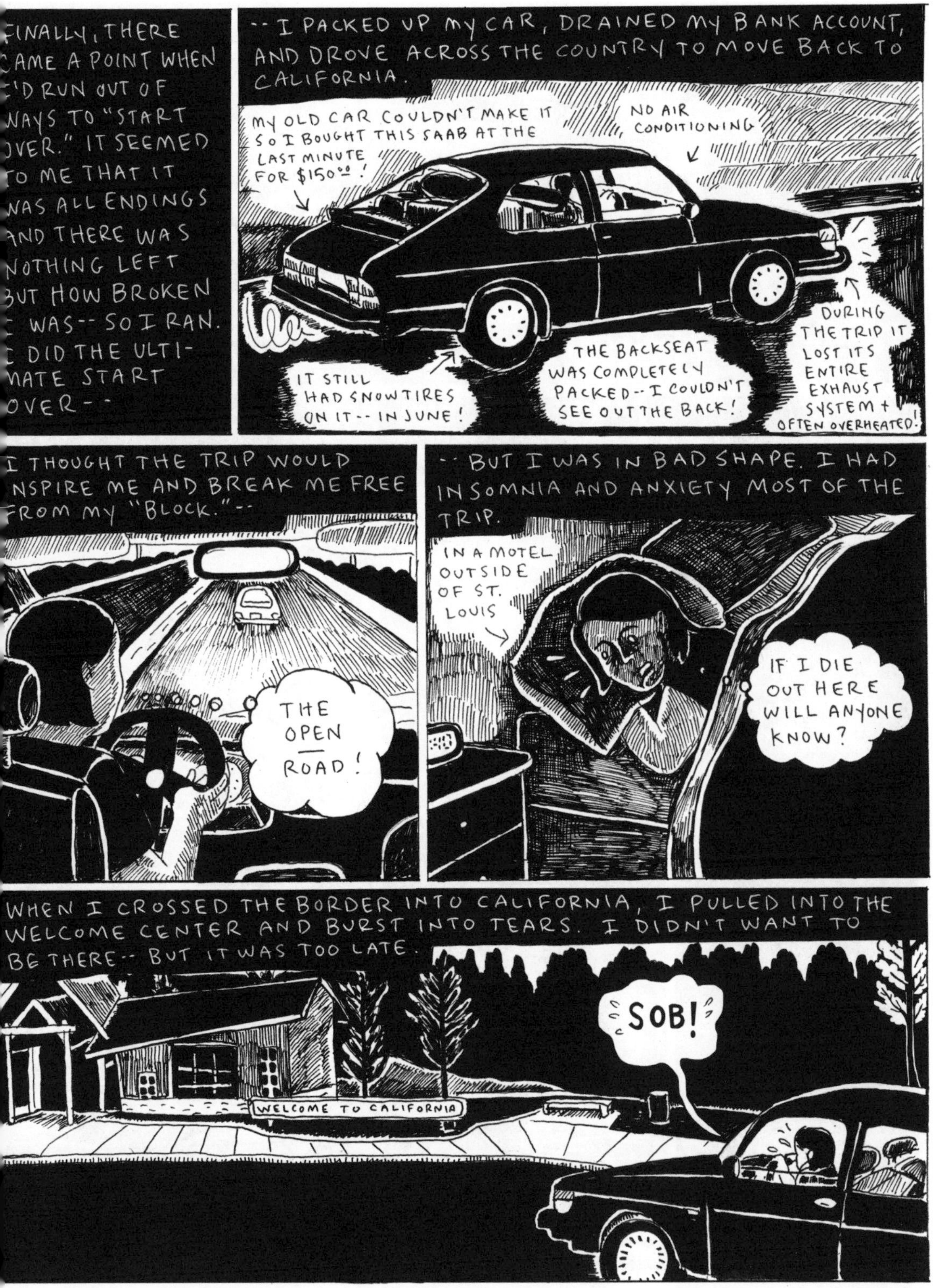
FINALLY, THERE CAME A POINT WHEN I'D RUN OUT OF WAYS TO "START OVER." IT SEEMED TO ME THAT IT WAS ALL ENDINGS AND THERE WAS NOTHING LEFT BUT HOW BROKEN I WAS -- SO I RAN. I DID THE ULTIMATE START OVER --
-- I PACKED UP MY CAR, DRAINED MY BANK ACCOUNT, AND DROVE ACROSS THE COUNTRY TO MOVE BACK TO CALIFORNIA.
MY OLD CAR COULDN'T MAKE IT SO I BOUGHT THIS SAAB AT THE LAST MINUTE FOR $150.00!
NO AIR CONDITIONING
IT STILL HAD SNOW TIRES ON IT -- IN JUNE!
THE BACKSEAT WAS COMPLETELY PACKED -- I COULDN'T SEE OUT THE BACK!
DURING THE TRIP IT LOST ITS ENTIRE EXHAUST SYSTEM + OFTEN OVERHEATED!
I THOUGHT THE TRIP WOULD INSPIRE ME AND BREAK ME FREE FROM MY "BLOCK." --
THE OPEN ROAD!
-- BUT I WAS IN BAD SHAPE. I HAD INSOMNIA AND ANXIETY MOST OF THE TRIP.
IN A MOTEL OUTSIDE OF ST. LOUIS
IF I DIE OUT HERE WILL ANYONE KNOW?
WHEN I CROSSED THE BORDER INTO CALIFORNIA, I PULLED INTO THE WELCOME CENTER AND BURST INTO TEARS. I DIDN'T WANT TO BE THERE -- BUT IT WAS TOO LATE.
WELCOME TO CALIFORNIA
SOB!

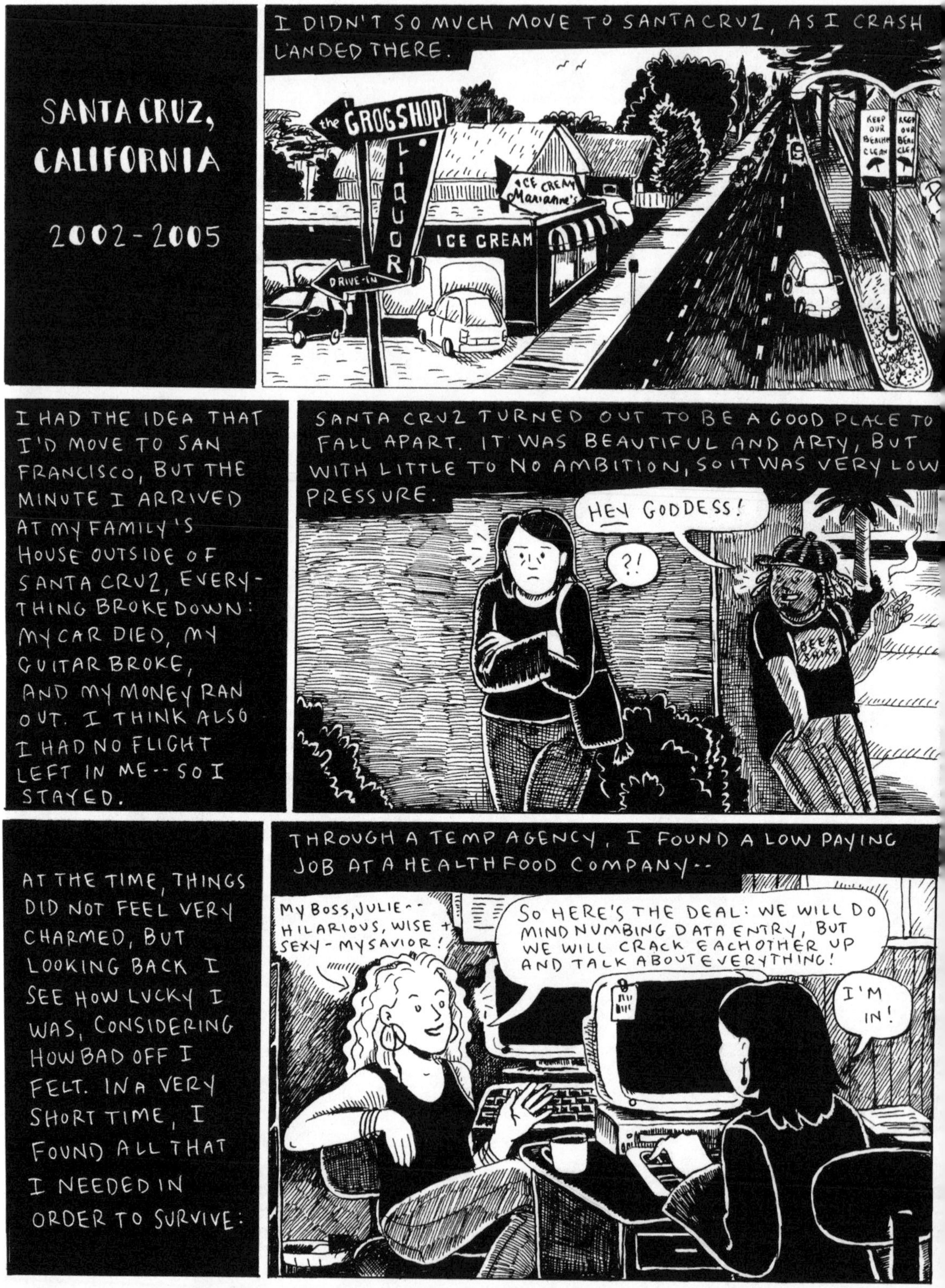
SANTA CRUZ, CALIFORNIA
2002-2005
I DIDN'T SO MUCH MOVE TO SANTA CRUZ, AS I CRASH LANDED THERE.
the GROGSHOP
LIQUOR
ICE CREAM Marianne's
ICE CREAM
DRIVE-IN
KEEP OUR BEACH CLEAN
I HAD THE IDEA THAT I'D MOVE TO SAN FRANCISCO, BUT THE MINUTE I ARRIVED AT MY FAMILY'S HOUSE OUTSIDE OF SANTA CRUZ, EVERYTHING BROKE DOWN: MY CAR DIED, MY GUITAR BROKE, AND MY MONEY RAN OUT. I THINK ALSO I HAD NO FLIGHT LEFT IN ME-- SO I STAYED.
SANTA CRUZ TURNED OUT TO BE A GOOD PLACE TO FALL APART. IT WAS BEAUTIFUL AND ARTY, BUT WITH LITTLE TO NO AMBITION, SO IT WAS VERY LOW PRESSURE.
HEY GODDESS!
?!
BEER SHIRT
AT THE TIME, THINGS DID NOT FEEL VERY CHARMED, BUT LOOKING BACK I SEE HOW LUCKY I WAS, CONSIDERING HOW BAD OFF I FELT. IN A VERY SHORT TIME, I FOUND ALL THAT I NEEDED IN ORDER TO SURVIVE:
THROUGH A TEMP AGENCY, I FOUND A LOW PAYING JOB AT A HEALTH FOOD COMPANY--
MY BOSS, JULIE-- HILARIOUS, WISE + SEXY - MY SAVIOR!
SO HERE'S THE DEAL: WE WILL DO MIND NUMBING DATA ENTRY, BUT WE WILL CRACK EACHOTHER UP AND TALK ABOUT EVERYTHING!
I'M IN!

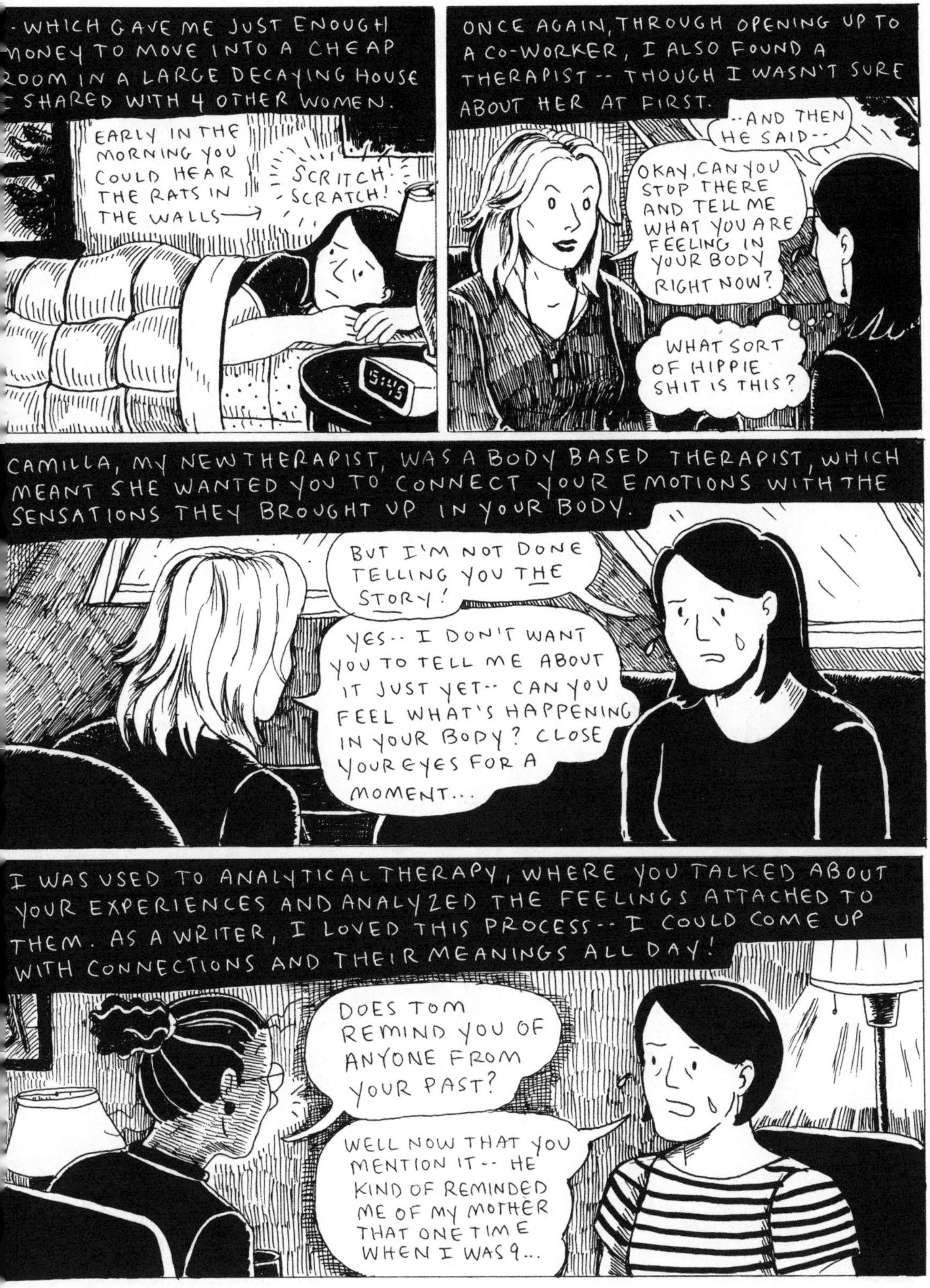
-WHICH GAVE ME JUST ENOUGH MONEY TO MOVE INTO A CHEAP ROOM IN A LARGE DECAYING HOUSE I SHARED WITH 4 OTHER WOMEN.
EARLY IN THE MORNING YOU COULD HEAR THE RATS IN THE WALLS
SCRITCH SCRATCH!
5:45
ONCE AGAIN, THROUGH OPENING UP TO A CO-WORKER, I ALSO FOUND A THERAPIST -- THOUGH I WASN'T SURE ABOUT HER AT FIRST.
--AND THEN HE SAID--
OKAY, CAN YOU STOP THERE AND TELL ME WHAT YOU ARE FEELING IN YOUR BODY RIGHT NOW?
WHAT SORT OF HIPPIE SHIT IS THIS?
CAMILLA, MY NEW THERAPIST, WAS A BODY BASED THERAPIST, WHICH MEANT SHE WANTED YOU TO CONNECT YOUR EMOTIONS WITH THE SENSATIONS THEY BROUGHT UP IN YOUR BODY.
BUT I'M NOT DONE TELLING YOU THE STORY!
YES-- I DON'T WANT YOU TO TELL ME ABOUT IT JUST YET-- CAN YOU FEEL WHAT'S HAPPENING IN YOUR BODY? CLOSE YOUR EYES FOR A MOMENT...
I WAS USED TO ANALYTICAL THERAPY, WHERE YOU TALKED ABOUT YOUR EXPERIENCES AND ANALYZED THE FEELINGS ATTACHED TO THEM. AS A WRITER, I LOVED THIS PROCESS-- I COULD COME UP WITH CONNECTIONS AND THEIR MEANINGS ALL DAY!
DOES TOM REMIND YOU OF ANYONE FROM YOUR PAST?
WELL NOW THAT YOU MENTION IT-- HE KIND OF REMINDED ME OF MY MOTHER THAT ONE TIME WHEN I WAS 9...

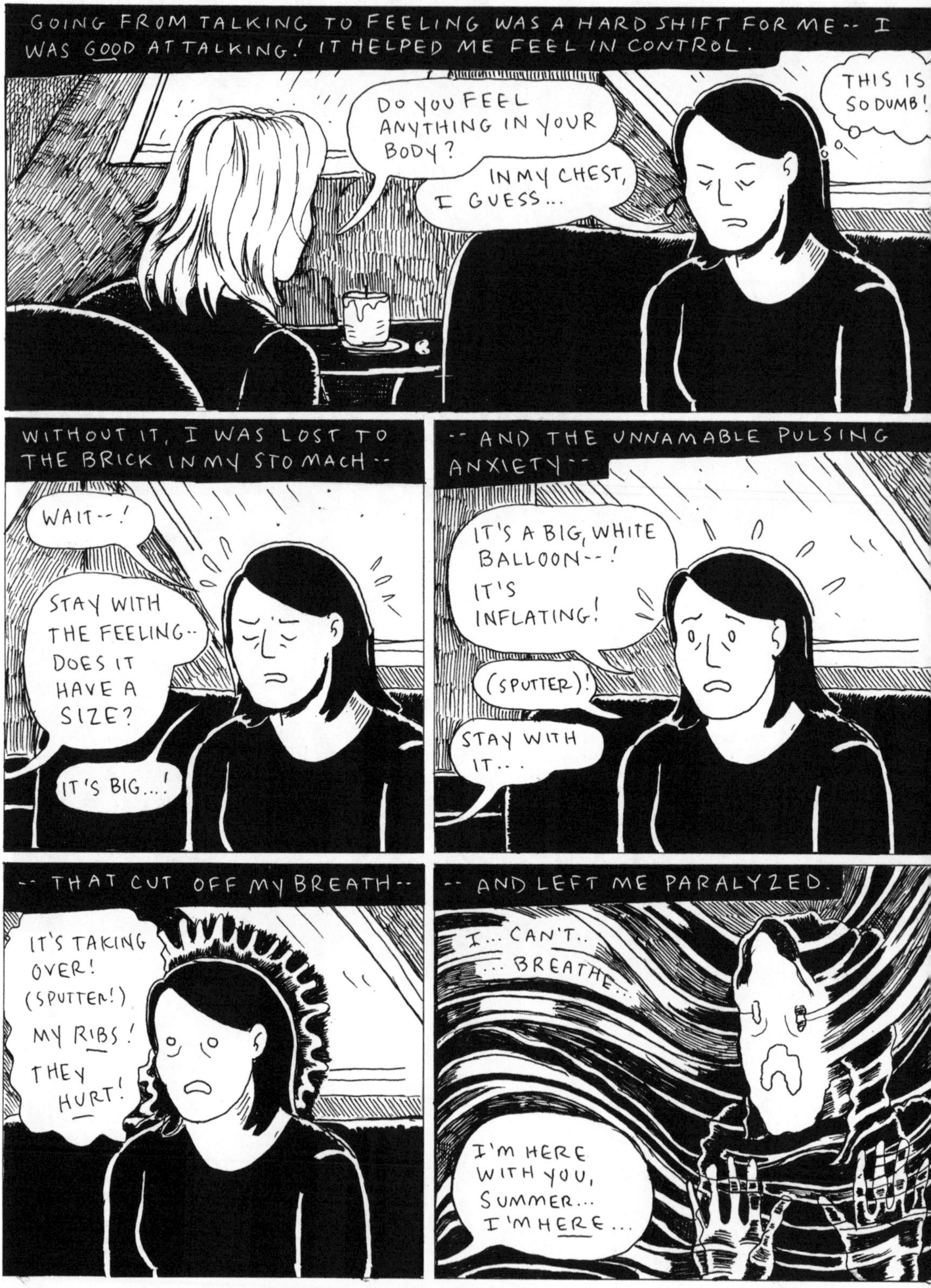

GOING FROM TALKING TO FEELING WAS A HARD SHIFT FOR ME -- I WAS GOOD AT TALKING! IT HELPED ME FEEL IN CONTROL.
DO YOU FEEL ANYTHING IN YOUR BODY?
IN MY CHEST, I GUESS...
THIS IS SO DUMB!
WITHOUT IT, I WAS LOST TO THE BRICK IN MY STOMACH --
WAIT--!
STAY WITH THE FEELING.. DOES IT HAVE A SIZE?
IT'S BIG...!
-- AND THE UNNAMABLE PULSING ANXIETY --
IT'S A BIG, WHITE BALLOON--! IT'S INFLATING!
(SPUTTER)!
STAY WITH IT...
-- THAT CUT OFF MY BREATH --
IT'S TAKING OVER! (SPUTTER!) MY RIBS! THEY HURT!
-- AND LEFT ME PARALYZED.
I... CAN'T.. ... BREATHE...
I'M HERE WITH YOU, SUMMER... I'M HERE...

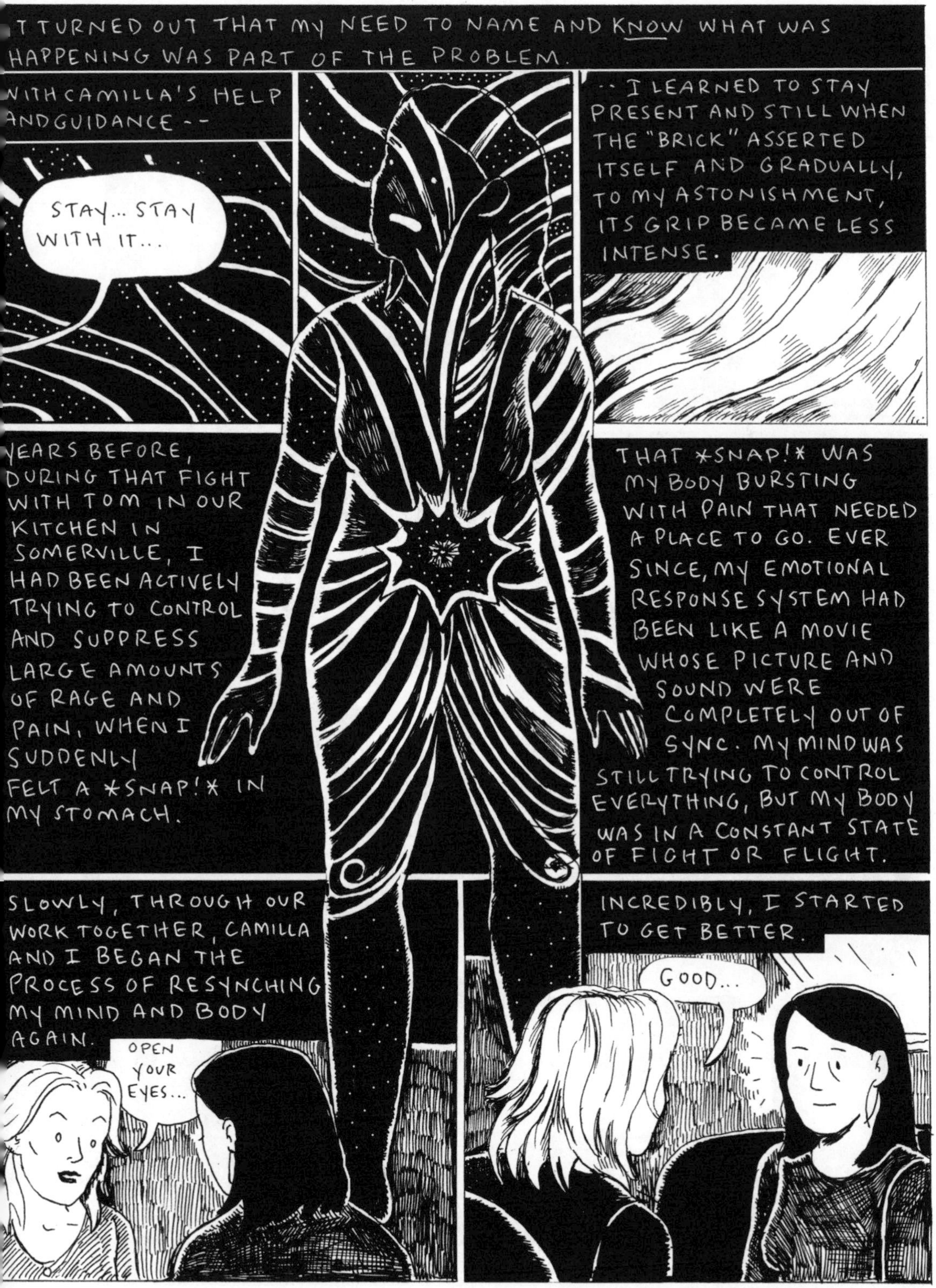
IT TURNED OUT THAT MY NEED TO NAME AND KNOW WHAT WAS HAPPENING WAS PART OF THE PROBLEM.
WITH CAMILLA'S HELP AND GUIDANCE --
STAY... STAY WITH IT...
-- I LEARNED TO STAY PRESENT AND STILL WHEN THE "BRICK" ASSERTED ITSELF AND GRADUALLY, TO MY ASTONISHMENT, ITS GRIP BECAME LESS INTENSE.
YEARS BEFORE, DURING THAT FIGHT WITH TOM IN OUR KITCHEN IN SOMERVILLE, I HAD BEEN ACTIVELY TRYING TO CONTROL AND SUPPRESS LARGE AMOUNTS OF RAGE AND PAIN, WHEN I SUDDENLY FELT A *SNAP!* IN MY STOMACH.
THAT *SNAP!* WAS MY BODY BURSTING WITH PAIN THAT NEEDED A PLACE TO GO. EVER SINCE, MY EMOTIONAL RESPONSE SYSTEM HAD BEEN LIKE A MOVIE WHOSE PICTURE AND SOUND WERE COMPLETELY OUT OF SYNC. MY MIND WAS STILL TRYING TO CONTROL EVERYTHING, BUT MY BODY WAS IN A CONSTANT STATE OF FIGHT OR FLIGHT.
SLOWLY, THROUGH OUR WORK TOGETHER, CAMILLA AND I BEGAN THE PROCESS OF RESYNCHING MY MIND AND BODY AGAIN.
OPEN YOUR EYES...
INCREDIBLY, I STARTED TO GET BETTER.
GOOD...

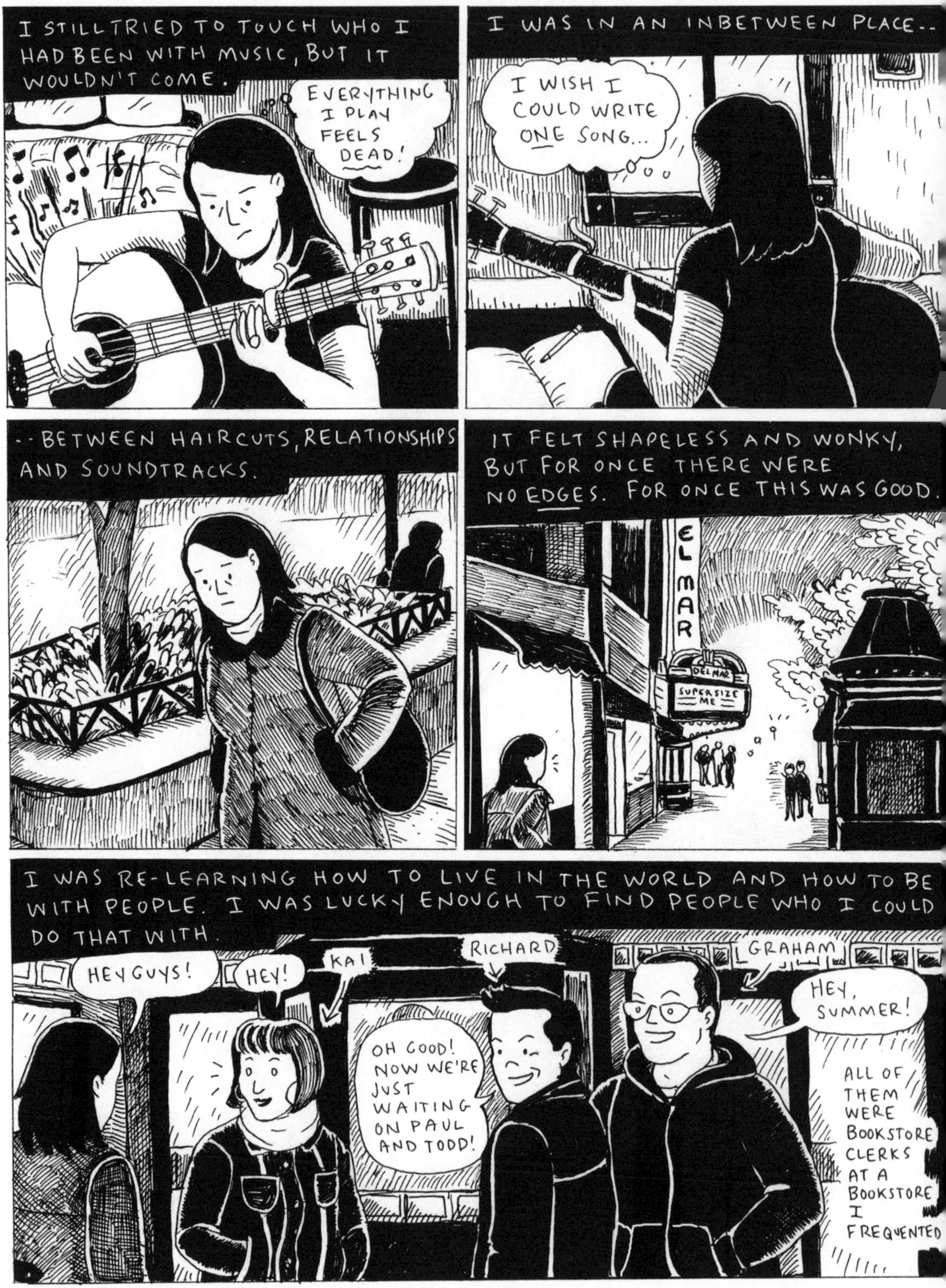
I STILL TRIED TO TOUCH WHO I HAD BEEN WITH MUSIC, BUT IT WOULDN'T COME.
EVERYTHING I PLAY FEELS DEAD!
I WAS IN AN INBETWEEN PLACE..
I WISH I COULD WRITE ONE SONG...
--BETWEEN HAIRCUTS, RELATIONSHIPS AND SOUNDTRACKS.
IT FELT SHAPELESS AND WONKY, BUT FOR ONCE THERE WERE NO EDGES. FOR ONCE THIS WAS GOOD.
EL MAR
DEL MAR
SUPERSIZE ME
I WAS RE-LEARNING HOW TO LIVE IN THE WORLD AND HOW TO BE WITH PEOPLE. I WAS LUCKY ENOUGH TO FIND PEOPLE WHO I COULD DO THAT WITH.
HEY GUYS!
HEY!
KAI
RICHARD
GRAHAM
HEY, SUMMER!
OH GOOD! NOW WE'RE JUST WAITING ON PAUL AND TODD!
ALL OF THEM WERE BOOKSTORE CLERKS AT A BOOKSTORE I FREQUENTED

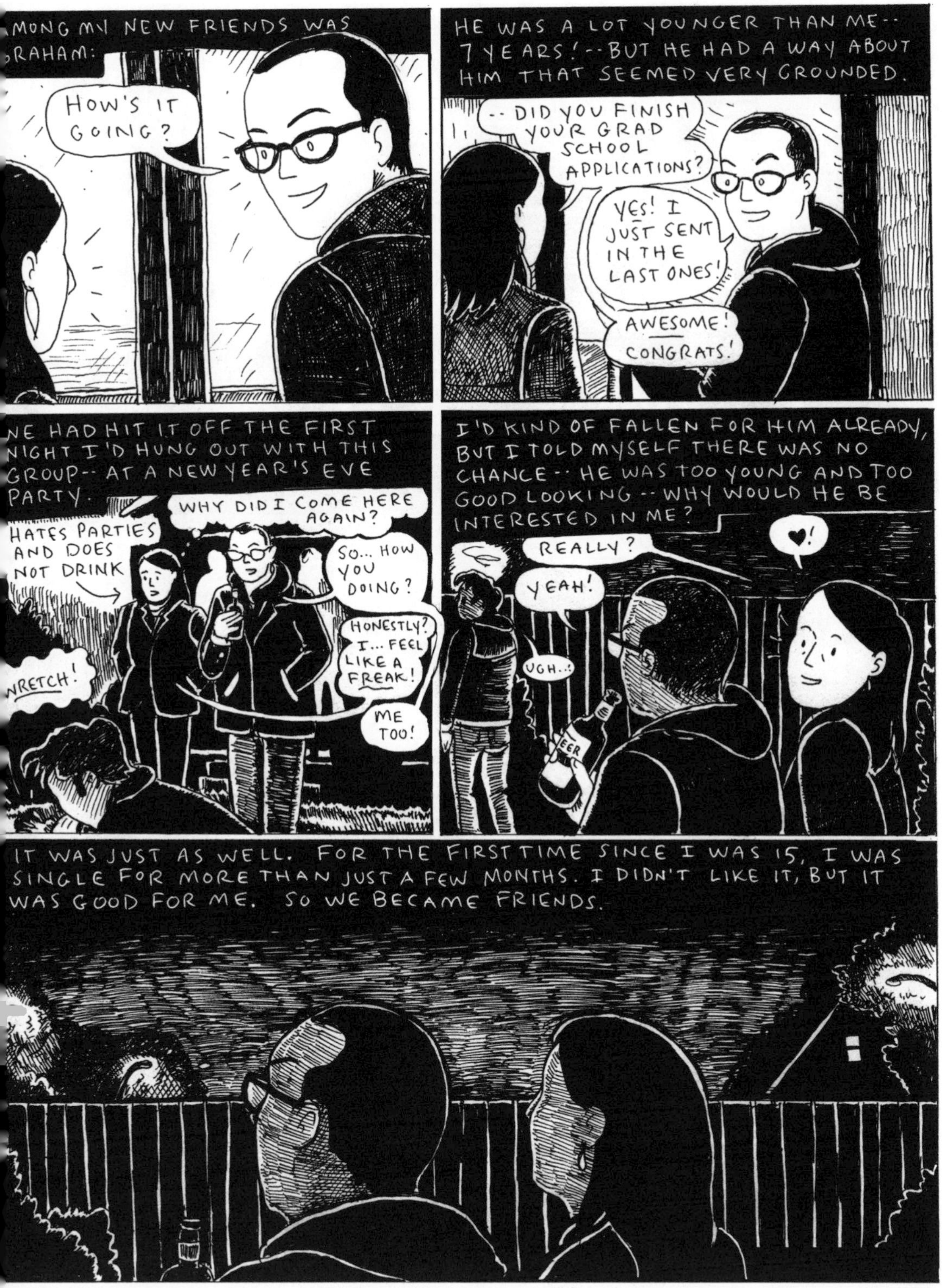
MONG MY NEW FRIENDS WAS GRAHAM:
HOW'S IT GOING?
HE WAS A LOT YOUNGER THAN ME-- 7 YEARS!--BUT HE HAD A WAY ABOUT HIM THAT SEEMED VERY GROUNDED.
--DID YOU FINISH YOUR GRAD SCHOOL APPLICATIONS?
YES! I JUST SENT IN THE LAST ONES!
AWESOME! CONGRATS!
WE HAD HIT IT OFF THE FIRST NIGHT I'D HUNG OUT WITH THIS GROUP-- AT A NEW YEAR'S EVE PARTY.
WHY DID I COME HERE AGAIN?
HATES PARTIES AND DOES NOT DRINK
SO... HOW YOU DOING?
HONESTLY? I... FEEL LIKE A FREAK!
ME TOO!
WRETCH!
I'D KIND OF FALLEN FOR HIM ALREADY, BUT I TOLD MYSELF THERE WAS NO CHANCE-- HE WAS TOO YOUNG AND TOO GOOD LOOKING--WHY WOULD HE BE INTERESTED IN ME?
REALLY?
YEAH!
♥!
UGH..!
IT WAS JUST AS WELL. FOR THE FIRST TIME SINCE I WAS 15, I WAS SINGLE FOR MORE THAN JUST A FEW MONTHS. I DIDN'T LIKE IT, BUT IT WAS GOOD FOR ME. SO WE BECAME FRIENDS.

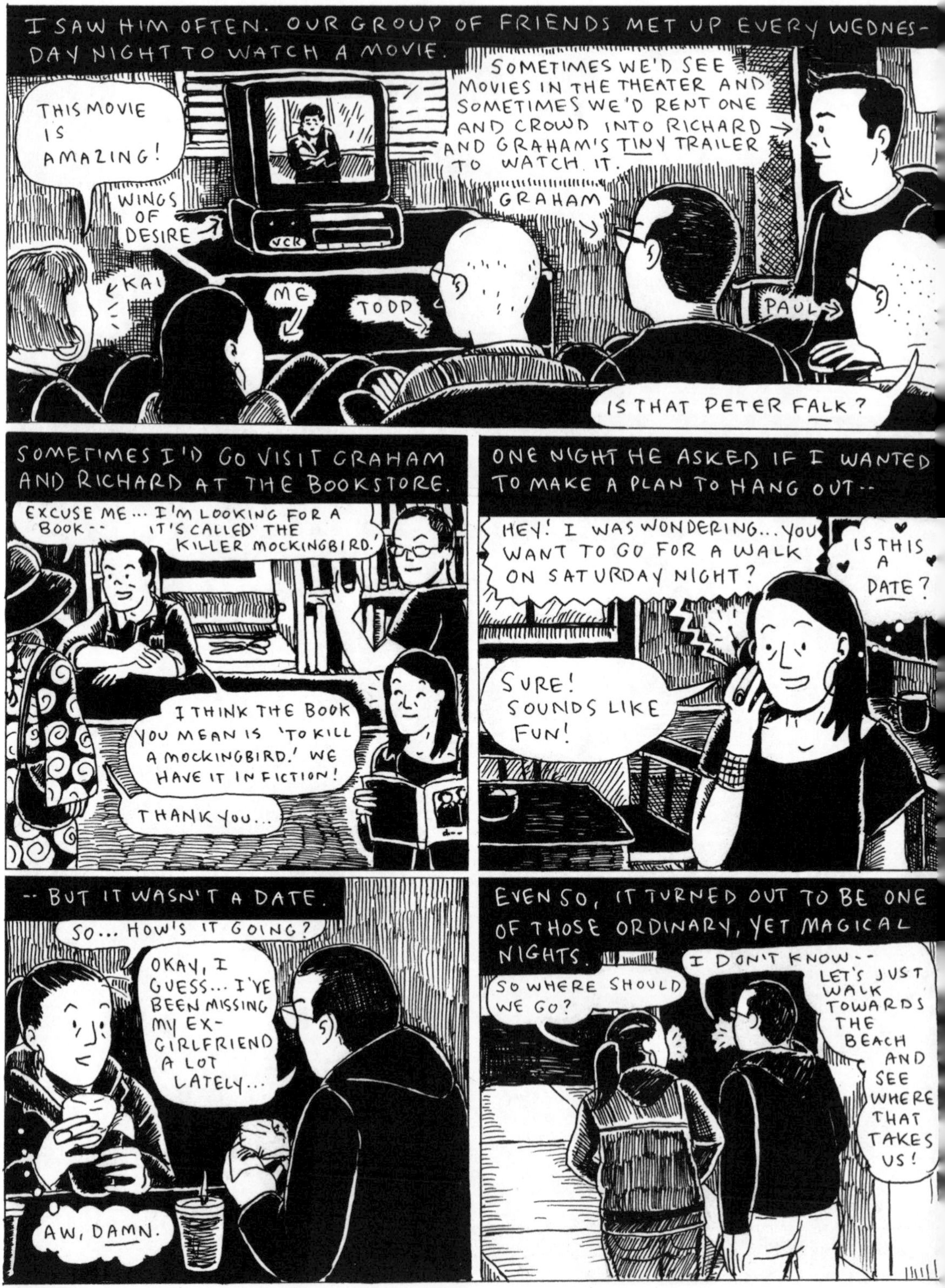
I SAW HIM OFTEN. OUR GROUP OF FRIENDS MET UP EVERY WEDNESDAY NIGHT TO WATCH A MOVIE.
SOMETIMES WE'D SEE MOVIES IN THE THEATER AND SOMETIMES WE'D RENT ONE AND CROWD INTO RICHARD AND GRAHAM'S TINY TRAILER TO WATCH IT.
THIS MOVIE IS AMAZING!
WINGS OF DESIRE
VCR
GRAHAM
KAI
ME
TODD
PAUL
IS THAT PETER FALK?
SOMETIMES I'D GO VISIT GRAHAM AND RICHARD AT THE BOOKSTORE.
EXCUSE ME... I'M LOOKING FOR A BOOK-- IT'S CALLED 'THE KILLER MOCKINGBIRD.'
I THINK THE BOOK YOU MEAN IS 'TO KILL A MOCKINGBIRD.' WE HAVE IT IN FICTION!
THANK YOU...
ONE NIGHT HE ASKED IF I WANTED TO MAKE A PLAN TO HANG OUT--
HEY! I WAS WONDERING... YOU WANT TO GO FOR A WALK ON SATURDAY NIGHT?
IS THIS A DATE?
SURE! SOUNDS LIKE FUN!
-- BUT IT WASN'T A DATE.
SO... HOW'S IT GOING?
OKAY, I GUESS... I'VE BEEN MISSING MY EX-GIRLFRIEND A LOT LATELY...
AW, DAMN.
EVEN SO, IT TURNED OUT TO BE ONE OF THOSE ORDINARY, YET MAGICAL NIGHTS.
SO WHERE SHOULD WE GO?
I DON'T KNOW-- LET'S JUST WALK TOWARDS THE BEACH AND SEE WHERE THAT TAKES US!

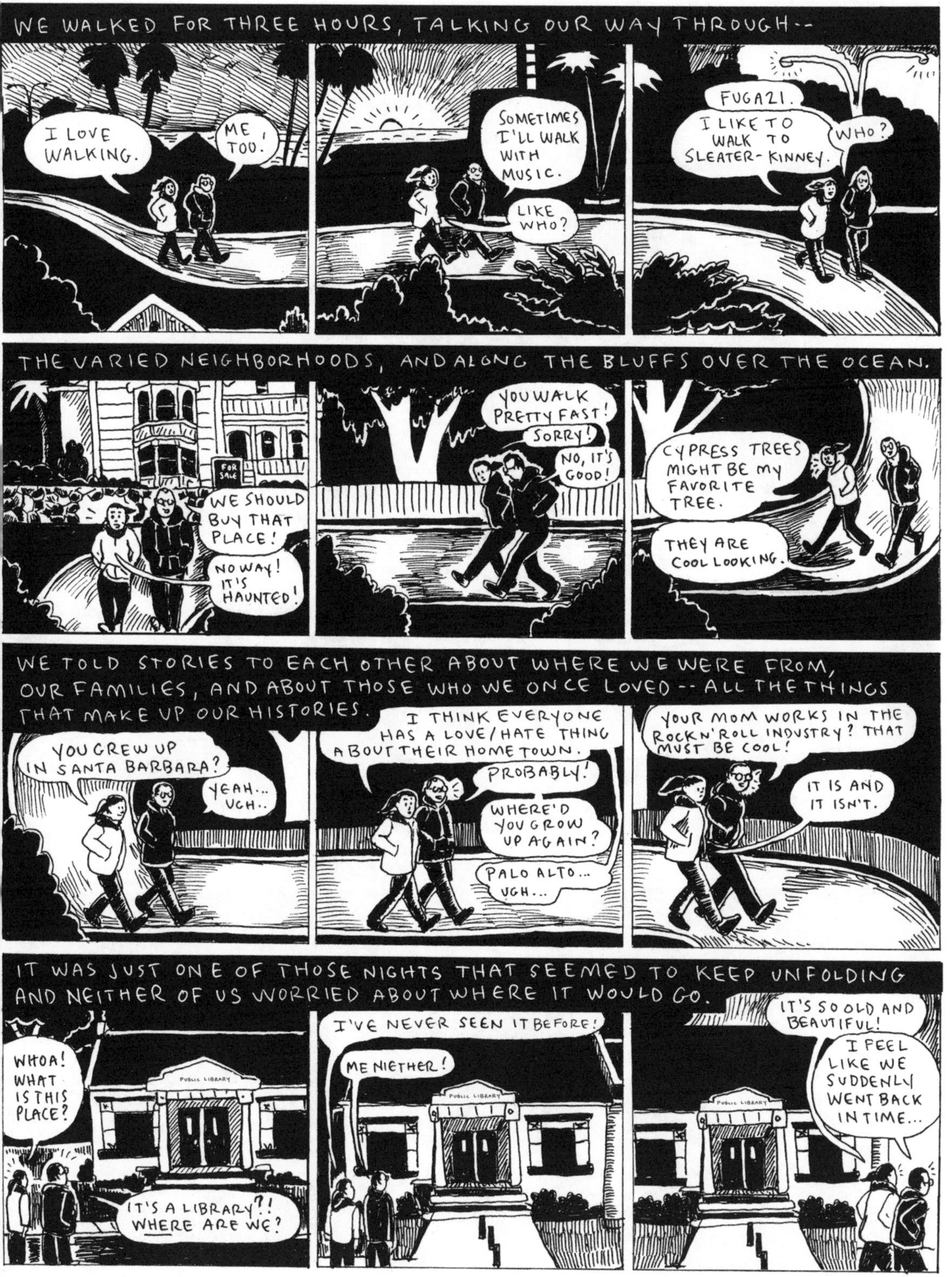
WE WALKED FOR THREE HOURS, TALKING OUR WAY THROUGH--
I LOVE WALKING.
ME TOO!
SOMETIMES I'LL WALK WITH MUSIC.
LIKE WHO?
FUGAZI.
I LIKE TO WALK TO SLEATER-KINNEY.
WHO?
THE VARIED NEIGHBORHOODS, AND ALONG THE BLUFFS OVER THE OCEAN.
FOR SALE
WE SHOULD BUY THAT PLACE!
NO WAY! IT'S HAUNTED!
YOU WALK PRETTY FAST!
SORRY!
NO, IT'S GOOD!
CYPRESS TREES MIGHT BE MY FAVORITE TREE.
THEY ARE COOL LOOKING.
WE TOLD STORIES TO EACH OTHER ABOUT WHERE WE WERE FROM, OUR FAMILIES, AND ABOUT THOSE WHO WE ONCE LOVED -- ALL THE THINGS THAT MAKE UP OUR HISTORIES.
YOU GREW UP IN SANTA BARBARA?
YEAH... UGH..
I THINK EVERYONE HAS A LOVE/HATE THING ABOUT THEIR HOMETOWN.
PROBABLY!
WHERE'D YOU GROW UP AGAIN?
PALO ALTO... UGH...
YOUR MOM WORKS IN THE ROCK N' ROLL INDUSTRY? THAT MUST BE COOL!
IT IS AND IT ISN'T.
IT WAS JUST ONE OF THOSE NIGHTS THAT SEEMED TO KEEP UNFOLDING AND NEITHER OF US WORRIED ABOUT WHERE IT WOULD GO.
WHOA! WHAT IS THIS PLACE?
PUBLIC LIBRARY
IT'S A LIBRARY?! WHERE ARE WE?
I'VE NEVER SEEN IT BEFORE!
ME NIETHER!
PUBLIC LIBRARY
IT'S SO OLD AND BEAUTIFUL!
I FEEL LIKE WE SUDDENLY WENT BACK IN TIME...
PUBLIC LIBRARY

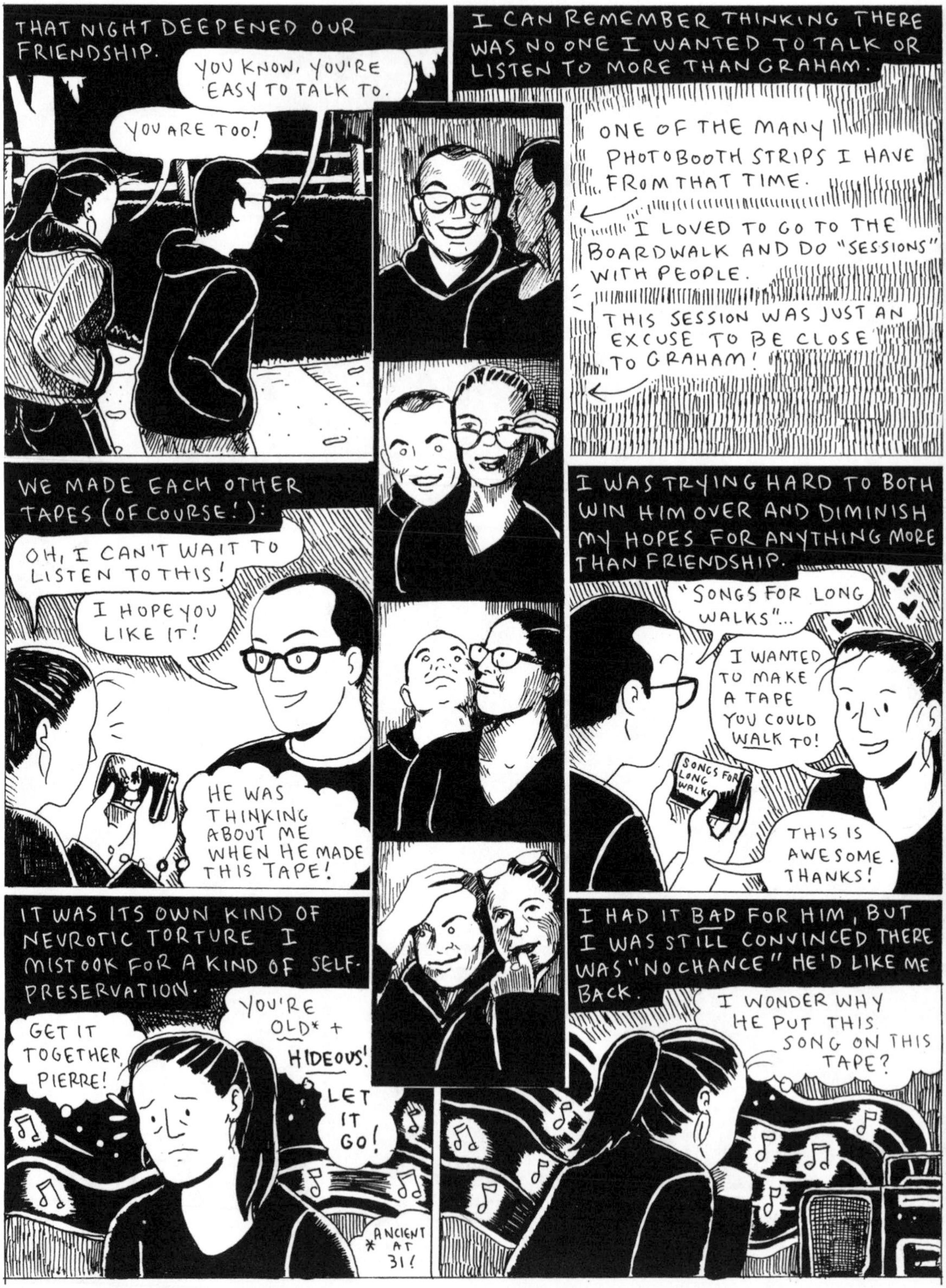
THAT NIGHT DEEPENED OUR FRIENDSHIP.
YOU KNOW, YOU'RE EASY TO TALK TO.
YOU ARE TOO!
I CAN REMEMBER THINKING THERE WAS NO ONE I WANTED TO TALK OR LISTEN TO MORE THAN GRAHAM.
ONE OF THE MANY PHOTOBOOTH STRIPS I HAVE FROM THAT TIME.
I LOVED TO GO TO THE BOARDWALK AND DO "SESSIONS" WITH PEOPLE.
THIS SESSION WAS JUST AN EXCUSE TO BE CLOSE TO GRAHAM!
WE MADE EACH OTHER TAPES (OF COURSE!):
OH, I CAN'T WAIT TO LISTEN TO THIS!
I HOPE YOU LIKE IT!
HE WAS THINKING ABOUT ME WHEN HE MADE THIS TAPE!
I WAS TRYING HARD TO BOTH WIN HIM OVER AND DIMINISH MY HOPES FOR ANYTHING MORE THAN FRIENDSHIP.
"SONGS FOR LONG WALKS"...
I WANTED TO MAKE A TAPE YOU COULD WALK TO!
SONGS FOR LONG WALKS
THIS IS AWESOME. THANKS!
IT WAS ITS OWN KIND OF NEUROTIC TORTURE I MISTOOK FOR A KIND OF SELF-PRESERVATION.
GET IT TOGETHER, PIERRE!
YOU'RE OLD* + HIDEOUS!
LET IT GO!
*ANCIENT AT 31!
I HAD IT BAD FOR HIM, BUT I WAS STILL CONVINCED THERE WAS "NO CHANCE" HE'D LIKE ME BACK.
I WONDER WHY HE PUT THIS SONG ON THIS TAPE?

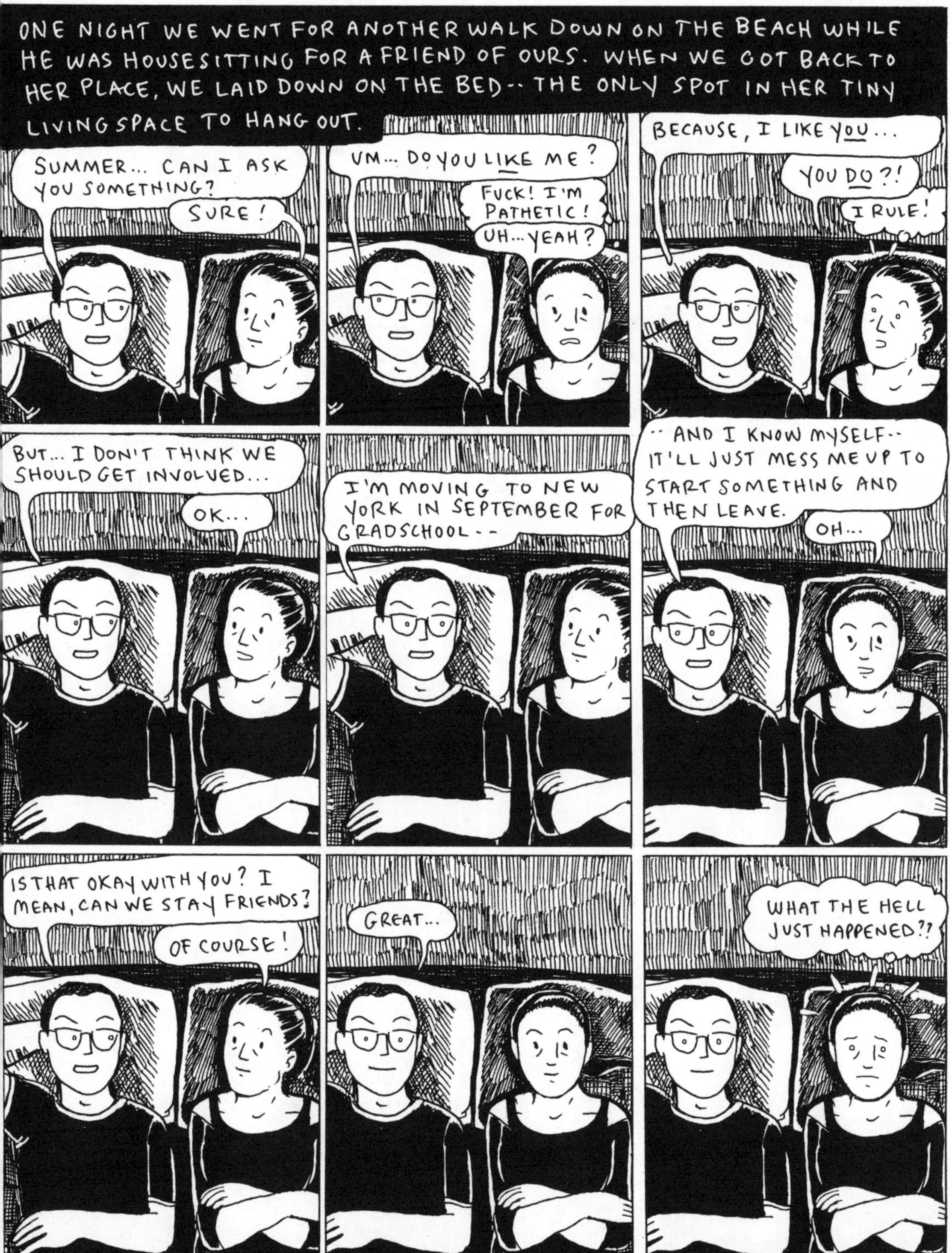
ONE NIGHT WE WENT FOR ANOTHER WALK DOWN ON THE BEACH WHILE HE WAS HOUSESITTING FOR A FRIEND OF OURS. WHEN WE GOT BACK TO HER PLACE, WE LAID DOWN ON THE BED -- THE ONLY SPOT IN HER TINY LIVING SPACE TO HANG OUT.
SUMMER... CAN I ASK YOU SOMETHING?
SURE!
UM... DO YOU LIKE ME?
FUCK! I'M PATHETIC!
UH... YEAH?
BECAUSE, I LIKE YOU...
YOU DO?!
I RULE!
BUT... I DON'T THINK WE SHOULD GET INVOLVED...
OK...
I'M MOVING TO NEW YORK IN SEPTEMBER FOR GRADSCHOOL --
-- AND I KNOW MYSELF -- IT'LL JUST MESS ME UP TO START SOMETHING AND THEN LEAVE.
OH...
IS THAT OKAY WITH YOU? I MEAN, CAN WE STAY FRIENDS?
OF COURSE!
GREAT...
WHAT THE HELL JUST HAPPENED??

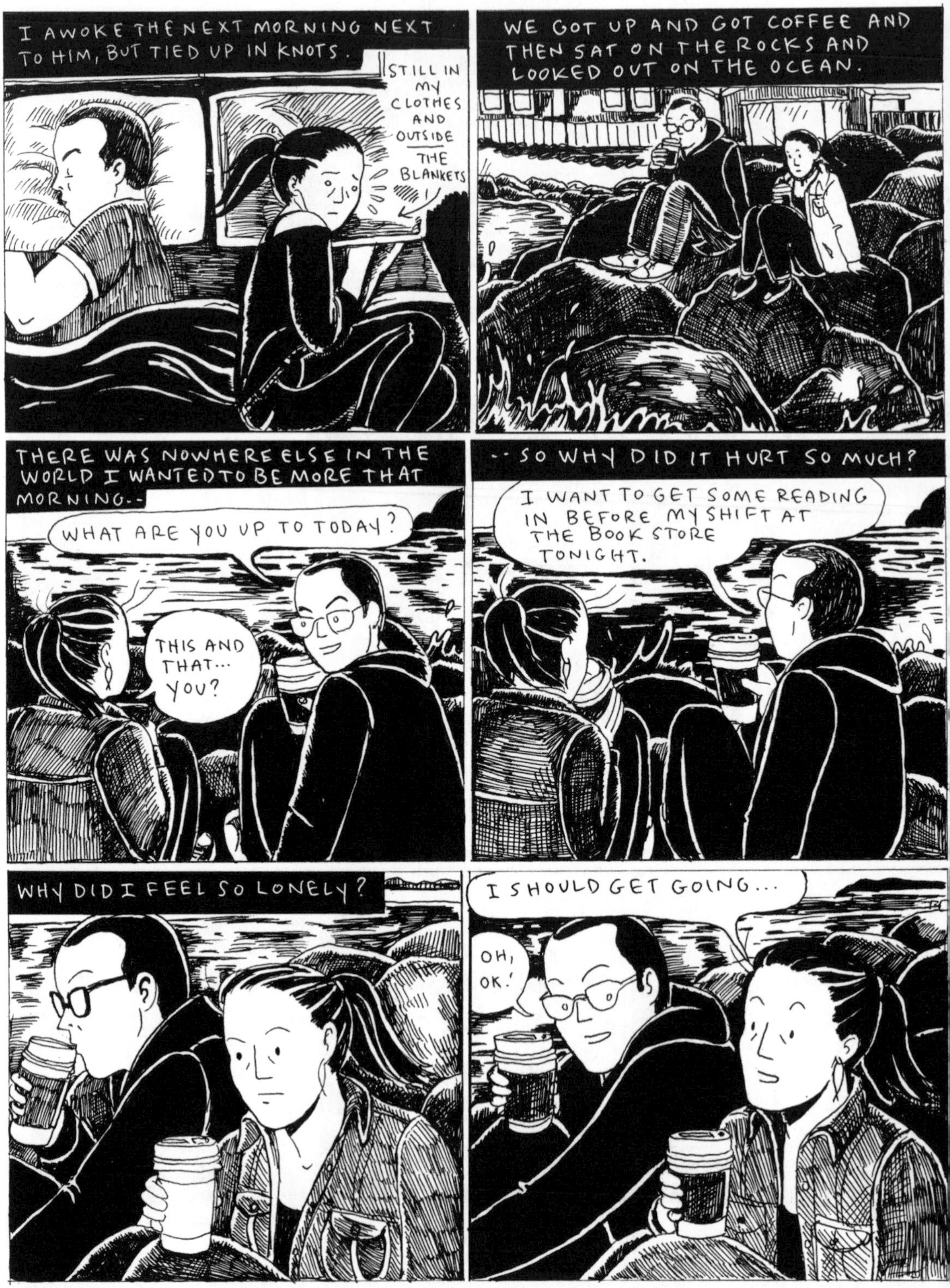
I AWOKE THE NEXT MORNING NEXT TO HIM, BUT TIED UP IN KNOTS.
STILL IN MY CLOTHES AND OUTSIDE THE BLANKETS!
WE GOT UP AND GOT COFFEE AND THEN SAT ON THE ROCKS AND LOOKED OUT ON THE OCEAN.
THERE WAS NOWHERE ELSE IN THE WORLD I WANTED TO BE MORE THAT MORNING.-
WHAT ARE YOU UP TO TODAY?
THIS AND THAT... YOU?
--SO WHY DID IT HURT SO MUCH?
I WANT TO GET SOME READING IN BEFORE MY SHIFT AT THE BOOK STORE TONIGHT.
WHY DID I FEEL SO LONELY?
I SHOULD GET GOING...
OH, OK.'

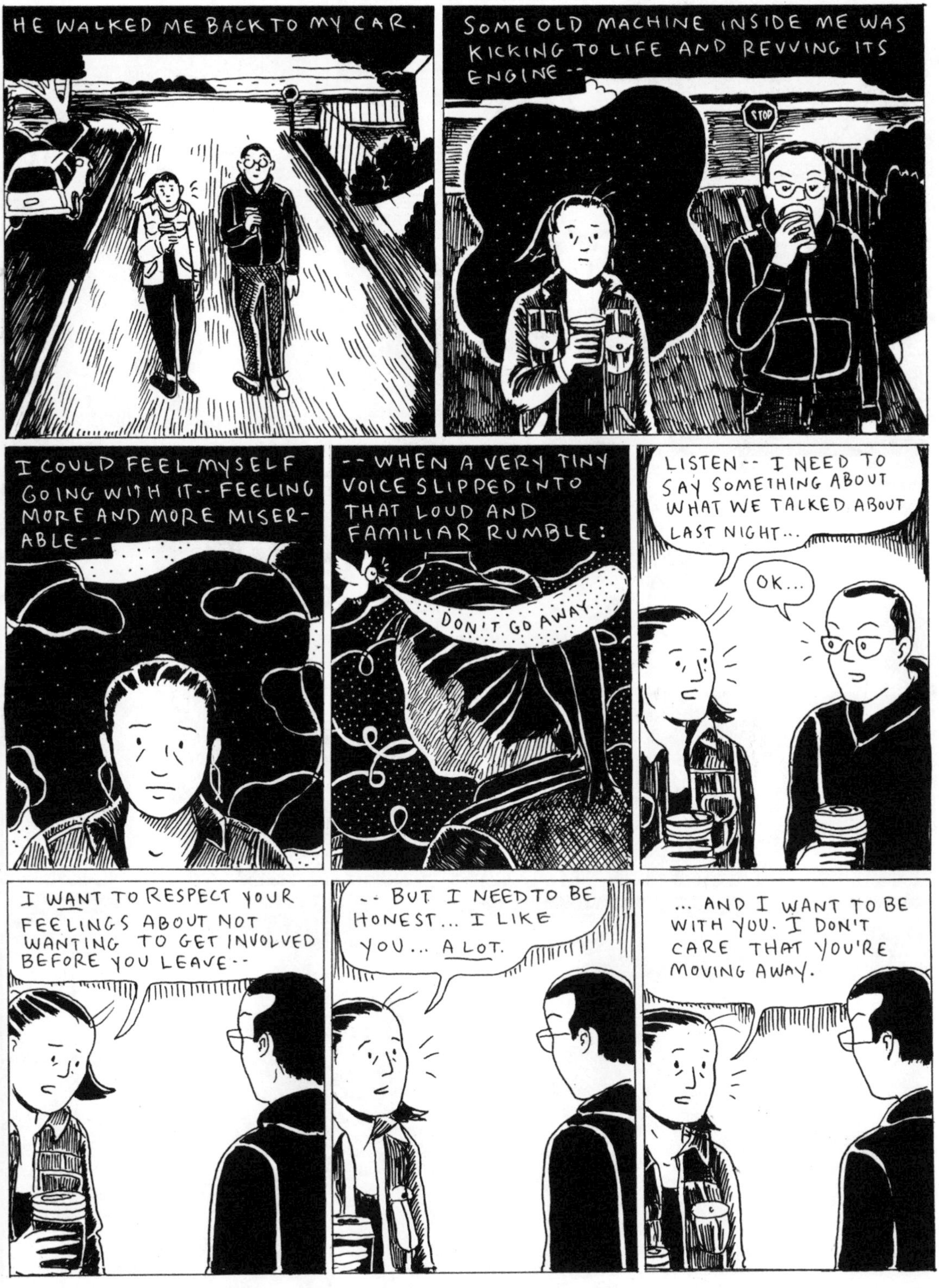

HE WALKED ME BACK TO MY CAR.
SOME OLD MACHINE INSIDE ME WAS KICKING TO LIFE AND REVVING ITS ENGINE--
STOP
I COULD FEEL MYSELF GOING WITH IT-- FEELING MORE AND MORE MISERABLE--
--WHEN A VERY TINY VOICE SLIPPED INTO THAT LOUD AND FAMILIAR RUMBLE:
DON'T GO AWAY.
LISTEN-- I NEED TO SAY SOMETHING ABOUT WHAT WE TALKED ABOUT LAST NIGHT...
OK...
I WANT TO RESPECT YOUR FEELINGS ABOUT NOT WANTING TO GET INVOLVED BEFORE YOU LEAVE--
--BUT I NEED TO BE HONEST... I LIKE YOU... A LOT.
... AND I WANT TO BE WITH YOU. I DON'T CARE THAT YOU'RE MOVING AWAY.

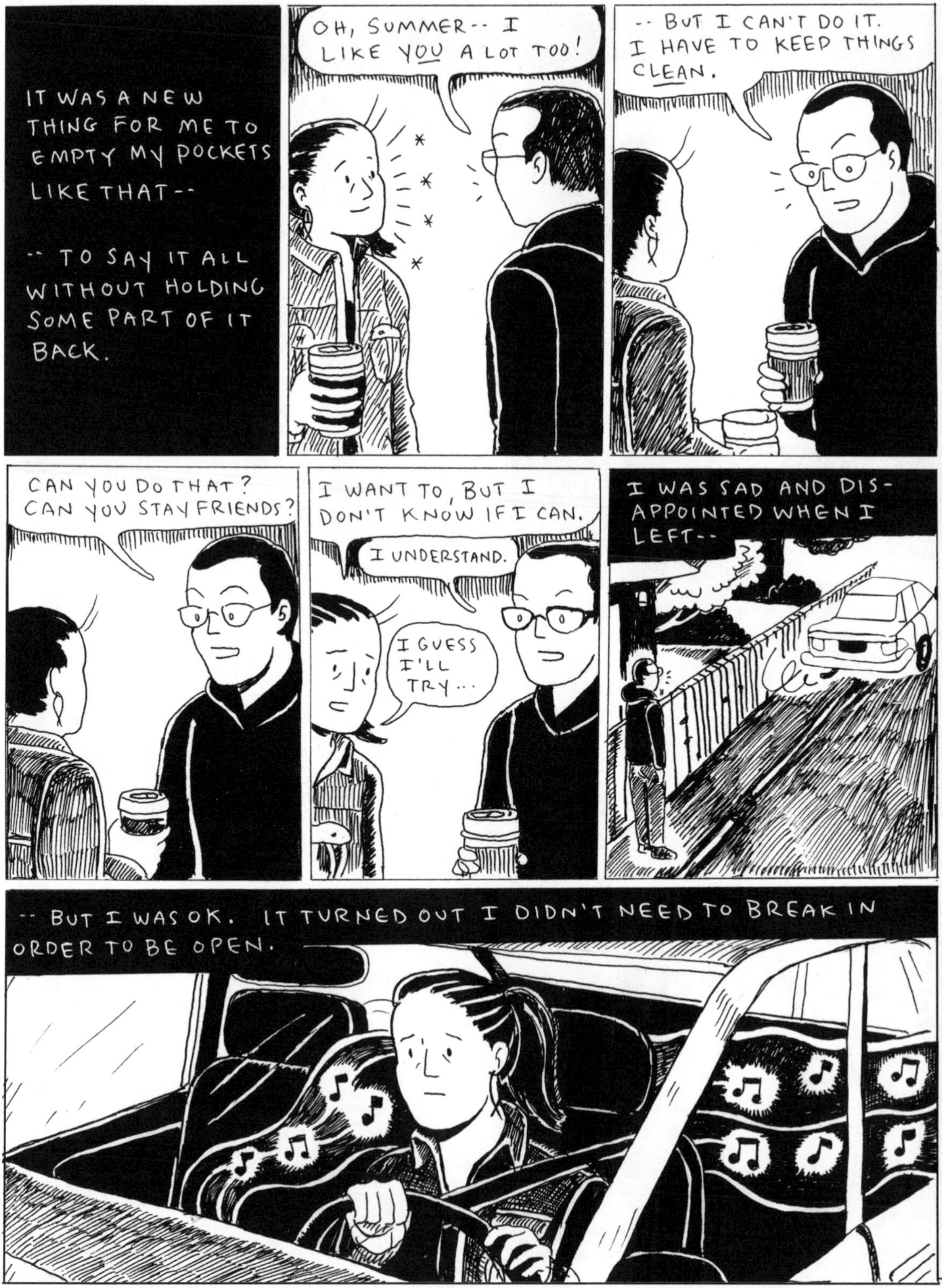
IT WAS A NEW THING FOR ME TO EMPTY MY POCKETS LIKE THAT--
-- TO SAY IT ALL WITHOUT HOLDING SOME PART OF IT BACK.
OH, SUMMER-- I LIKE YOU A LOT TOO!
-- BUT I CAN'T DO IT. I HAVE TO KEEP THINGS CLEAN.
CAN YOU DO THAT? CAN YOU STAY FRIENDS?
I WANT TO, BUT I DON'T KNOW IF I CAN.
I UNDERSTAND.
I GUESS I'LL TRY...
I WAS SAD AND DIS-APPOINTED WHEN I LEFT--
-- BUT I WAS OK. IT TURNED OUT I DIDN'T NEED TO BREAK IN ORDER TO BE OPEN.

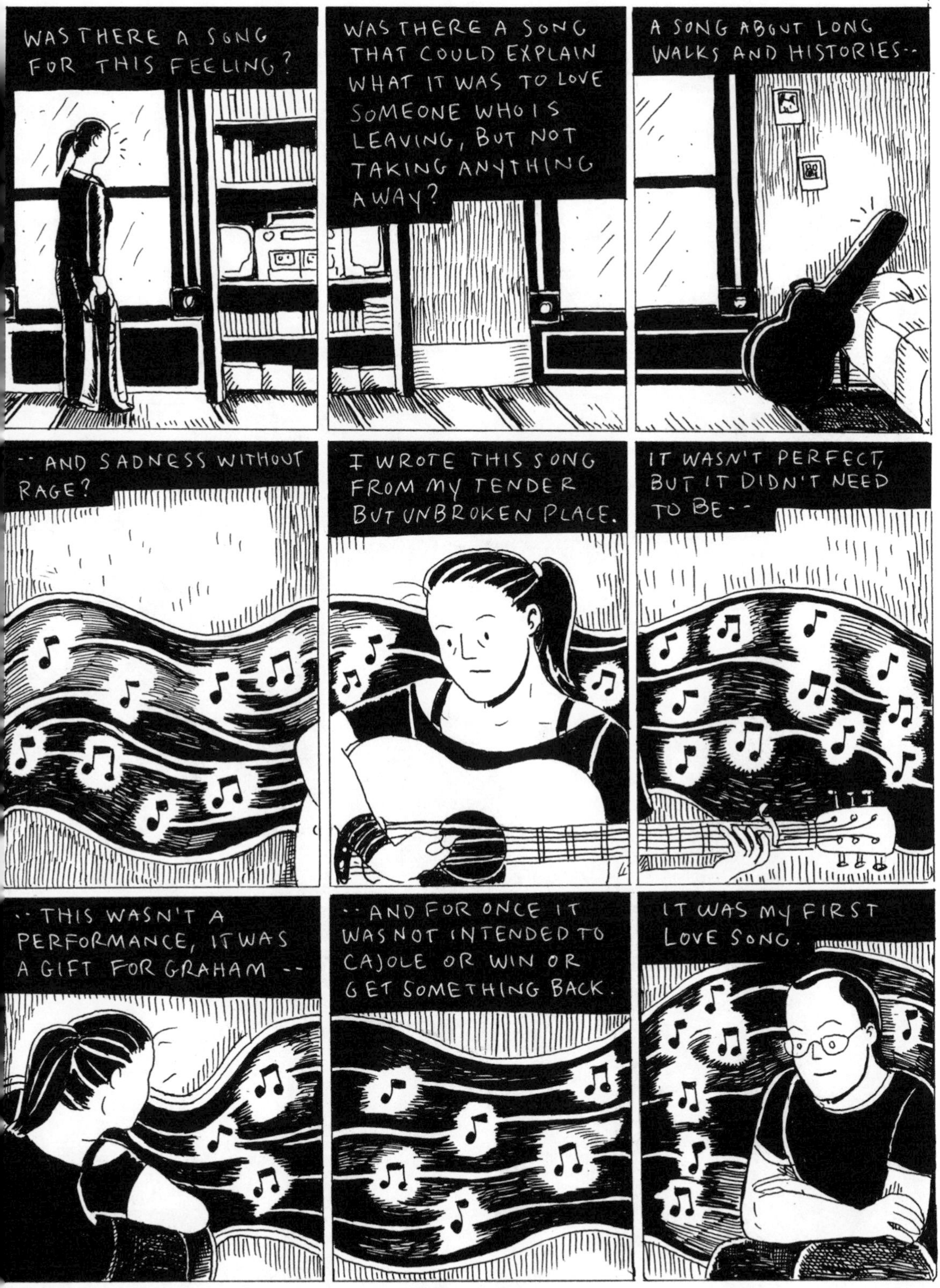
WAS THERE A SONG FOR THIS FEELING?
WAS THERE A SONG THAT COULD EXPLAIN WHAT IT WAS TO LOVE SOMEONE WHO IS LEAVING, BUT NOT TAKING ANYTHING AWAY?
A SONG ABOUT LONG WALKS AND HISTORIES--
--AND SADNESS WITHOUT RAGE?
I WROTE THIS SONG FROM MY TENDER BUT UNBROKEN PLACE.
IT WASN'T PERFECT, BUT IT DIDN'T NEED TO BE--
--THIS WASN'T A PERFORMANCE, IT WAS A GIFT FOR GRAHAM--
--AND FOR ONCE IT WAS NOT INTENDED TO CAJOLE OR WIN OR GET SOMETHING BACK.
IT WAS MY FIRST LOVE SONG.

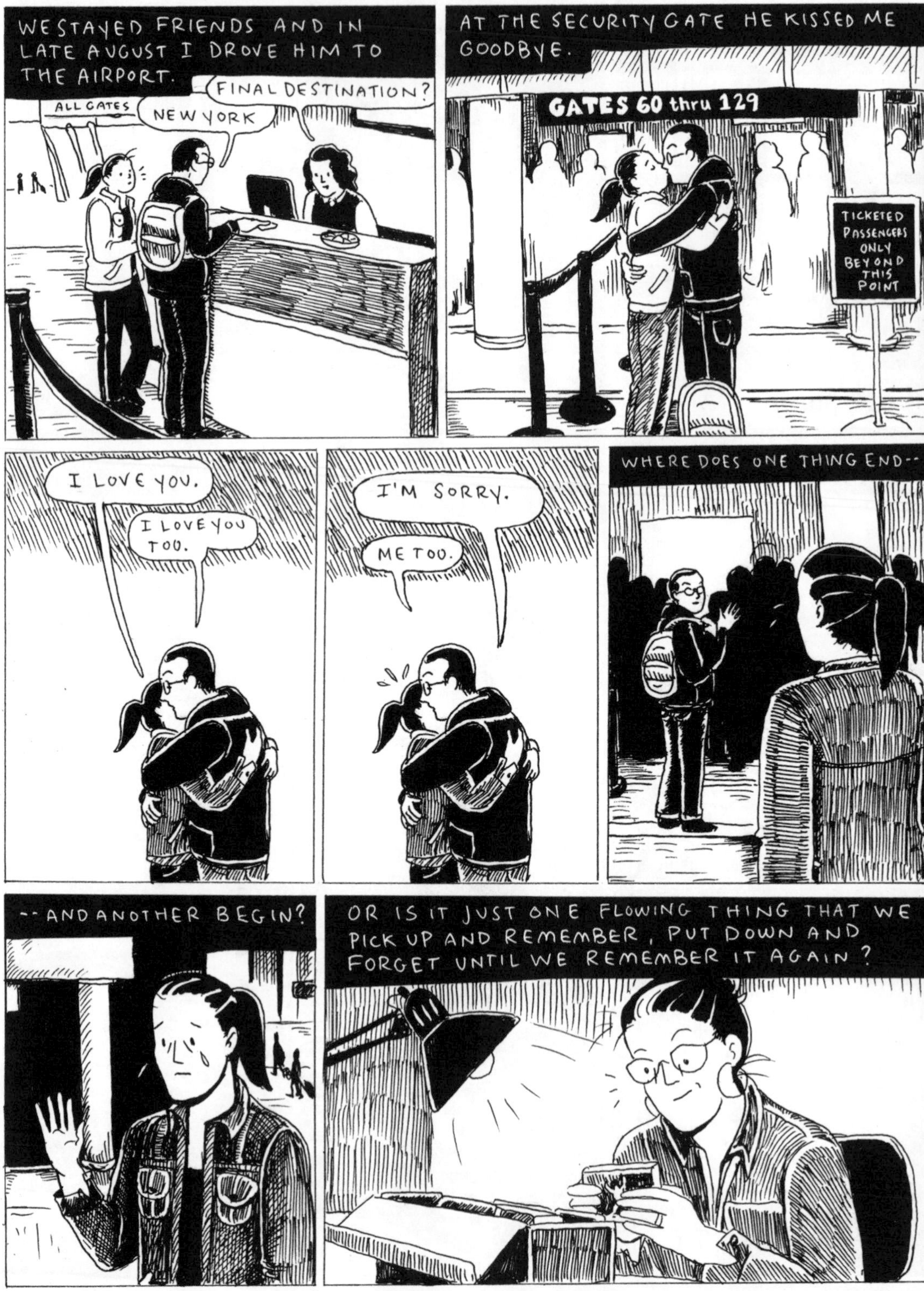

WE STAYED FRIENDS AND IN LATE AUGUST I DROVE HIM TO THE AIRPORT.
ALL GATES
FINAL DESTINATION?
NEW YORK
AT THE SECURITY GATE HE KISSED ME GOODBYE.
GATES 60 thru 129
TICKETED PASSENGERS ONLY BEYOND THIS POINT
I LOVE YOU.
I LOVE YOU TOO.
I'M SORRY.
ME TOO.
WHERE DOES ONE THING END--
--AND ANOTHER BEGIN?
OR IS IT JUST ONE FLOWING THING THAT WE PICK UP AND REMEMBER, PUT DOWN AND FORGET UNTIL WE REMEMBER IT AGAIN?

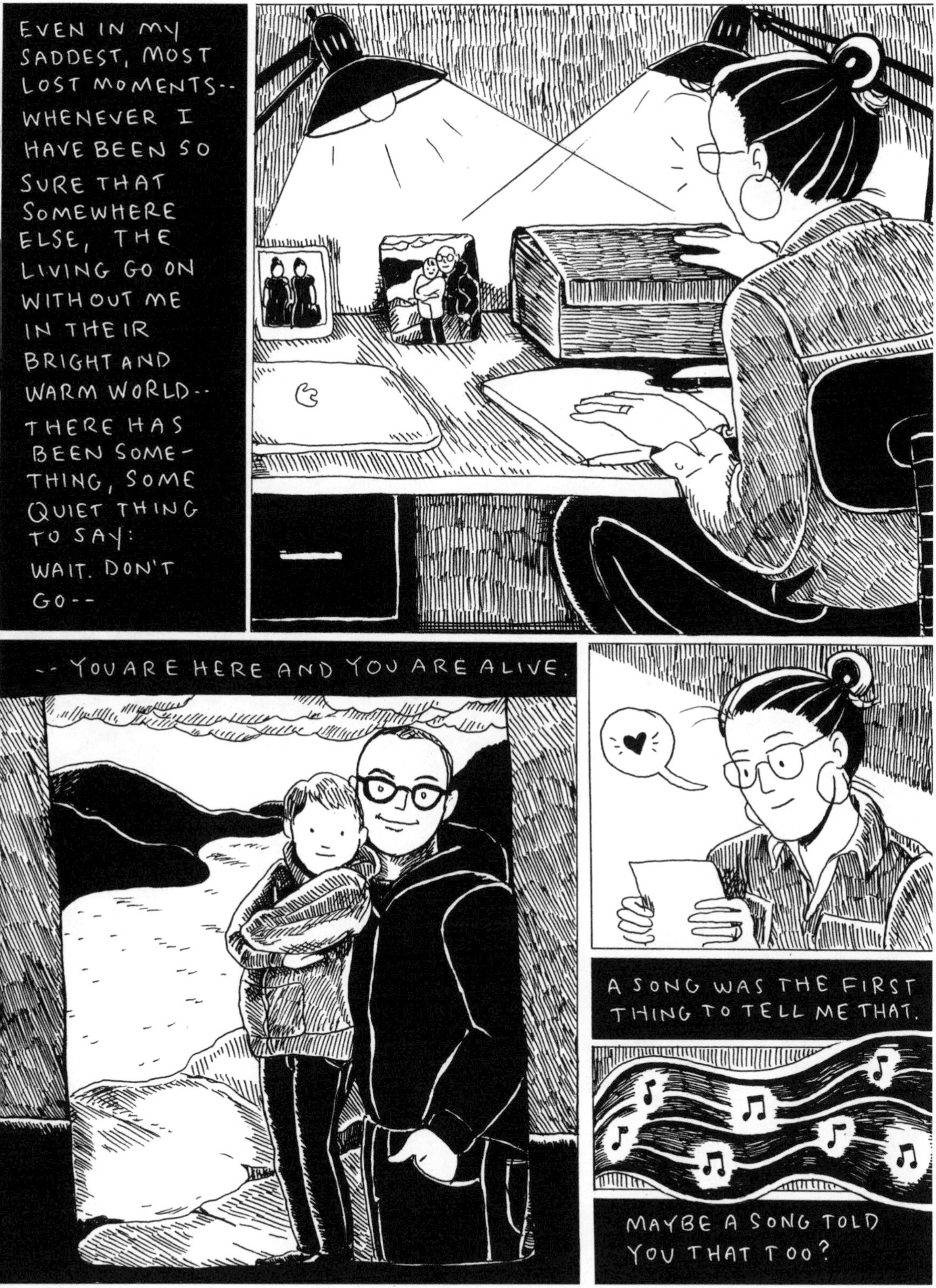
EVEN IN MY SADDEST, MOST LOST MOMENTS-- WHENEVER I HAVE BEEN SO SURE THAT SOMEWHERE ELSE, THE LIVING GO ON WITHOUT ME IN THEIR BRIGHT AND WARM WORLD-- THERE HAS BEEN SOME-THING, SOME QUIET THING TO SAY: WAIT. DON'T GO--
--YOU ARE HERE AND YOU ARE ALIVE.
A SONG WAS THE FIRST THING TO TELL ME THAT.
MAYBE A SONG TOLD YOU THAT TOO?

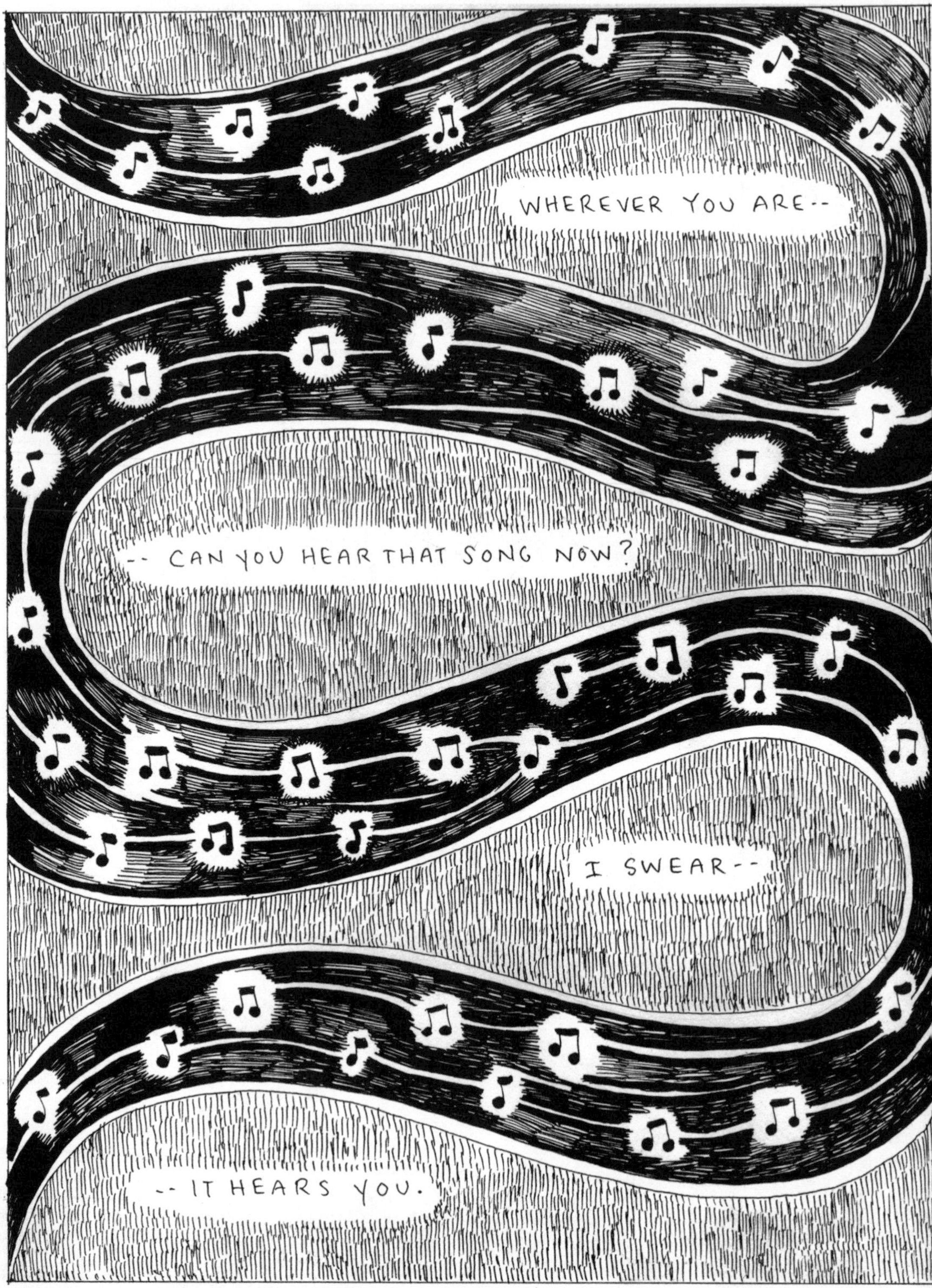
WHEREVER YOU ARE--
-- CAN YOU HEAR THAT SONG NOW?
I SWEAR--
-- IT HEARS YOU.

SELECTED SOUNDTRACK

THE TAPE I MADE HIM

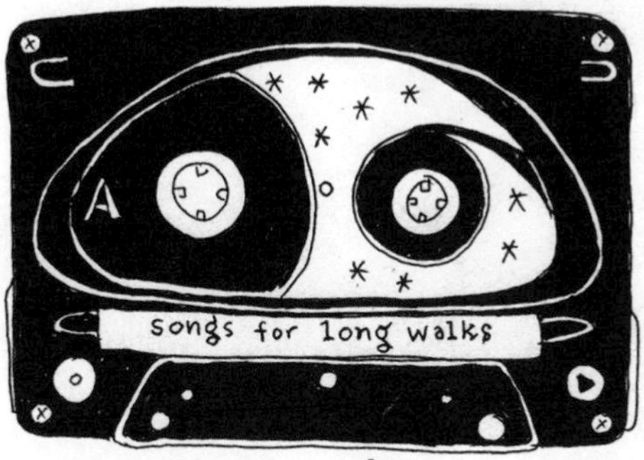
A
songs for long walks

A RIPE- BABES IN TOYLAND* • ONE MORE HOUR - SLEATER- KINNEY • AARON + MARIA - AMERICAN ANALOG SET • LETTERS + DRAWINGS - DAMIEN JURADO • THE TROUBLE WITH PUBLIC PLACES - CADALLACA • HAPPINESS - ELLIOTT SMITH • STUTTER - ELASTICA • MEET ZE MONSTER - PJ HARVEY • PLEASE LET THAT BE YOU - THE RENTALS • REMOTE CONTROL - THE CLASH • HOTEL YORBA - THE WHITE STRIPES • BEAT ON THE BRAT - THE RAMONES • PROVE MY LOVE - VIOLENT FEMMES • PITSELEH - ELLIOTT SMITH

B SOUL KITCHEN - X • LITTLE BABIES - SLEATER-KINNEY • PRINCESS + THE PONY - SEAN NANA • OHIO - DAMIEN JURADO • THE SATURDAY BOY - BILLY BRAGG • I WANNA BE YOUR BOYFRIEND - THE RAMONES • GOT ALL THIS WAITING - THE GOSSIP • ROCK & ROLL - THE VELVET UNDERGROUND • O-STELLA - PJ HARVEY • I FOUGHT THE LAW - THE CLASH • OH! - SLEATER-KINNEY • THE SKY LIT UP - PJ HARVEY • JOHNNY HIT & RUN PAULENE - X • JUST SOMEBODY I USED TO KNOW - ELLIOTT SMITH • THE OTHER ICE AGE - THE PEECHEES • I THINK WE ARE GOING TO BE FRIENDS - THE WHITE STRIPES

THE TAPE HE MADE ME

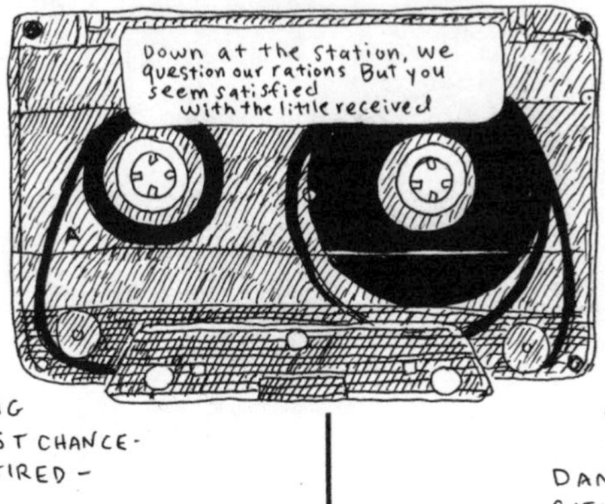
Down at the station, we question our rations But you seem satisfied with the little received
A

A GUILFORD HALL - FUGAZI • NO, NO, NO - THE GOSSIP • ALEC EIFFEL - THE PIXIES • THE DEVIL IN MISS JONES - MIKE NESS • BETTER - GOOD RIDDANCE • NO SURPRISE - FUGAZI • RUB 'TIL IT BLEEDS - PJ HARVEY • 364 DAYS - MURDER CITY DEVILS • RECONCILIATION POLICY - THREADBARE • KISS ME DEADLY - GENERATION X • LOOKING AT YOU - MC5 • LAST CHANCE - FUGAZI • I'M SO TIRED - FUGAZI

B THIS IS LOVE - PJ HARVEY • TELLING THEM - SOCIAL DISTORTION • LET ME GET WHAT I WANT - THE SMITHS • FAST CAR - TRACY CHAPMAN • BED FOR THE SCRAPING - FUGAZI • COME DANCING - GOOD RIDDANCE • HOLIDAYS IN THE SUN - THE SEX PISTOLS • LOST IN THE SUPERMARKET - THE CLASH • GRAVEYARD - THE DEVIL MAKES THREE • SOUTHERN BELLE - ELLIOTT SMITH • WELCOME TO THE TERRORDOME - PUBLIC ENEMY • DANCN' SHOES - MURDER CITY DEVILS • REPRODUCTION OF DEATH - INTERNATIONAL NOISE CONSPIRACY

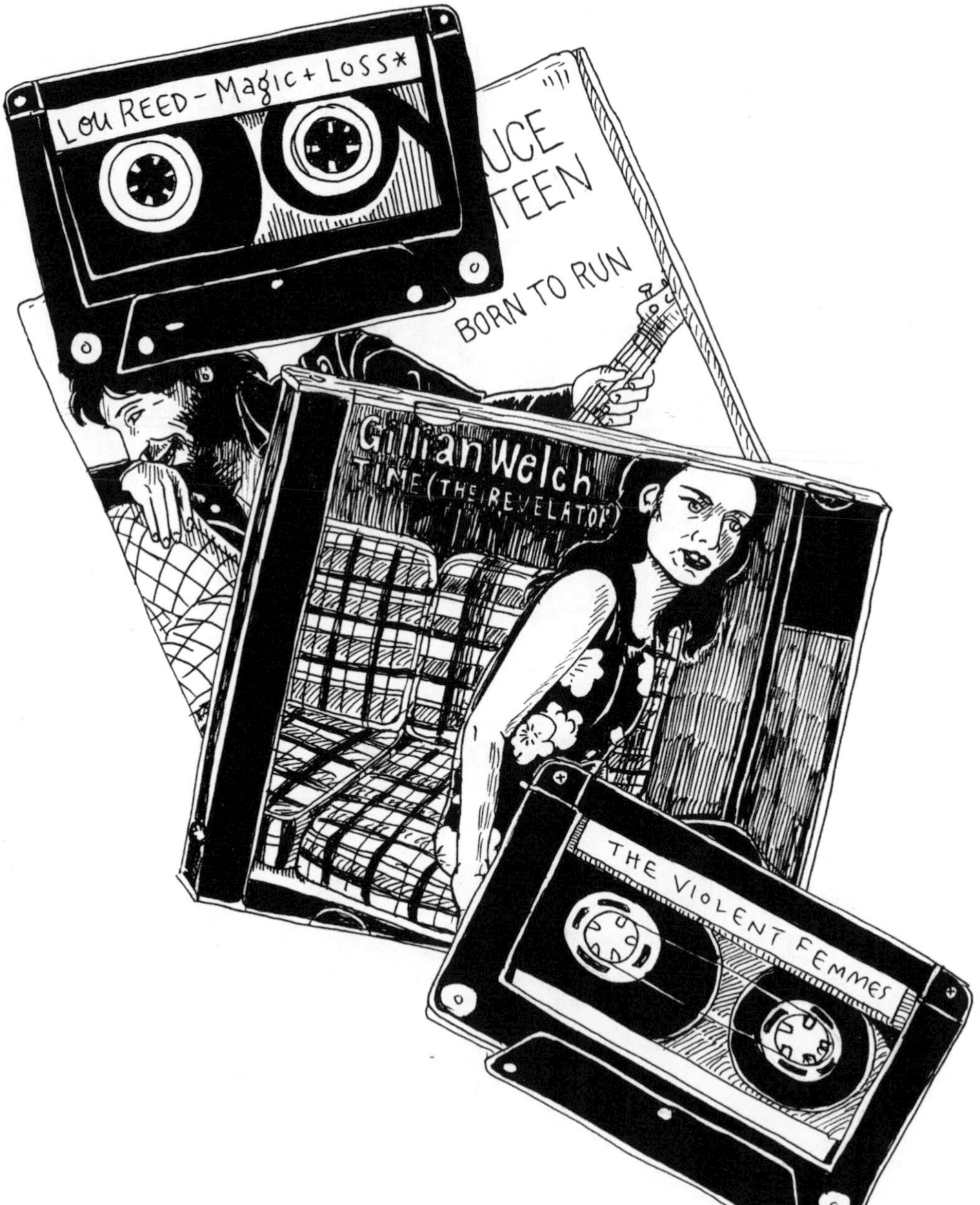

Lou REED - Magic + LOSS*
UCE
TEEN
BORN TO RUN
Gillian Welch
TIME (THE REVELATOR)
THE VIOLENT FEMMES

ACKNOWLEDGEMENTS

Thank you Graham & Gus Parsons
Box Brown & Jared Smith
Chris Duffy
Glynnis Fawkes & Jennifer Hayden & Gabrielle Bell
Anne Hyson & Nathan Pyritz
Gary Starkweather, Pam Shaw, Jake Pierre & Bee Oliver
Jennifer & John Parsons
Members of the ACHH: Charles, Deb, Cheryl, Jen & Chris

Special Thanks to:
Michelle Ollie & all at The Center for Cartoon Studies

Thank you to the songwriters whose work has traveled with me
in the many places I have lived--especially (but not limited to):
Tom Waits, Bruce Springsteen, Lou Reed, Neil Young,
Gillian Welch & David Rawlings

A special tip of the hat to Tim Luntzel:
a beautiful person & gifted musician.
He was on my mind a lot when I was making this book & I had hoped
to share it with him, but he died before I was able to.
Tim, you are loved & missed.

Author's Note:
Some names and descriptions of poeple
have been changed in order to protect privacy.

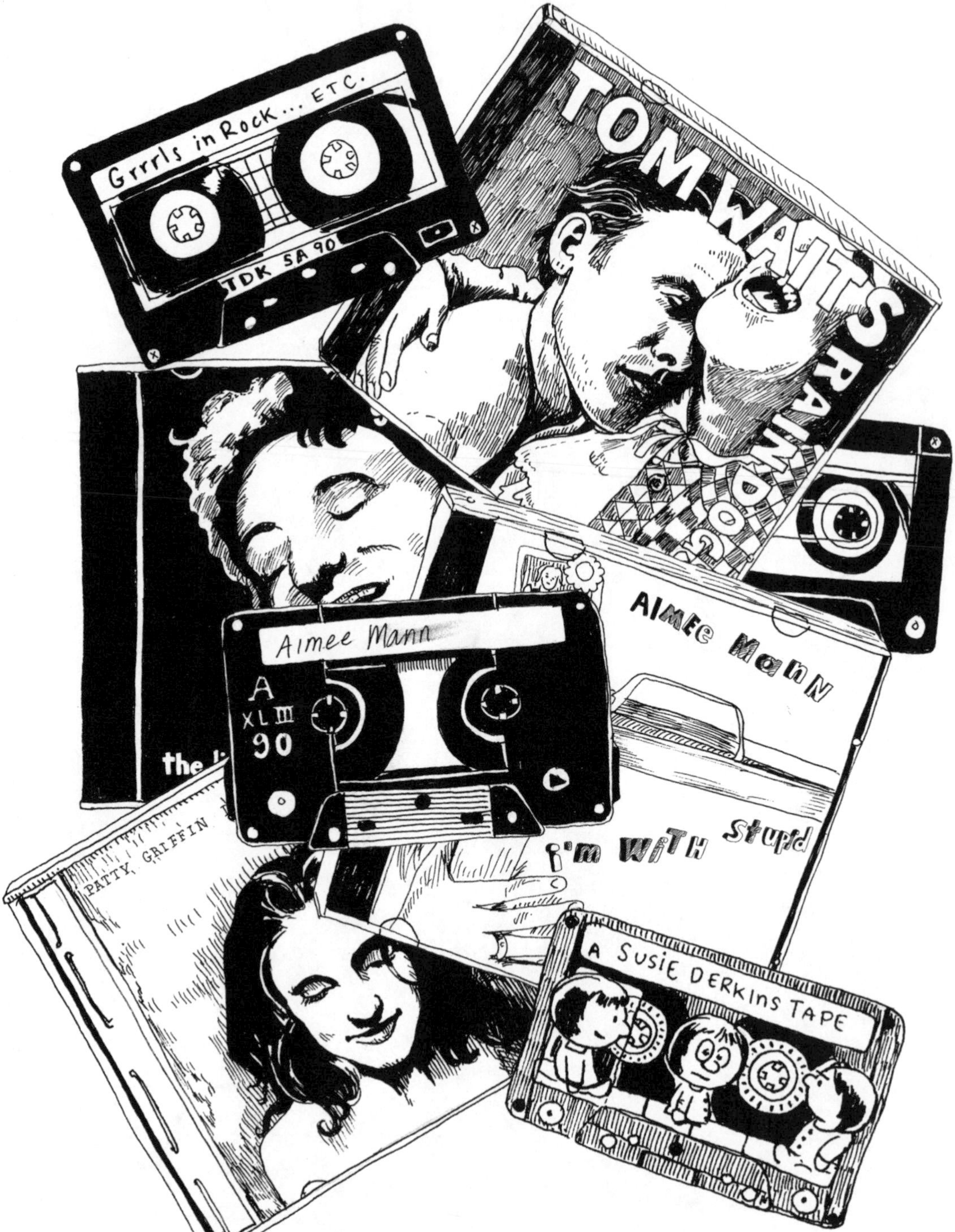

Grrrls in Rock... ETC.
TDK SA 90
TOM WAITS
RAIN DOGS
Aimee Mann
A
XL III
90
AIMEE MANN
i'm WiTH Stupid
PATTY GRIFFIN
A SUSIE DERKINS TAPE

Summer Pierre is the creator of the acclaimed autobiographical comic series *Paper Pencil Life*. She lives in the Hudson Valley of New York with her husband and son.

Find more at summerpierre.com